Published by High Pines Press, PO Box 42, Reigate, Surrey, RH2 8YW

First published in 1986
New edition 1989

ISBN 0 948792 01 9

Series devised and designed by Peter Phillips
Gesture drawings by Alison Archbald
Electronic page make-up by HyperText Limited

Printed by Richard Clay Ltd, Crane House Lavington St, London, SE1 0NX

Other languages in this series: French, Italian, Spanish
In preparation: Greek

SPEAKEASY
PHRASEMAKER

Introduction

The aim of Speakeasy Phrasemakers is quick and easy communication rather than unattainable linguistic perfection.

By choosing from a collection of key words for particular subjects you can make an almost infinite number of simple tailor-made phrases, and foreigners can communicate back in a similar manner by pointing However, the concept does accept that often inaccurate grammar is the price that has to be paid for this flexibility. The pronunciation system, with only two simple rules to remember, is especially designed for ease of use by English speakers and also aims for adequate comprehension rather than accuracy.

In addition to the usual subjects, also included are Family Relations, Jobs, Sports, Hobbies, and the Countryside, all handy for small talk or for expanding the scope of other sections. There's also a unique page of Gesture language.

Layout of the Phrasemaker

For quick reference useful words and phrases are on the inside front cover. Even if Germans you meet understand English, most will appreciate your attempting a few words of greeting in their own language.

Subjects are in alphabetical order throughout the book, and there is a detailed index at the back. Most subjects are spread over double pages. More complex ones, like 'Eating Out' have additional pages following them, generally with lists of nouns, but you should always start any conversation at the 'starter' double page.

The 'starter' pages of all subjects are laid out in a consistent pattern. The left-hand page has a column of words such as I, you, which, what, by, etc. and a column of verbs in a tinted box. The right-hand page has lists of other words relevant to the subject, set out in logical groupings.

Across the bottom of most pages are useful cross-references to other related subjects.

Phrasemaking

Make up phrases by pointing to words that have the nearest meaning to what you want to say. You can speak the translations as you point using the phonetic pronunciation in italics above the German. If you prefer not to speak, just point to the words. If you prefer to say the English whilst you are pointing that's fine too. Use whatever technique you find suits you best. Even if you attempt to speak German, it would still help to let the other person see what you are doing so that they will catch onto the idea and perhaps answer back using the same technique. There are a few simple instructions similar to these in German on the back cover which you can point to, to show people before inviting a reply.

Don't worry about the grammar, it will usually sound pigeon-English and will invariably sound pigeon-German to the listener, but if you keep

...rases short, use appropriate intonations and sometimes a bit of sign ...guage as well, you should be understood.

...hould be noted that the letter 'ß' is sometimes used in small lettering ...German but when written in capitals it usually changes to a double S ...S). The letter 'ß' will not be found in this translator as all the German is ...capital lettering for clarity.

...re are examples of phrases using " HOTEL - Checking in & out" on page ...:—

is there • inexpensive • guest house • near • here
do you have • double room • for • 2 *(use fingers)* • night
how much is • bed & breakfast • per • night
do you have • better • room • with • private • bathroom

...erbs

...l verbs are grouped in a tinted box for clarity. They always start with ...ould likes' 'haves' 'is/ares' and 'cans' followed by a list of other verbs ...levant to the subject. If you want to use an infinitive eg. "I would like ...pay", don't use "to" if it is listed elsewhere, just say "I would like pay". ...member, keep it simple!

...egatives

...e word for 'no' on its own (i.e. the opposite of yes) is **NEIN**. The 'no' on ...bject 'starter' pages – **KEIN** – has the following type of meaning; "we have ...) tickets for today".

...ronunciation

...e phonetic pronunciation is in italics above the German. There are only ...o simple rules to remember:—
Read out the pronunciation as if it were English but stress the syllables in bold type.
The special double letter combination '**sh**' should be pronounced like the 'ch' in the Scottish 'loch', however if you forget and say 'sh' instead, you should still be understood.

...you can put a little German intonation into your speech - all the better! ...on't be afraid to have a go!

...eople with Scottish accents (who tend to roll their 'r's) should try not to ...ound single 'r's that follow an 'a', for example as in **nar**-*mer* (name). ...he 'r' is there just to distinguish the 'a' as being like that in 'father' rather ...an as in 'cat'.

...pdating

...uch careful consideration has gone into the content and layout of this ...ook but we welcome any constructive comments and suggestions that ...ou think might help us improve future editions.

...on voyage!

I	*ish* **ICH**		I would like	*ish* **mersh**-ter **ICH MÖCHTE**
my	*mine* **MEIN**		we would like	*veer* **mersh**-tern **WIR MÖCHTEN**
he	*air* **ER**		do you want	*vol-ern zee* **WOLLEN SIE**
she	*zee* **SIE**			
we	*veer* **WIR**		I have	*ish* **har**-ber **ICH HABE**
our	**oon**-ser **UNSER**		he / she has	*air / zee hat* **ER/SIE HAT**
you	*zee* **SIE**		we have	*veer* **har**-bern **WIR HABEN**
your	*eeyer* **IHR**		do you have	**har**-bern zee **HABEN SIE**
they	*zee* **SIE**			
			there has been	*ess var* **ES WAR**
friends	**froyn**-der **FREUNDE**			
somebody	**yay**-mant **JEMAND**		can I	*kan ish* **KANN ICH**
some people	**iy**-nigger **loy**-ter **EINIGE LEUTE**		can we	**ker**-nen veer **KÖNNEN WIR**
			can you	**ker**-nen zee **KÖNNEN SIE**
not	*nisht* **NICHT**			
no	*kine* **KEIN**		am	*bin* **BIN**
			is	*isst* **IST**
which	**vel**-shyer **WELCHER**		are	*zint* **SIND**
where	*voh* **WO**		is there	*gipt ess* **GIBT ES**
when	*van* **WANN**		is it	*ist ess* **IST ES**
what	*vass* **WAS**			
what time	*uhm vee-**feel** ooer* **UM WIEVIEL UHR**		get	ber-**kom**-mern **BEKOMMEN**
			give	**gay**-bern **GEBEN**
how long	*vee **lang**-er* **WIE LANGE**		go	**far**-rern **FAHREN**
how many	*vee-**fee**-ler* **WIEVIELE**		had	*gair-**hapt*** **GEHABT**
			have	**har**-bern **HABEN**
and	*oont* **UND**		help me	**hel**-fern zee meer **HELFEN SIE MIR**
at	*an* **AN**		help us	**hel**-fern zee oonss **HELFEN SIE UNS**
for	*foor* **FÜR**		move	ber-**vay**-gurn **BEWEGEN**
in	*in* **IN**		need	**brow**-shern **BRAUCHEN**
of	*fon* **VON**		phone	telefon-**nee**-rern **TELEFONIEREN**
to	*tsoo* **ZU**		stop	**an**-haltern **ANHALTEN**

nearest	*nex-ster* **NÄCHSTER**		very	*zair* **SEHR**
near	*in dair nay-er fon* **IN DER NÄHE VON**		serious	*airnst* **ERNST**
here	*here* **HIER**		seriously	*airnst* **ERNST**
there	*dar* **DA**		badly	*shvair* **SCHWER**
			probably	*var-shine-lish* **WAHRSCHEINLICH**
ambulance	*kran-kern-var-gurn* **KRANKENWAGEN**			
fire brigade	*foy-yer-vair* **FEUERWEHR**		broken	*gur-brosh-ern* **GEBROCHEN**
hospital	*kran-kern-house* **KRANKENHAUS**		burnt	*gur-brant* **GEBRANNT**
police	*pollit-tsigh* **POLIZEI**		choking	*air-shtick-ernd* **ERSTICKEND**
			collapsed	*tsoo-zam-ern-gur-brosh-ern* **ZUSAMMENGEBROCHEN**
dentist	*tsarn-artst* **ZAHNARZT**		drowned	*air-troon-kern* **ERTRUNKEN**
doctor	*artst* **ARZT**		fallen	*gur-fal-lern* **GEFALLEN**
witness	*tsoy-gur* **ZEUGE**		(a) fit	*an-fal* **ANFALL**
			hurt	*fair-letst* **VERLETZT**
			injured	*fair-letst* **VERLETZT**
			run over	*oober-far-rern* **ÜBERFAHREN**
accident	*oon-fal* **UNFALL**		(in) shock	*shock* **SCHOCK**
emergency	*note-fal* **NOTFALL**		trapped	*gur-fang-ern* **GEFANGEN**
fire	*brant* **BRAND**		unconscious	*ber-voost-lows* **BEWUSSTLOS**
help	*hill-fer* **HILFE**		started	*an-gur-fang-ern* **ANGEFANGEN**
			stopped	*owf-gur-hurt* **AUFGEHÖRT**
quick	*shnel* **SCHNELL**		suddenly	*plerts-lish* **PLÖTZLICH**
quickly	*shnel* **SCHNELL**		happened	*pah-seert* **PASSIERT**
			ago	*hair* **HER**
be careful	*pas-sern zee owf* **PASSEN SIE AUF**			
carefully	*zorg-fel-tig* **SORGFÄLTIG**		first aid	*air-ster hill-fer* **ERSTE HILFE**
			insulin	*inzoo-leen* **INSULIN**
			pain reliever	*shmairts-shtill-enders-mitterl* **SCHMERZSTILLENDES MITTEL**
	EMERGENCY PHONE Nos:		sedative	*be-roo-igoongs-mitterl* **BERUHIGUNGSMITTEL**
Austria	fire -122 police -133		something	*et-varss tsoom* **ETWAS ZUM**
Germany	fire -112 police -110		to keep warm	*varm-bligh-bern* **WARMBLEIBEN**
Switzerland	fire -118 police -117			

parts of the body: 44   telephone: 120

I	*ish* **ICH**	I would like	*ish mersh-ter* **ICH MÖCHTE**	
my	*mine* **MEIN**	we would like	*veer mersh-tern* **WIR MÖCHTEN**	
we	*veer* **WIR**	do you want	*vol-ern zee* **WOLLEN SIE**	
our	*oon-ser* **UNSER**			
you	*zee* **SIE**	I have	*ish har-ber* **ICH HABE**	
your	*eeyer* **IHR**	we have	*veer har-bern* **WIR HABEN**	
it	*ess* **ES**	do you have	*har-bern zee* **HABEN SIE**	
not	*nisht* **NICHT**	can I	*kan ish* **KANN ICH**	
no	*kine* **KEIN**	can we	*ker-nen veer* **KÖNNEN WIR**	
		can you	*ker-nen zee* **KÖNNEN SIE**	
which	*vel-shyer* **WELCHER**			
where	*voh* **WO**	is	*isst* **IST**	
when	*van* **WANN**	are	*zint* **SIND**	
what	*vass* **WAS**	is there	*gipt ess* **GIBT ES**	
what time	*uhm vee-feel ooer* **UM WIEVIEL UHR**	is it	*ist ess* **IST ES**	
how long	*vee lang-er* **WIE LANGE**	arrive	*an-kommern* **ANKOMMEN**	
how many	*vee-fee-ler* **WIEVIELE**	change	*oom-shtigh-gurn* **UMSTEIGEN**	
how much is (that)	*vass koss-tert (das)* **WAS KOSTET (DAS)**	depart	*ap-far-rern* **ABFAHREN**	
		get	*ber-kom-mern* **BEKOMMEN**	
nearest	*nex-ster* **NÄCHSTER**	go	*far-rern* **FAHREN**	
near	*in dair nay-er fon* **IN DER NÄHE VON**	have	*har-bern* **HABEN**	
here	*here* **HIER**	hire	*mee-tern* **MIETEN**	
		do you know	*viss-ern zee* **WISSEN SIE**	
and	*oont* **UND**	reserve	*rezair-vee-rern* **RESERVIEREN**	
at	*an* **AN**	show me	*tsigh-gurn zee meer* **ZEIGEN SIE MIR**	
by	*by* **BEI**	transfer	*oom-shtiy-gurn* **UMSTEIGEN**	
for	*foor* **FÜR**	wait	*var-tern* **WARTEN**	
from	*fon* **VON**			
in	*in* **IN**	flight	*floog* **FLUG**	
to	*narsh* **NACH**	airline ticket	*tee-ket* **TICKET**	

person	*pair-zone* **PERSON**	flight number	*floog noo-mer* **FLUG–NR.**	
child	*kint* **KIND**	early	*frooh* **FRÜH**	
children	*kin-der* **KINDER**	late	*shpayt* **SPÄT**	
baby	baby **BABY**	on time	*poonk-tlish* **PÜNKTLICH**	
age	*al-ter* **ALTER**	cancelled	*ent-felt* **ENTFÄLLT**	
name	*nar-mer* **NAME**			
		open	*owff* **AUF**	
single	*iyn-fash* **EINFACH**	closed	*tsoo* **ZU**	
return	*hin oont tsoo-rook* **HIN UND ZURÜCK**			
non-stop	*dee-rect* **DIREKT**	aircraft	*floog-tsoyg* **FLUGZEUG**	
		check-in	*check-in* **CHECK-IN**	
seat	*zits* **SITZ**	connection	*an-shlooss* **ANSCHLUSS**	
first class	*air-ster klass-ser* **ERSTE KLASSE**	gate no.	*owss-gang noo-mer* **AUSGANG NR.**	
business class	*biz-ness-klass-ser* **BUSINESS-KLASSE**	luggage	*gur-peck* **GEPÄCK**	
economy class	*too-riss-tern-klass-ser* **TOURISTEN-KLASSE**	take off	*shtart* **START**	
smoking	*raoo-sher* **RAUCHER**	nothing to declare	*nishts tsoo fair-tsol-lern* **NICHTS ZU VERZOLLEN**	
non-smoking	*nisht-rau-sher* **NICHTRAUCHER**	passport	*pas* **PASS**	
window	*fen-ster* **FENSTER**	visa	*vee-zoom* **VISUM**	
aisle	*gang* **GANG**			
		arrivals hall	*an-koonfts-hal-ler* **ANKUNFTSHALLE**	
front	*for-ner* **VORNE**	bank	*bank* **BANK**	
back	*hin-tern* **HINTEN**	departure lounge	*ap-floog-hal-ler* **ABFLUGHALLE**	
middle	*mit-ter* **MITTE**	accommodation bureau	*tsim-mer-narsh-vice* **ZIMMERNACHWEIS**	
		tourist information	*too-ristern-ows-koonft* **TOURISTENAUSKUNFT**	
first	*airst* **ERST**	toilets	*twal-let-tern* **TOILETTEN**	
last	*letst* **LETZT**			
next	*next* **NÄCHST**	airport bus	*floog-harfern-booss* **FLUGHAFENBUS**	
		car	*var-gurn* **WAGEN**	
minutes	*min-noo-tern* **MINUTEN**	taxi	*taxi* **TAXI**	
hours	*shtoon-dern* **STUNDEN**	train	*tsoog* **ZUG**	
		city centre	*shtat-mitter* **STADTMITTE**	

local transport: 100   time & meeting: 122

I	*ish* **ICH**	I would like	*ish* **mersh**-ter **ICH MÖCHTE**
my	*mine* **MEIN**	we would like	*veer* **mersh**-tern **WIR MÖCHTEN**
we	*veer* **WIR**	do you want	*vol*-ern *zee* **WOLLEN SIE**
our	**oon**-ser **UNSER**		
you	*zee* **SIE**	I have	*ish* **har**-ber **ICH HABE**
your	*eeyer* **IHR**	we have	*veer* **har**-bern **WIR HABEN**
it	*ess* **ESS**	do you have	**har**-bern *zee* **HABEN SIE**
not	*nisht* **NICHT**	can I	*kan ish* **KANN ICH**
no	*kine* **KEIN**	can we	**ker**-nen *veer* **KÖNNEN WIR**
		can you	**ker**-nen *zee* **KÖNNEN SIE**
which	**vel**-shyer **WELCHER**		
where	*voh* **WO**	is	*isst* **IST**
when	*van* **WANN**	are	*zint* **SIND**
what	*vass* **WAS**	is there	*gipt ess* **GIBT ES**
what time	*uhm* vee-**feel** *ooer* **UM WIEVIEL UHR**	is it	*ist ess* **IST ES**
how long	vee **lang**-er **WIE LANGE**	get	ber-**kom**-mern **BEKOMMEN**
how many	vee-**fee**-ler **WIEVIELE**	have	**har**-bern **HABEN**
how much is (that)	*vass* **koss**-tert *(das)* **WAS KOSTET (DAS)**	repair	rep-par-**ree**-rern **REPARIEREN**
		will be ready	*veert* **fair**-tig **WIRD FERTIG**
near	in dair **nay**-er fon **IN DER NÄHE VON**	see	**zay**-ern **SEHEN**
here	*here* **HIER**	send	**shick**-ern **SCHICKEN**
		show me	**tsigh**-gurn *zee meer* **ZEIGEN SIE MIR**
and	*oont* **UND**	wrap	**iyn**-packern **EINPACKEN**
at	*an* **AN**		
by	*by* **BEI**	how works....	vee foonk-tseo-**neert** **WIE FUNKTIONIERT....**
for	*foor* **FÜR**		
from	*fon* **VON**	receipt	**kvit**-toong **QUITTUNG**
in	*in* **IN**	deposit	*an*-tsar-loong **ANZAHLUNG**
on	*owf* **AUF**	included	**iyn**-shlees-lish **EINSCHLIESSLICH**
to	*tsoo* **ZU**	insurance	fair-**zish**-er-roong **VERSICHERUNG**

name	*nar-mer* **NAME**	**ANTIQUE SHOP**	*antick-vee-tay-tern-gur-sheft* **ANTIQUITÄTENGESCHÄFT**
address	*ad-dress-ser* **ADRESSE**	bric a brac	*nip-zash-ern* **NIPPSACHEN**
artist	*koonst-ler* **KÜNSTLER**	bronzes	*bron-tser-gay-gurn-shten-der* **BRONZEGEGENSTÄNDE**
		china	*port-sel-larn* **PORZELLAN**
good	*goot* **GUT**	coins	*moon-tsern* **MÜNZEN**
expensive	*price-goon-stig* **PREISGÜNSTIG**	dolls & toys	*poo-pern oont shpeel-tsoygur* **PUPPEN UND SPIELZEUGE**
		figures	*fig-goo-ree-nern* **FIGURINEN**
alternative	*al-tairna-tee-ver* **ALTERNATIVE**	furniture	*mur-berl* **MÖBEL**
cheaper	*bill-ligger* **BILLIGER**	glass	*glarss* **GLAS**
better	*bess-ser* **BESSER**	militaria	*millee-tair-zash-ern* **MILITÄRSACHEN**
similar	*ayn-lish* **ÄHNLICH**	musical instruments	*mo-zeek-instroo-menter* **MUSIKINSTRUMENTE**
simpler	*iyn-fasher* **EINFACHER**	scientific instruments	*viss-sern-shaft-lisher* instroo-men-ter **WISSENSCHAFTLICHE** **INSTRUMENTE**
bigger	*grer-ser* **GRÖSSER**	silverware	*zil-ber-var-rern* **SILBERWAREN**
smaller	*kliy-ner* **KLEINER**	veteran cars	*old-timer-var-gurn* **OLDTIMER-WAGEN**
thicker	*dick-er* **DICKER**		
thinner	*doo-ner* **DÜNNER**	**ART GALLERY**	*koonst-gallaree* **KUNSTGALERIE**
wider	*brigh-ter* **BREITER**	architecture	*arshee-teck-toor* **ARCHITEKTUR**
narrower	*shmar-ler* **SCHMALER**	ceramic	*kair-rar-meek* **KERAMIK**
		drawing	*tsiysh-noong* **ZEICHNUNG**
broken	*gur-brosh-ern* **GEBROCHEN**	etching	*koop-fer-shtish* **KUPFERSTICH**
cracked	*gur-shproong-ern* **GESPRUNGEN**	frame	*rar-mern* **RAHMEN**
		landscape	*lant-shaft* **LANDSCHAFT**
(very) old	*(zair) alt* **(SEHR) ALT**	miniature	*minnia-toor-gur-melder* **MINIATURGEMÄLDE**
modern	*moh-dairn* **MODERN**	oil painting	*erl-gur-melder* **ÖLGEMÄLDE**
genuine	*esht* **ECHT**	painting	*gur-mel-der* **GEMÄLDE**
original	*orree-ghee-narl* **ORIGINAL**	portrait	*bilt-niss* **BILDNIS**
production	*ray-pro-dook-tsee-yohn* **REPRODUKTION**	pottery	*shtine-goot* **STEINGUT**
copy	*kop-pee* **KOPIE**	print	*shtish* **STICH**
		sculpture	*plass-teek* **PLASTIK**
open	*owff* **AUF**	still life	*shtil-laybern* **STILLEBEN**
closed	*tsoo* **ZU**	watercolour	*akva-rell* **AQUARELL**

artist's materials: 119   fabrics: 28   colours: 28

I	*ish* **ICH**		I would like	*ish* **mersh**-ter **ICH MÖCHTE**
my	*mine* **MEIN**		do you want	*vol*-ern zee **WOLLEN SIE**
you	*zee* **SIE**			
your	*eeyer* **IHR**		I have	*ish* **har**-ber **ICH HABE**
it	*ess* **ESS**		do you have	**har**-bern zee **HABEN SIE**
not	*nisht* **NICHT**		can I	*kan ish* **KANN ICH**
no	*kine* **KEIN**		can you	**ker**-nen zee **KÖNNEN SIE**
which	**vel**-*shyer* **WELCHER**		is	*isst* **IST**
where	*voh* **WO**		are	*zint* **SIND**
when	*van* **WANN**		is there	*gipt ess* **GIBT ES**
what	*vass* **WAS**		is it	*ist ess* **IST ES**
what time	*uhm* vee-**feel** *ooer* **UM WIEVIEL UHR**			
			accept	**nay**-mern **NEHMEN**
how	*vee* **WIE**		arrange	*organee*-**zee**-rern **ORGANISIEREN**
how long	*vee* **lang**-er **WIE LANGE**		cash	*iyn*-lerzern **EINLÖSEN**
how many	vee-**fee**-ler **WIEVIELE**		change	**veck**-serln **WECHSELN**
how much is (that)	*vass* **koss**-tert *(das)* **WAS KOSTET (DAS)**		charge	**koss**-tern **KOSTEN**
			come back	*tsoo*-**rook**-kommern **ZURÜCKKOMMEN**
nearest	**nex**-ster **NÄCHSTER**		have	**har**-bern **HABEN**
near	*in dair* **nay**-*er fon* **IN DER NÄHE VON**		pay	**tsar**-lern **ZAHLEN**
here	*here* **HIER**		receive	*emp*-**fang**-ern **EMPFANGEN**
			will be ready	*veert* **fair**-tig **WIRD FERTIG**
and	*oont* **UND**		send	**shick**-ern **SCHICKEN**
at	*an* **AN**		sign	*oonter*-**shriy**-bern **UNTERSCHREIBEN**
by	*by* **BEI**		will take	*nimmt* **NIMMT**
for	*foor* **FÜR**		transfer	*oober*-**viy**-zern **ÜBERWEISEN**
from	*fon* **VON**		wait	**var**-tern **WARTEN**
in	*in* **IN**			
to	*tsoo* **ZU**		this	**dee**-zer **DIESE**
with	*mit* **MIT**		these	**dee**-zer **DIESE**

names of English-speaking countries: 121

English	Pronunciation	German
money	*gelt*	**GELD**
cash	*bar*	**BAR**
notes	*shiy-ner*	**SCHEINE**
small change	*kline-gelt*	**KLEINGELD**
receipt	*kvit-toong*	**QUITTUNG**
exchange rate	*veck-serl-koors*	**WECHSELKURS**
buying	*an-cowf*	**ANKAUF**
selling	*fair-cowf*	**VERKAUF**
commission	*gur-boor*	**GEBÜHR**
Deutsche Marks	*doytch-mark*	**DEUTSCHMARK**
Pfennigs	*pfen-neesh*	**PFENNIG**
Francs	*fran-kern*	**FRANKEN**
Rappen	*rap-pern*	**RAPPEN**
Schillings	*shilling*	**SCHILLING**
Groschen	*grosh-ern*	**GROSCHEN**
Dollars	*dollar*	**DOLLAR**
Pounds	*pfoont*	**PFUND**
Rands	*rant*	**RAND**
account	*kon-toh*	**KONTO**
number	*noo-mer*	**NUMMER**
name	*nar-mer*	**NAME**
address	*ad-dress-ser*	**ADRESSE**
identification	*owss-vice*	**AUSWEIS**
passport	*pas*	**PASS**
open	*owf*	**AUF**
closed	*tsoo*	**ZU**
now	*yetst*	**JETZT**
sooner	*froo-er*	**FRÜHER**
later	*shpay-ter*	**SPÄTER**
before	*for*	**VOR**
after	*narsh*	**NACH**
yesterday	*guest-ern*	**GESTERN**
today	*hoy-ter*	**HEUTE**
tomorrow	*more-gurn*	**MORGEN**
Monday	*morn-targ*	**MONTAG**
morning	*for-mittarg*	**VORMITTAG**
lunchtime	*mit-arg*	**MITTAG**
afternoon	*narsh-mittarg*	**NACHMITTAG**
bank	*bank*	**BANK**
savings bank	*shpar-kasser*	**SPARKASSE**
cash machine	*ghelt-ow-toe-mart*	**GELDAUTOMAT**
change bureau	*veck-serl-shoober*	**WECHSELSTUBE**
bank card	*bank-karter*	**BANKKARTE**
cashiers' cheque	*bank-an-viy-zoong*	**BANKANWEISUNG**
personal cheque	*bar-sheck*	**BARSCHECK**
credit card	*kred-deet-karter*	**KREDITKARTE**
Eurocheque card	*oy-roh-sheck-karter*	**EUROSCHECKKARTE**
intl. money order	*inter-natseeyo-nar-ler tsar-loongs-shine*	**INTERNATIONALER ZAHLUNGSSCHEIN**
letter of credit	*ack-kreddee-teef*	**AKKREDITIF**
pension	*ren-ter*	**RENTE**
statement	*kon-toh-owss-tsoog*	**KONTOAUSZUG**
travellers' cheque	*riy-zer-sheck*	**REISESCHECK**

I	*ish* **ICH**	I would like	*ish **mersh**-ter* **ICH MÖCHTE**
my	*mine* **MEIN**	we would like	*veer **mersh**-tern* **WIR MÖCHTEN**
we	*veer* **WIR**	do you want	*vol-ern zee* **WOLLEN SIE**
our	***oon**-ser* **UNSER**		
you	*zee* **SIE**	I have	*ish **har**-ber* **ICH HABE**
your	*eeyer* **IHR**	we have	*veer **har**-bern* **WIR HABEN**
it	*ess* **ES**	do you have	***har**-bern zee* **HABEN SIE**
not	*nisht* **NICHT**	can I	*kan ish* **KANN ICH**
no	*kine* **KEIN**	can we	*ker-nen veer* **KÖNNEN WIR**
		can you	*ker-nen zee* **KÖNNEN SIE**
which	***vel**-shyer* **WELCHER**		
where	*voh* **WO**	is	*isst* **IST**
when	*van* **WANN**	are	*zint* **SIND**
what	*vass* **WAS**	is there	*gipt ess* **GIBT ES**
what time	*uhm vee-**feel** ooer* **UM WIEVIEL UHR**	is it	*ist ess* **IST ES**
how long	*vee **lang**-er* **WIE LANGE**	buy	*cow-fern* **KAUFEN**
how many	*vee-**fee**-ler* **WIEVIELE**	camp	*tsel-tern* **ZELTEN**
how much is (that)	*vass **koss**-tert (das)* **WAS KOSTET (DAS)**	come back	*tsoo-**rook**-komme* **ZURÜCKKOMMEN**
		go	*far-rern* **FAHREN**
near	*in dair **nay**-er fon* **IN DER NÄHE VON**	have	*har-bern* **HABEN**
nearest	***nex**-ster* **NÄCHSTER**	hire	*mee-tern* **MIETEN**
		leave *(things)*	*lass-ern* **LASSEN**
and	*oont* **UND**	light *(fire)*	*mash-ern* **MACHEN**
at	*an* **AN**	do you know	*viss-ern zee* **WISSEN SIE**
by	*by* **BEI**	pitch	*owf-shlar-gurn* **AUFSCHLAGEN**
for	*foor* **FÜR**	stay	*bligh-bern* **BLEIBEN**
from	*fon* **VON**	wash	*vash-ern* **WASCHEN**
in	*in* **IN**		
on	*owf* **AUF**	here	*here* **HIER**
to	*tsoo* **ZU**	there	*dar* **DA**

the charge	*dair price* **DER PREIS**		bicycle	*far-rard* **FAHRRAD**
per	*pro* **PRO**		car	*ow-toh* **AUTO**
night	*narsht* **NACHT**		caravan	*vone-var-gurn* **WOHNWAGEN**
person	*pair-zone* **PERSON**		trailer	*an-henger* **ANHÄNGER**
tent	*tselt* **ZELT**		motorcycle	*moh-tor-rard* **MOTORRAD**
vehicle	*far-tsoyg* **FAHRZEUG**			
			barn	*shoy-ner* **SCHEUNE**
deposit	*an-tsar-loong* **ANZAHLUNG**		camping ground	*cam-ping-plats* **CAMPINGPLATZ**
receipt	*kvit-toong* **QUITTUNG**		farm	*baoo-wern-horf* **BAUERNHOF**
camping carnet	*cum-ping-shine-heft* **CAMPINGSCHEINHEFT**		(farmer)	*baoo-wer* **BAUER**
passport	*pas* **PASS**		field	*vee-zer* **WIESE**
reservation	*rezzair-vee-roong* **RESERVIERUNG**		site (pitch)	*plats* **PLATZ**
name	*nar-mer* **NAME**			
address	*ad-dress-ser* **ADRESSE**			
			clubhouse	*kloob-house* **KLUBHAUS**
a place	*iyn ort* **EIN ORT**		facilities	*iyn-rish-toong-ern* **EINRICHTUNGEN**
anywhere	*eer-goon-tvoh* **IRGENDWO**		a fire	*iyn foy-yer* **EIN FEUER**
away from	*fairn fon* **FERN VON**		freezer	*teef-cool-an-largur* **TIEFKÜHLANLAGE**
			fridge	*cool-shrank* **KÜHLSCHRANK**
quiet	*roo-wig* **RUHIG**		groceries	*lay-berns-mitterl* **LEBENSMITTEL**
sheltered	*gur-shootst* **GESCHÜTZT**		main gate	*howpt-iyn-gang* **HAUPTEINGANG**
alternative	*al-tairna-tee-ver* **ALTERNATIVE**		power supply	*shtrome* **STROM**
quieter	*roo-wigger* **RUHIGER**		security safe	*tray-zor* **TRESOR**
			shop	*lar-dern* **LADEN**
open	*owf* **AUF**		showers	*doo-shern* **DUSCHEN**
closed	*tsoo* **ZU**		tent	*tselt* **ZELT**
			toilets	*twal-let-tern* **TOILETTEN**
before	*for* **VOR**		valuables	*vairt-zash-ern* **WERTSACHEN**
after	*narsh* **NACH**		washroom	*vash-rowm* **WASCHRAUM**
all day	*den gant-sern targ* **DEN GANZEN TAG**		(for dishes)	*foor gur-shair* **FÜR GESCHIRR**
early	*froo* **FRÜH**		water	*vas-ser* **WASSER**
late	*shpayt* **SPÄT**		(drinking water)	*trink-vasser* **TRINKWASSER**

EQUIPMENT	*owss-roo-stoong*
	AUSRÜSTUNG
aluminium	*aloo-min-yoom*
	ALUMINIUM
canvas	*line-vant*
	LEINWAND
paper	*pap-peer*
	PAPIER
plastic	*plar-stick*
	PLASTIK
glass	*glars*
	GLAS
stainless steel	*rost-fryer shtarl*
	ROSTFREIER STAHL
lightweight	*liysht*
	LEICHT
heavy duty	*hosh-liy-stoongs*
	HOCHLEISTUNGS
large	*gross*
	GROSS
small	*kline*
	KLEIN
air mattress	*looft-mattrat-ser*
	LUFTMATRAZE
air pump	*looft-poomper*
	LUFTPUMPE
axe	*ark-st*
	AXT
back pack	*rook-sack*
	RUCKSACK
bottle	*flash-er*
	FLASCHE
bottle opener	*flash-ern-erfner*
	FLASCHENÖFFNER
brush	*boor-ster*
	BÜRSTE
bucket	*iy-mer*
	EIMER
butane gas	*boo-tarn-garz*
	BUTANGAS
camp bed	*felt-bet*
	FELDBETT
can opener	*book-sern-erfner*
	BÜCHSENÖFFNER
candles	*kairt-sern*
	KERZEN
chair	*shtool*
	STUHL
(folding chair)	*clap-shtool*
	KLAPPSTUHL
compass	*kom-pass*
	KOMPASS
corkscrew	*kor-kern-tsee-yer*
	KORKENZIEHER
crockery	*gur-sheer*
	GESCHIRR
cup	*tass-ser*
	TASSE

cutlery	*ber-shteck*
	BESTECK
dehydrated food	*trock-kern-layberns-mit..*
	TROCKENLEBENSMITTEL
first aid kit	*fair-bant-kass-tern*
	VERBANDKASTEN
flask	*flash-er*
	FLASCHE
food box	*pro-vee-arnt-kister*
	PROVIANTKISTE
fork	*gar-berl*
	GABEL
frying pan	*brart-pfanner*
	BRATPFANNE
ground sheet	*tselt-boh-dern*
	ZELTBODEN
guy line	*tselt-shnoor*
	ZELTSCHNUR
hammer	*ham-mer*
	HAMMER
ice bag	*ice-ber-helter*
	EISBEHÄLTER
ice box	*iyz-shrank*
	EISSCHRANK
kerosene	*pay-troh-layum*
	PETROLEUM
kettle	*kess-erl*
	KESSEL
knapsack	*tor-niss-ter*
	TORNISTER
knife	*mess-ser*
	MESSER
lamp	*lam-per*
	LAMPE
light bulb	*gloo-beerner*
	GLÜHBIRNE
mallet	*holts-hammer*
	HOLZHAMMER
matches	*shtrysh-herl-tser*
	STREICHHÖLZER
mattress	*mar-trart-ser*
	MATRATZE
methylated spirits	*bren-shpee-ree-toos*
	BRENNSPIRITUS
mosquito net	*moss-kee-toh-nets*
	MOSKITONETZ
mug	*besh-er*
	BECHER
paraffin	*pet-troh-layoom*
	PETROLEUM
pen knife	*tash-ern-messer*
	TASCHENMESSER
picnic case	*pick-nick-koffer*
	PICKNICKKOFFER
plate	*tel-ler*
	TELLER
pressure cooker	*dampf-kosh-topf*
	DAMPFKOCHTOPF
primus stove	*pree-moos-kosh-er*
	PRIMUSKOCHER
pump	*poom-per*
	PUMPE
rope	*ziyl*
	SEIL

rucksack	*rook-sack* **RUCKSACK**	cheaper	*bill-ligger* **BILLIGER**
saucepan	*kosh-topf* **KOCHTOPF**	better	*bess-er* **BESSER**
saucer	*oonter-tasser* **UNTERTASSE**	bigger	*grur-ser* **GRÖSSER**
scissors	*shay-rer* **SCHERE**	smaller	*kliy-ner* **KLEINER**
screwdriver	*shrow-burn-tsee-her* **SCHRAUBENZIEHER**		
sheath knife	*far-tern-mair-ser* **FAHRTENMESSER**	lighter	*liysh-ter* **LEICHTER**
sleeping bag	*shlarf-zack* **SCHLAFSACK**	heavier duty	*shtair-ker* **STÄRKER**
pace blanket	*al-loo-decker* **ALU-DECKE**		
spoon	*ler-ferl* **LÖFFEL**		
stove	*kosh-er* **KOCHER**		
table	*tish* **TISCH**		
(folding table)	*clap-tish* **KLAPPTISCH**		
teaspoon	*tay-ler-ferl* **TEELÖFFEL**		
tent	*tselt* **ZELT**		
tent peg	*hair-ring* **HERING**		
tent pole	*tselt-shtanger* **ZELTSTANGE**		
thermos flask	*tair-moss-flasher* **THERMOSFLASCHE**		
tin opener	*book-sern-erfner* **BÜCHSENÖFFNER**		
torch	*tash-ern-lamper* **TASCHENLAMPE**		
tool kit	*vairk-tsoyg-kar-stern* **WERKZEUGKASTEN**		
trowel	*hole-shpat-erl* **HOHLSPATEL**		
water carrier	*vass-ser-kannister* **WASSERKANISTER**		

I	*ish* **ICH**	I would like	*ish mersh-ter* **ICH MÖCHTE**
me	*mish* **MICH**	do you want	*vol-ern zee* **WOLLEN SIE**
my	*mine* **ME**		
he	*air* **ER**	I have	*ish har-ber* **ICH HABE**
his	*zine* **SEIN**	he / she has	*air / zee hut* **ER / SEI HAT**
she	*zee* **SIE**	do you have	*har-bern zee* **HABEN SIE**
her	*eeyer* **IHR**		
you	*zee* **SIE**	can I	*kan ish* **KANN ICH**
your	*eeyer* **IHR**	can you	*ker-nen zee* **KÖNNEN SIE**
who	*vair* **WER**		
it	*ess* **ES**	is	*isst* **IST**
them	*zee* **SIE**	are	*zint* **SIND**
		is there	*gipt ess* **GIBT ES**
not	*nisht* **NICHT**	is it	*ist ess* **IST ES**
no	*kine* **KEIN**		
		come back	*tsoo-rook-kommern* **ZURÜCKKOMMEN**
where	*voh* **WO**	have	*har-bern* **HABEN**
when	*van* **WANN**	will be ready	*veert fair-tig* **WIRD FERTIG**
what	*vass* **WAS**	recommend	*emp-fay-lern* **EMPFEHLEN**
what time	*uhm vee-feel ooer* **UM WIEVIEL UHR**	see	*zay-ern* **SEHEN**
		show me	*tsigh-gurn zee meer* **ZEIGEN SIE MIR**
how many	*vee-fee-ler* **WIEVIELE**	take	*nay-mern* **NEHMEN**
how often	*vee oft* **WIE OFT**	tell me	*zar-gurn zee meer* **SAGEN SIE MIR**
how much is (that)	*vass koss-tert (das)* **WAS KOSTET (DAS)**	wait	*var-tern* **WARTEN**
and	*oont* **UND**	nearest	*nex-ster* **NÄCHSTER**
at	*an* **AN**	near	*in dair nay-er fon* **IN DER NÄHE VON**
by	*by* **BEI**	here	*here* **HIER**
for	*foor* **FÜR**		
in	*in* **IN**	open	*owff* **AUF**
on	*owf* **AUF**	closed	*tsoo* **ZU**
to	*tsoo* **ZU**	all night	*mit narsht-deenst* **MIT NACHTDIENST**

prescription	*rayt-**sept*** **REZEPT**	water	*vass-ser* **WASSER**
name	*nar-mer* **NAME**	meals	*marl-tsightern* **MAHLZEITEN**
doctor	*artst* **ARZT**	in morning	*more-gurns* **MORGENS**
dentist	*tsarn-artst* **ZAHNARZT**	at night	*narshts* **NACHTS**
		using toilet	*twal-**let**-ter ber-**noot**-sern* **TOILETTE BENUTZEN**
husband	*man* **MANN**		
wife	*fraoo* **FRAU**	.... times daily	*...marl **tay**-glish* **....MAL TÄGLICH**
friend	*froynt* **FREUND**	swallow whole	*oh-ner tsoo cow-ern shlook-ern* **OHNE ZU KAUEN SCHLUCKEN**
child	*kint* **KIND**		
		SYMPTOMS	*zoomp-**toh**-mer* **SYMPTOME**
some	*et-vars* **ETWAS**	asthma	*ast-mar* **ASTHMA**
something	*et-vars* **ETWAS**	chapped skin	*gur-**shproong**-erner howt* **GESPRUNGENE HAUT**
safe	*zish-er* **SICHER**	(a) cold	*air-kel-toong* **ERKÄLTUNG**
		constipation	*fair-**shtop**-foong* **VERSTOPFUNG**
much	*feel* **VIEL**	cough	*hoo-stern* **HUSTEN**
more	*mair* **MEHR**	diarrhoea	*doorsh-fal* **DURCHFALL**
less	*vay-nigger* **WENIGER**	hay fever	*hoy-shnoop-fern* **HEUSCHNUPFEN**
too	*tsoo* **ZU**	headache	*kopf-shmairt-sern* **KOPFSCHMERZEN**
		indigestion	*mar-gurn-fair-stimmoong* **MAGENVERSTIMMUNG**
(a) temperature	*fee-ber* **FIEBER**	infection	*infektsee-**yown*** **INFEKTION**
high	*hosh* **HOCH**	inflammation	*ent-**soon**-doong* **ENTZÜNDUNG**
low	*teef* **TIEF**	insect bite	*in-**zek**-tern-shtish* **INSEKTENSTICH**
hot	*hice* **HEISS**	itch	*yoo-kern* **JUCKEN**
cold	*kalt* **KALT**	nausea	*oo-berl-kite* **ÜBELKEIT**
		pain	*shmairt-sern* **SCHMERZEN**
STRUCTIONS	*an-viy-zoongern* **ANWEISUNGEN**	rash	*owss-shlarg* **AUSSCHLAG**
dosage	*doh-ziss* **DOSIS**	sunburn	*zon-nern-brant* **SONNENBRAND**
teaspoonfuls	*tay-lurferl* **TEELÖFFEL**	sore throat	*halss-shmairt-sern* **HALSSCHMERZEN**
		stomach ache	*mar-gurn-shmairt-sern* **MAGENSCHMERZEN**
before	*for* **VOR**	(a) temperature	*fee-ber* **FIEBER**
after	*narsh* **NACH**	toothache	*tsarn-shmairt-sern* **ZAHNSCHMERZEN**
with	*mit* **MIT**	travel sickness	*riy-zer-krank-hite* **REISEKRANKHEIT**

wounds & damage: 46   pharmaceuticals & toiletries: overleaf ☞

PHARMA-	*far*-mar-prod-ook-ter
CEUTICALS	**PHARMA-PRODUKTE**
analgesic	*annral-gay-tee-koom*
	ANALGETIKUM
antihistamine	*anti-hissta-meen*
	ANTIHISTAMIN
antiseptic	*anti-zep-tee-koom*
	ANTISEPTIKUM
aspirins	*asspee-ze-nern*
	ASPIRINEN
bandages	*fair-ben-der*
	VERBÄNDE
(crepe)	*ay-lass-tisher*
	ELASTISCHE
(gauze)	*mool*
	MULL
band aids	*heft-pflaster*
	HEFTPFLASTER
calamine	*cal-lammeen*
	CALAMIN
contraceptives	*fair-hoo-toongs-mitterl*
	VERHÜTUNGSMITTEL
(the pill)	*dee pill-ler*
	DIE PILLE
(sheaths)	*con-dom-mer*
	KONDOME
corn plasters	*hoo-ner-owgurn-pflaster*
	HÜHNERAUGENPFLASTER
cotton wool	*vat-ter*
	WATTE
cough drops	*hoo-stern-bonbons*
	HUSTENBONBONS
decongestant	*nar-zern-shpray*
	NASENSPRAY
diabetic lozenges	*deeya-bay-ticker-pastillern*
	DIABETIKERPASTILLEN
disinfectant	*day-zinfect-see-yowns-mitterl*
	DESINFEKTIONSMITTEL
ear drops	*or-rern-trop-fern*
	OHRENTROPFEN
elastoplast	*heft-pflaster*
	HEFTPFLASTER
eye drops	*ow-gurn-trop-fern*
	AUGENTROPFEN
gargle	*goor-gurl-vasser*
	GURGELWASSER
gauze	*fair-bant-mool*
	VERBANDMULL
insect repellent	*in-zeck-tern-shoots-mitterl*
	INSEKTENSCHUTZMITTEL
insulin	*inzoo-leen*
	INSULIN
iodine	*yoht*
	JOD
laxative	*ap-foor-mitterl*
	ABFÜHRMITTEL
medicine	*maydee-kar-ment*
	MEDIKAMENT
mouthwash	*moont-vasser*
	MUNDWASSER
sedative	*ber-roo-igoongs-mitterl*
	BERUHIGUNGSMITTEL
sleeping pills	*shlarf-tab-lettern*
	SCHLAFTABLETTEN

thermometer	*tair-moh-may-te*
	THERMOMETER
throat lozenges	*halss-pastillern*
	HALSPASTILLEN
vitamins	*veeta-mee-nern*
	VITAMINEN

FORM OF	*dar-riysh-oongs*
MEDICINES	*formern*
	DARREICHUN•
	FORMEN
capsules	*kap-zerln*
	KAPSELN
cream	*kraym*
	CREME
drops	*trop-fern*
	TROPFEN
lozenges	*pas-tillern*
	PASTILLEN
lotion	*loatsee-yown*
	LOTION
ointment	*zal-ber*
	SALBE
powder	*poo-der*
	PUDER
suppositories	*tsepf-shyern*
	ZÄPFCHEN
tablets	*tab-let-tern*
	TABLETTEN
tonic	*toh-nickoom*
	TONIKUM

HAIR	*har-pflay-gur*
CARE	**HAARPFLEGE**
brush	*boor-ster*
	BÜRSTE
comb	*kamm*
	KAMM
curlers	*lock-ern-vickler*
	LOCKENWICKLER
hair dye	*har-fair-ber-mitt*
	HAARFÄRBEMITTEL
hair grips	*har-clammern*
	HAARKLAMMERN
hair lacquer	*har-lack*
	HAARLACK
hair oil	*har-rurl*
	HAARÖL
hair pins	*har-nar-derln*
	HAARNADELN
rollers	*lock-ern-vickler*
	LOCKENWICKLER
scissors	*shay-rer*
	SCHERE
setting lotion	*har-festigger*
	HAARFESTIGER
shampoo	*sham-poo*
	SHAMPOO
tint	*tur-noongs-mitter*
	TÖNUNGSMITTEL

English	Pronunciation	German
TOILETRIES	*twal-let-tern-artickerl*	**TOILETTENARTIKEL**
aftershave	*ra-zeer-vasser*	**RASIERWASSER**
astringent	*ard-string-erns*	**ADSTRINGENS**
bath salts	*bar-der-zalts*	**BADESALZ**
bib	*lets-shern*	**LÄTZCHEN**
cleansing cream	*riy-niggoongs-craym*	**REINIGUNGSCREME**
cologne	*curl-nish-vasser*	**KÖLNSCHWASSER**
cuticle cream	*nar-gurl-howt-craym*	**NAGELHAUTCREME**
cuticle remover	*nar-gurl-howt-ent-fairner*	**NAGELHAUTENTFERNER**
deodorant	*dayzo-doh-rans*	**DESODORANS**
emery board	*zant-pap-peer-fiy-ler*	**SANDPAPIERFEILE**
eye liner	*leed-shtift*	**LIDSTIFT**
eye pencil	*ow-gurn-browern-shtift*	**AUGENBRAUENSTIFT**
eye shadow	*leet-shattern*	**LIDSCHATTEN**
face powder	*gur-ziyshts-pooder*	**GESICHTSPUDER**
foot cream	*fooss-craym*	**FUSSCREME**
foot powder	*fooss-pooder*	**FUSSPUDER**
foundation cream	*groon-dee-roongs-craym*	**GRUNDIERUNGSCREME**
hand cream	*hant-craym*	**HANDCREME**
hand lotion	*hant-loatsee-yoan*	**HANDLOTION**
lipsalve	*lip-ern-pom-marder*	**LIPPENPOMADE**
lipstick	*lip-pern-shtift*	**LIPPENSTIFT**
make-up rem. pads	*ap-shmink-vatter*	**ABSCHMINKWATTE**
mascara	*vim-pern-toosher*	**WIMPERNTUSCHE**
mirror	*shpee-gurl*	**SPIEGEL**
moisturiser	*foysh-tig-kites-craym*	**FEUCHTIGKEITSCREME**
nail brush	*nar-gurl-boor-ster*	**NAGELBÜRSTE**
nail clippers	*nar-gurl-tsanger*	**NAGELZANGE**
nail file	*nar-gurl-fiyler*	**NAGELFEILE**
nail polish	*nar-gurl-lack*	**NAGELLACK**
polish remover	*nar-gurl-lackent-fairner*	**NAGELLACKENTFERNER**
nail scissors	*nar-gurl-share-rer*	**NAGELSCHERE**
nail varnish	*nar-gurl-lack*	**NAGELLACK**
nail varnish rem.	*nar-gurlack-entfairner*	**NAGELLACKENTFERNER**
nappies	*vin-derln*	**WINDELN**
(disposable nappies)	*pap-peer-vin-derln*	**PAPIERWINDELN**
night cream	*narsht-craym*	**NACHTCREME**
perfume	*par-foom*	**PARFÜM**
plastic pants	*plass-tik-hur-shern*	**PLASTIKHÖSCHEN**
powder	*poo-der*	**PUDER**
pumice	*bim-shtiyn*	**BIMSSTEIN**
razor	*ra-zeer-appar-rart*	**RASIERAPPARAT**
razor blades	*ra-zeer-clingern*	**RASIERKLINGEN**
rouge	*rouge*	**ROUGE**
safety pins	*sish-er-heights-naderln*	**SICHERHEITSNADELN**
sanitary towels	*dar-mern-binnder*	**DAMENBINDE**
shaving brush	*rah-zeer-pinzerl*	**RASIERPINSEL**
shaving cream	*ra-zeer-craym*	**RASIERCREME**
soap	*ziy-fer*	**SEIFE**
sponge	*shvamm*	**SCHWAMM**
sunglasses	*zon-nern-briller*	**SONNENBRILLE**
suntan cream	*zon-nern-craym*	**SONNENCREME**
suntan oil	*zon-nern-erl*	**SONNENÖL**
(mild)	*mit nee-drig-em shoots*	**MIT NIEDRIGEM SCHUTZ**
(medium)	*mit mit-ler-room shoots*	**MIT MITTLEREM SCHUTZ**
(strong)	*mit hoe-oom shoots*	**MIT HOHEM SCHUTZ**
talcum powder	*tal-koom-pooder*	**TALKUMPUDER**
tampons	*bin-dern*	**BINDEN**
tissues	*pa-peer-tooshyer*	**PAPIERTÜCHER**
toilet paper	*twal-let-tern-pappeer*	**TOILETTENPAPIER**
toilet water	*twal-let-tern-vasser*	**TOILETTENWASSER**
toothbrush	*tsarn-boorster*	**ZAHNBÜRSTE**
toothpaste	*tsarn-paster*	**ZAHNPASTA**
tweezers	*pin-tset-ter*	**PINZETTE**

I	*ish* **ICH**		I would like	*ish* **mersh**-ter **ICH MÖCHTE**
my	*mine* **MEIN**		we would like	veer **mersh**-tern **WIR MÖCHTEN**
we	*veer* **WIR**		do you want	*vol-ern zee* **WOLLEN SIE**
our	***oon**-ser* **UNSER**			
you	*zee* **SIE**		I have	*ish* **har**-ber **ICH HABE**
your	*eeyer* **IHR**		we have	*veer* **har**-bern **WIR HABEN**
it	*ess* **ES**		do you have	**har**-bern *zee* **HABEN SIE**
them	*zee* **SIE**			
			can I	*kan ish* **KANN ICH**
not	*nisht* **NICHT**		can we	***ker**-nen veer* **KÖNNEN WIR**
no	*kine* **KEIN**		can you	***ker**-nen zee* **KÖNNEN SIE**
where	*voh* **WO**		is	*isst* **IST**
when	*van* **WANN**		are	*zint* **SIND**
what	*vass* **WAS**		is there	*gipt ess* **GIBT ES**
what time	*uhm* vee-**feel** *ooer* **UM WIEVIEL UHR**		is it	*ist ess* **IST ES**
how long	*vee* **lang**-er **WIE LANGE**		clean	*riy-niggern* **REINIGEN**
how much is (that)	*vass* **koss**-tert *(das)* **WAS KOSTET (DAS)**		do	*mash-ern* **MACHEN**
			dryclean	*shay-mish riy-nigger* **CHEMISCH REINIGEN**
nearest	**nex**-ster **NÄCHSTER**		have	*har-bern* **HABEN**
near	*in dair* **nay**-er *fon* **IN DER NAHE VON**		iron	*boo-gurln* **BÜGELN**
here	*here* **HIER**		patch	*flick-ern* **FLICKEN**
			pay	*tsar-lern* **ZAHLEN**
and	*oont* **UND**		press	*boo-gurln* **BÜGELN**
at	*an* **AN**		will be ready	*veert* **fair**-tig **WIRD FERTIG**
for	*foor* **FÜR**		remove	*ent-**fair**-nern* **ENTFERNEN**
from	*fon* **VON**		repair	*reppar-**ree**-rern* **REPARIEREN**
in	*in* **IN**		sew	**an**-nay-ern **ANNÄHEN**
on	*owf* **AUF**		stitch	*nay-ern* **NÄHEN**
to	*tsoo* **ZU**		wash	*vash-ern* **WASCHEN**
with	*mit* **MIT**		will take	*nimmt* **NIMMT**

this	*dee*-zer	**CLOTHES**	*kliy-doong*
	DIESER		**KLEIDUNG**
these	*dee*-zer	cleaners	*riy-niggoong*
	DIESE		**REINIGUNG**
		dry-cleaners	*shay-misher riy-niggoong*
			CHEMISCHE REINIGUNG
new	*noy*	tailor	*shniy-der*
	NEU		**SCHNEIDER**
placement	*air-zats*		
	ERSATZ		
		cleaned	*gur-riy-neesht*
			GEREINIGT
open	*owff*	dry-cleaned	*shay-mish gur-riy-neesht*
	AUF		**CHEMISCH GEREINIGT**
closed	*tsoo*	ironed	*boo-gurln*
	ZU		**BÜGELN**
		invisible mending	*koonst-shtop-fern*
			KUNSTSTOPFEN
now	*yetst*	repaired	*ray-par-reert*
	JETZT		**REPARIERT**
quickly	*shnell*		
	SCHNELL		
soon	*balt*	fabric	*shtoff*
	BALD		**STOFF**
sooner	*froo-er*	(non-iron)	*boo-gurl-fry*
	FRÜHER		**BÜGELFREI**
		button	*knopf*
			KNOPF
before	*for*	patch	*flick-ern*
	VOR		**FLICKEN**
after	*narsh*		
	NACH		
		grease	*fet*
			FETT
today	*hoy-ter*	hole	*losh*
	HEUTE		**LOCH**
tomorrow	*more-gurn*	stain	*fleck*
	MORGERN		**FLECK**
morning	*for-mittarg*	tear	*riss*
	VORMITTAG		**RISS**
midday	*mit-targ*	worn	*fair-shliss-ern*
	MITTAG		**VERSCHLISSEN**
afternoon	*narsh-mittarg*		
	NACHMITTAG		
evening	*ar-bent*	needle	*nar-derl*
	ABEND		**NADEL**
		thread	*garn*
			GARN
		soap powder	*vash-poolver*
			WASCHPULVER
deposit	*an-tsarloong*		
	ANZAHLUNG		
receipt	*kvit-toong*	**SHOES**	*shoo-er*
	QUITTUNG		**SCHUHE**
on my bill	*das gayt owf my-ner*	shoe repairer	*shoe-masher*
	resh-noong		**SCHUHMACHER**
	DAS GEHT AUF MEINE	boots	*shtee-ferl*
	RECHNUNG		**STIEFEL**
		sandals	*zan-dar-lern*
			SANDALEN
room	*tsim-mer*	heel	*ap-zet-ser*
	ZIMMER		**ABSÄTZE**
number	*noo-mer*	sole	*zoh-lern*
	NUMMER		**SOHLEN**

I	*ish* ICH	I would like	*ish mersh-ter* ICH MÖCHTE
my	*mine* MEIN	we would like	*veer mersh-tern* WIR MÖCHTEN
we	*veer* WIR	do you want	*vol-ern zee* WOLLEN SIE
our	*oon-ser* UNSER		
you	*zee* SIE	I have	*ish har-ber* ICH HABE
your	*eeyer* IHR	we have	*veer har-bern* WIR HABEN
it	*ess* ESS	do you have	*har-bern zee* HABEN SIE
them	*zee* SIE		
		can I	*kan ish* KANN ICH
not	*nisht* NICHT	can we	*ker-nen veer* KÖNNEN WIR
no	*kine* KEIN	can you	*ker-nen zee* KÖNNEN SIE
which	*vel-shyer* WELCHER	is	*isst* IST
where	*voh* WO	are	*zint* SIND
when	*van* WANN	is there	*gipt ess* GIBT ES
what	*vass* WAS	is it	*ist ess* IST ES
what time	*uhm vee-feel ooer* UM WIEVIEL UHR		
		alter	*en-dern* ÄNDERN
how long	*vee lang-er* WIE LANGE	have	*har-bern* HABEN
how many	*vee-fee-ler* WIEVIELE	help me	*hel-fern zee meer* HELFEN SIE MIR
how much is (that)	*vass koss-tert (das)* WAS KOSTET (DAS)	like	*mer-gurn* MÖGEN
		measure	*mess-ern* MESSEN
near	*in dair nay-er fon* IN DER NÄHE VON	will be ready	*veerd fair-tig* WIRD FERTIG
here	*here* HIER	return *(things)*	*tsoo-rook-nay-mern* ZURÜCKNEHMEN
		see	*zay-ern* SEHEN
and	*oont* UND	send	*shick-ern* SCHICKEN
at	*an* AN	try on	*an-pro-beer-ern* ANPROBIEREN
for	*foor* FÜR		
from	*fon* VON	each	*yay* JE
in	*in* IN	per metre	*pro may-ter* PRO METER
on	*owf* AUF	receipt	*kvit-toong* QUITTUNG
to	*tsoo* ZU	refund	*tsoo-rook-air-shat-to•* ZURÜCKERSTATTUNG

something	*et-vars* **ETWAS**	top	*oh-bern* **OBEN**
		bottom	*oon-tern* **UNTEN**
simple	*iyn-fash* **EINFACH**	middle	*mit-ter* **MITTE**
similar	*ayn-lish* **ÄHNLICH**	side	*zigh-ter* **SEITE**
same	*gliysh* **GLEICH**		
different	*an-ders* **ANDERS**	cheaper	*bill-ligger* **BILLIGER**
matching	*pas-sernt* **PASSEND**	better	*bess-er* **BESSER**
		more	*mair* **MEHR**
expensive	*price-goonstig* **PREISGÜNSTIG**	less	*vay-nigger* **WENIGER**
od quality	*ho-er kval-lee-tate* **HOHE QUALITÄT**		
		larger	*groor-ser* **GRÖSSER**
small	*kline* **KLEIN**	smaller	*kliy-ner* **KLEINER**
medium	*mit-terl-gross* **MITTELGROSS**	wider	*brigh-ter* **BREITER**
large	*gross* **GROSS**	narrower	*shmar-ler* **SCHMALER**
wide	*brite* **BREIT**	longer	*leng-er* **LÄNGER**
narrow	*eng* **ENG**	shorter	*koort-ser* **KÜRZER**
long	*lang* **LANG**		
short	*koorts* **KURZ**	hand-made	*hant-ar-bight* **HANDARBEIT**
		made in this country	*heer-tsoolander hair-gurshtelt* **HIERZULANDE HERGESTELLT**
thick	*dick* **DICK**		
thin	*doon* **DÜNN**	display case	*vee-tree-ner* **VITRINE**
loose	*lock-er* **LOCKER**	fitting room	*oom-kliyder-cab-beener* **UMKLEIDEKABINE**
tight	*eng* **ENG**	mirror	*shpee-gurl* **SPIEGEL**
ightweight	*liysht* **LEICHT**	shop window	*shaoo-fenster* **SCHAUFENSTER**
light	*hell* **HELL**	department store	*var-rern-house* **WARENHAUS**
dark	*doong-kerl* **DUNKEL**	draper	*tex-teel-gur-sheft* **TEXTILGESCHÄFT**
colour	*far-ber* **FARBE**	menswear shop	*hair-rern-ber-kliydoongs-gur-sheft* **HERREN-BEKLEIDUNGSGESCHÄFT**
fabric	*shtoff* **STOFF**	shoe shop	*shoe-gur-sheft* **SCHUHGESCHÄFT**
size	*grur-ser* **GRÖSSE**	womens' shop	*dar-mern-berkliydoongs-gursheft* **DAMEN-BEKLEIDUNGSGESCHÄFT**
style	*shteel* **STIL**		

abrics & colours: 28 ☞   sizes: 29 ☞   clothes & accessories: overleaf ☞

men's	*hair*-rern
	HERREN–
women's	*dar*-mern
	DAMEN–
boy's	*yoon*-gurn
	JUNGEN–
girl's	*maid*-<u>shey</u>rn
	MÄDCHEN–
baby's	*baby*
	BABY–

CLOTHES	*kliy*-doong
	KLEIDUNG
anorak	*an*-norrak
	ANORAK
bath robe	*bar*-der-manterl
	BADEMANTEL
bathing cap	*bar*-der-capper
	BADEKAPPE
belt	*goor*-tel
	GÜRTEL
bikini	*bikini*
	BIKINI
blouse	*bloo*-zer
	BLUSE
boots	*shtee*-ferln
	STIEFELN
bow tie	*flee*-gur
	FLIEGE
bra	*booss*-tern-hal-ter
	BÜSTENHALTER
braces	*ho*-zern-traygur
	HOSENTRÄGER
briefs	*slip*
	SLIP
button	*knopf*
	KNOPF
cap	*moot*-ser
	MÜTZE
cape	*oom*-hang
	UMHANG
cardigan	*shtrick*-yacker
	STRICKJACKE
coat	*man*-terl
	MANTEL
dinner jacket	*smoking*
	SMOKING
dress	*klight*
	KLEID
dressing gown	*shlarf*-rock
	SCHLAFROCK
evening dress	*ar*-bent-klight
	ABENDKLEID
flip flops	*goo*-mee-latchern
	GUMMILATSCHEN
frock	*klight*
	KLEID
girdle	*hooft*-hal-ter
	HÜFTHALTER
gloves	*hant*-shoo-er
	HANDSCHUHE

handbag	*hant*-tasher
	HANDTASCHE
handkerchief	*tash*-ern-too<u>sh</u>
	TASCHENTUCH
hat	*hoot*
	HUT
jacket	*yack*-er
	JACKE
jeans	*jeans*-hozer
	JEANS-HOSE
jersey	*pull-oh*-ver
	PULLOVER
negligé	*negligé*
	NEGLIGE
nightdress	*nar<u>sht</u>*-hemt
	NACHTHEMD
overalls	*ar*-bights-antsoog
	ARBEITSANZUG
overcoat	*man*-terl
	MANTEL
panties	*shloop*-fer
	SCHLÜPFER
panty girdle	*shtroomf*-hal-ter-hers-<u>she</u>
	STRUMPFHALTERHÖSCHEN
panty hose	*shtroomf*-hozer
	STRUMPFHOSE
petticoat	*oon*-ter-rock
	UNTERROCK
pullover	*pull-oh*-ver
	PULLOVER
purse	*gelt*-boyterl
	GELDBEÜTEL
pyjamas	*shlarf*-antsoog
	SCHLAFANZUG
raincoat	*ray*-gurn-manterl
	REGENMANTEL
sandals	*zan-dar*-lern
	SANDALEN
scarf	*halss*-too<u>sh</u>
	HALSTUCH
shirt	*hemt*
	HEMD
shoes	*shoo*-er
	SCHUHE
short sleeved shirt	*koorts*-airmer-lishes-hemt
	KURZÄRMELIGES HEMD
shorts	*shorts*
	SHORTS
skirt	*rock*
	ROCK
slip	*oon*-ter-rock
	UNTERROCK
slippers	*house*-shoo-er
	HAUSSCHUHE
socks	*zock*-ern
	SOCKEN
sports jacket	*shport*-yacker
	SPORTJACKE
stockings	*shtroom*-pfer
	STRÜMPFE
suit (man's)	*an*-tsoog
	ANZUG
suit (woman's)	*koss-toom*
	KOSTÜM

cosmetics: 20-21

sweater	*pull-**oh**-ver*	
	PULLOVER	
sweatshirt	*sweatshirt*	
	SWEATSHIRT	
swimsuit	*bar-der-antsoog*	
	BADEANZUG	
imming trunks	*bar-der-hozer*	
	BADEHOSE	
tennis shoes	*ten-nis-shoo-er*	
	TENNISSCHUHE	
tie	*kra-**vat**-ter*	
	KRAWATTE	
tights	*stroompf-hozer*	
	STRUMPFHOSE	
towel	*hant-too**sh***	
	HANDTUCH	
track suit	***train**-nings-antsoog*	
	TRAININGSANZUG	
trainers	*shport-shoo-er*	
	SPORTSCHUHE	
trousers	*ho-zer*	
	HOSE	
T shirt	*T-shirt*	
	T-SHIRT	
underpants	*oon-ter-hozer*	
	UNTERHOSE	
vest	*oon-ter-hemt*	
	UNTERHEMD	

CLEANING	*riy-nee-goongs-met-toh-der*	
METHOD	**REINIGUNGSMETHODE**	
dryclean only	*noor **shay**-mish riy-niggern*	
	NUR CHEMISCH REINIGEN	
hand wash only	*noor hant-vesher*	
	NUR HANDWÄSCHE	
non-iron	*boo-gurl-fry*	
	BÜGELFREI	

ACCESSORIES *tsoo-ber-her*
ZUBEHÖR

bangle	***arm**-riyff*	
	ARMREIF	
beads	*pair-lern-shnoor*	
	PERLENSCHNUR	
belt	*goor-terl*	
	GÜRTEL	
bracelet	***arm**-bant*	
	ARMBAND	
braces	*hozen-tray-gur*	
	HOSENTRÄGER	
brooch	*brosh-er*	
	BROSCHE	
buckle	*shnal-ler*	
	SCHNALLE	
button	*knopf*	
	KNOPF	
chain	*ket-**shyern***	
	KETTCHEN	
charm	*amoo-**let***	
	AMULETT	
clip	*tsvick-er*	
	ZWICKE	
cuffs	*man-**shet**-tern*	
	MANSCHETTEN	
cuff links	*man-**shet**-tern-knerp-fer*	
	MANSCHETTENKNÖPFE	
earings	*or-ringer*	
	OHRRINGE	
elastic	*goo-mee-tsoog*	
	GUMMIZUG	
handbag	*hant-tasher*	
	HANDTASCHE	
necklace	*hals-ketter*	
	HALSKETTE	
pendant	*an-henger*	
	ANHÄNGER	
pin	***an**-shteck-nardel*	
	ANSTECKNADEL	
pocket	*tash-er*	
	TASCHE	
purse	*gelt-boyterl*	
	GELDBEUTEL	
ring	*ring*	
	RING	
shoe brush	*shoo-boor-ster*	
	SCHUHBÜRSTE	
shoe cream	*shoo-kraym*	
	SCHUHKREM	
shoe laces	*shnoor-zenkerl*	
	SCHNÜRSENKEL	
shoe polish	*shoe-kraym*	
	SCHUHCREME	
strap	*ree-men*	
	RIEMEN	
sunglasses	*zon-ern-brill-er*	
	SONNENBRILLE	
umbrella	*ray-gurn-sheerm*	
	REGENSCHIRM	
wallet	*breef-tasher*	
	BRIEFTASCHE	
zip	*rice-fair-shlooss*	
	REISSVERSCHLUSS	

with	*mit*	
	MIT	
without	*oh-ner*	
	OHNE	

FABRIC	*shtoff*	COLOUR	*far-ber*
	STOFF		**FARBE**
chiffon	*chif-fon*	beige	*beige*
	CHIFFON		**BEIGE**
corduroy	*kord*	black	*shvarts*
	KORD		**SCHWARZ**
cotton	***baooom***-*voller*	blue	*blaoo*
	BAUMWOLLE		**BLAU**
crepe	*krep*	brown	*brown*
	KREPP		**BRAUN**
denim	***drill***-*li__sh__ jeans*	cream	*kraym*
	DRILLICH, JEANS		**CREME**
felt	*filts*	crimson	*kar-__meen__-rowt*
	FILZ		**KARMINROT**
flannel	*fla-__nell__*	emerald	*smah-__ragd__-groon*
	FLANELL		**SMARAGDGRÜN**
fur	*pelts*	fawn	***hell***-*brown*
	PELZ		**HELLBRAUN**
gabardine	***gab***-*ardeen*	gold	***gol***-*dern*
	GABARDINE		**GOLDEN**
lace	***shpit***-*ser*	green	*groon*
	SPITZE		**GRÜN**
leather	***lay***-*der*	grey	*graoo*
	LEDER		**GRAU**
linen	***liy***-*nern*	mauve	***lee***-*lar*
	LEINEN		**LILA**
needlecord	***fine***-*cort*	orange	*or-__ran__-jern-farbern*
	FEINKORD		**ORANGENFARBEN**
nylon	*nylon*	pink	*ro-zar*
	NYLON		**ROSA**
polyester	*polloo-__ess__-ter*	purple	***poor***-*poor-roat*
	POLYESTER		**PURPURROT**
poplin	*popper-__leen__*	red	*roat*
	POPELINE		**ROT**
rubber	***goo***-*mee*	silver	*zil-bern*
	GUMMI		**SILBERN**
satin	*sa-__teen__*	tan	***gelp***-*brown*
	SATIN		**GELBBRAUN**
silk	***ziy***-*der*	turquoise	*toor-__keess__-farbern*
	SEIDE		**TÜRKISFARBEN**
serge	*serge*	white	*viyss*
	SERGE		**WEISS**
suede	***vilt***-*layder*	yellow	*gelp*
	WILDLEDER		**GELB**
terrytowelling	*frot-__tay__*		
	FROTTEE		
terylene	*terry-__layn__*	too	*tsoo*
	TERYLENE		**ZU**
tweed	*tveet*	bright	*hell*
	TWEED		**HELL**
velvet	*zamt*	dull	***far***-*der*
	SAMT		**FADE**
wool	***vol***-*ler*		
	WOLLE		
worsted	***kam***-*garn*	plain	*oo-nee*
	KAMMGARN		**UNI**
		patterned	*gur-__mooss__-tert*
			GEMUSTERT
artificial	*zoon-__tay__-ti__sh__*	spotted	***poonk***-*ter*
	SYNTHETISCH		**PUNKTE**
crease resistant	***knitter***-*fry*	check	*kah-__reert__*
	KNITTERFREI		**KARIERT**
wash & wear	***boo***-*gurl-fry*	striped	***shtrigh***-*fern*
	BÜGELFREI		**STREIFEN**

SIZES

Because imperial and metric sizes do not all exactly coincide, these sizes are only near equivalents.

Dresses Suits Trousers Jackets - *Ladies*

GB	32	34	36	38	40	42
USA	10	12	14	16	18	20
Metric	38	40	42	44	46	48

Stockings -*Ladies*

B / USA	8	8½	9	9½	10	10½
Metric	0	1	2	3	4	5

Sweaters - *Ladies*

B / USA	32	34	36	38	40	42
Metric	36	38	40	42	44	46

Hats - *Ladies & Mens*

GB	6⅝	6¾	6⅞	7	7⅛	7¼	7⅜	7½	7⅝
USA	6¾	6⅞	7	7⅛	7¼	7⅜	7½	7⅝	7¾
Metric	54	55	56	57	58	59	60	61	62

Shoes - *Ladies & Mens*

GB	4	4½	5	5½	6	6½	7	7½	8	8½	9	10	11
USA	5½	6	6½	7	7½	8	8½	9	9½	10	10½	11½	12½
Metric	36½		38		39		41		42		43	44	45

Socks - *Ladies & Mens*

B / USA	9½	10	10½	11	11½
Metric	38-39	39-40	40-41	41-42	42-43

Suits & Overcoats - *Mens*

B / USA	36	38	40	42	44	46
Metric	46	48	50	52	54	56

Shirts - *Mens*

B / USA	14	14½	15	15½	16	16½	17
Metric	36	37	38	39	41	42	43

General measurements

inches	24	26	28	30	32	34	36	38	40	42	44	46	48
centimetres	61	66	71	76	81	86	91	96	101	106	111	117	121

other conversion tables: 138

I	*ish* **ICH**	I would like	*ish* **mersh**-ter **ICH MÖCHTE**
my	*mine* **MEIN**	we would like	*veer* **mersh**-tern **WIR MÖCHTEN**
we	*veer* **WIR**	do you want	*vol-ern zee* **WOLLEN SIE**
our	*oon-ser* **UNSER**		
you	*zee* **SIE**	I have	*ish* **har**-ber **ICH HABE**
your	*eeyer* **IHR**	we have	*veer* **har**-bern **WIR HABEN**
it	*ess* **ES**	do you have	*har-bern zee* **HABEN SIE**
they	*zee* **SIE**		
		can I	*kan ish* **KANN ICH**
not	*nisht* **NICHT**	can we	*ker-nen veer* **KÖNNEN WIR**
no	*kine* **KEIN**	can you	*ker-nen zee* **KÖNNEN SIE**
which	*vel-shyer* **WELCHER**	am	*bin* **BIN**
where	*voh* **WO**	is	*isst* **IST**
when	*van* **WANN**	are	*zint* **SIND**
what	*vass* **WAS**	is there	*gipt ess* **GIBT ES**
what time	*uhm vee-feel ooer* **UM WIEVIEL UHR**	is it	*ist ess* **IST ES**
how long	*vee lang-er* **WIE LANGE**	was born	*gur-bor-rern* **GEBOREN**
how many	*vee-fee-ler* **WIEVIELE**	come back	*tsoo-rook-kommerr* **ZURÜCKKOMMEN**
how much is (that)	*vass koss-tert (das)* **WAS KOSTET (DAS)**	come from	*shtam-mern owss* **STAMMEN AUS**
		go	*far-rern* **FAHREN**
near	*in dair nay-er fon* **IN DER NÄHE VON**	have	*har-bern* **HABEN**
		like	*mur-gurn* **MÖGEN**
at	*an* **AN**	live	*voh-nern* **WOHNEN**
by	*by* **BEI**	stay	*bligh-bern* **BLEIBEN**
for	*foor* **FÜR**	study	*shtoo-dee-rern* **STUDIEREN**
from	*fon* **VON**	visit	*ber-zoosh-ern* **BESUCHEN**
in	*in* **IN**	work	*ar-bight-ern* **ARBEITEN**
on	*owf* **AUF**		
to	*narsh* **NACH**	here	*here* **HIER**
with	*mit* **MIT**	there	*dar* **DA**

name	*nar*-mer **NAME**	near	*in dair **nay**-er fon* **IN DER NÄHE VON**
address	*ad-**dress**-ser* **ADRESSE**	nearest	*nex*-ster **NÄCHSTER**
		meters	*may*-ter **METER**
family	*fa-**meel**-yer* **FAMILIE**	kilometres	*keelo-**may**-ter* **KILOMETER**
friend	*froynt* **FREUND**		
friends	*froyn*-der **FREUNDE**	large	*growss* **GROSS**
relations	*fair-**van**-ter* **VERWANDTE**	small	*kline* **KLEIN**
		medium sized	*mit*-terl-growss **MITTELGROSS**
home	*tsoo **how**-zer* **ZU HAUSE**		
place	*ort* **ORT**	flat	*voh*-noong **WOHNUNG**
		house	*house* **HAUS**
business	*gur-**sheft*** **GESCHÄFT**	campus	*cam*-pooss **CAMPUS**
tour	*toor* **TOUR**		
vacation	*oor*-laoob **URLAUB**	city	*shtat* **STADT**
		coast	*koo*-ster **KÜSTE**
studying	*shtoo*-dyum **STUDIUM**	country	*lant* **LAND**
visiting	*owf ber-**zoosh*** **AUF BESUCH**	countryside	*lend*-lisher **gay**-gunt **LÄNDLICHE GEGEND**
working	*im ber-**roof*** **IM BERUF**	suburb	*for*-ort **VORORT**
		town	*shtat* **STADT**
before	*for* **VOR**	village	*dorf* **DORF**
now	*yetst* **JETZT**		
during	*vair*-runt **WÄHREND**	north	*nort* **NORD**
after	*narsh* **NACH**	south	*zood* **SÜD**
		east	*ost* **OST**
perhaps	*fee-**liysht*** **VIELLEICHT**	west	*vest* **WEST**
a few	*iyn par* **EIN PAAR**		
more	*mair* **MEHR**	very	*zair* **SEHR**
days	*tar*-gur **TAGE**	beautiful	*shern* **SCHÖN**
weeks	*vosh*-ern **WOCHEN**	busy	*gur-**shef**-tig* **GESCHÄFTIG**
months	*moh*-natter **MONATE**	industrial	*in-dooss-**tree*** **INDUSTRIE**
years	*yar*-rer **JAHRE**	noisy	*lowt* **LAUT**
		quiet	*roo*-wig **RUHIG**

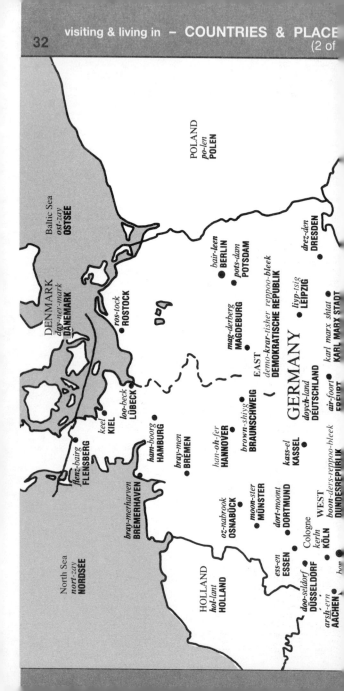

POLAND
po-len
POLEN

Baltic Sea
ost-zay
OSTSEE

DENMARK
day-ner-mark
DÄNEMARK

bair-leen
● **BERLIN**

pots-dam
POTSDAM

ros-tock
● **ROSTOCK**

mag-derberg
● **MAGDEBURG**

demo-krar-tisher reppoo-bleek
DEMOKRATISCHE REPUBLIK

drez-den
DRESDEN

liyp-tsig
● **LEIPZIG**

EAST

keel
● **KIEL**

loo-beck
● **LÜBECK**

brown-shiyg
● **BRAUNSCHWEIG**

GERMANY
doych-land
DEUTSCHLAND

karl marx shtat
● **KARL MARX STADT**

air-foort
● **ERFURT**

flenz-bairg
FLENSBERG

ham-boorg
● **HAMBURG**

bray-men
● **BREMEN**

han-oh-fer
HANNOVER

kass-el
● **KASSEL**

bray-merharven
BREMERHAVEN

North Sea
nort-zay
NORDSEE

oz-nabrook
● **OSNABRÜCK**

moon-ster
● **MÜNSTER**

dort-moont
● **DORTMUND**

WEST

Cologne
kerln
● **KÖLN**

boon-ders-reppoo-bleek
BUNDESREPUBLIK

ess-en
● **ESSEN**

HOLLAND
hol-lant
HOLLAND

doo-seldorf
● **DÜSSELDORF**

arsh-ern
● **AACHEN**

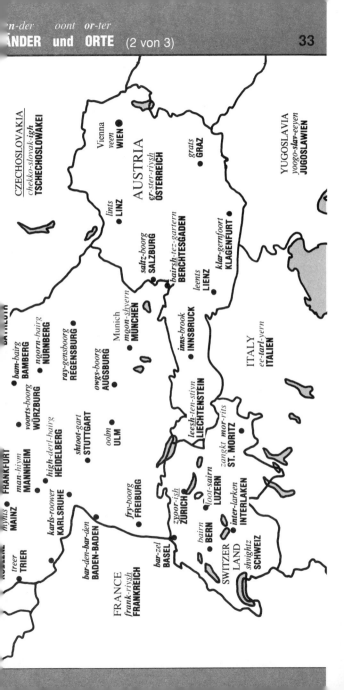

CZECHOSLOVAKIA
chekko-slovak-igh
TSCHECHOSLOWAKEI

Vienna
veen
WIEN ●

AUSTRIA
er-ster-riysh
ÖSTERREICH

grats
GRAZ ●

YUGOSLAVIA
yoogo-slav-eeyen
JUGOSLAWIEN

lints
LINZ ●

saltz-boorg
SALZBURG

hairsh-te-gartern
BERCHTESGADEN

klar-gernfoort
KLAGENFURT ●

leents
LIENZ ●

bam-bairg
● **BAMBERG**

ngorn-bairg
NÜRNBERG ●

ray-gensboorg
REGENSBURG ●

Munich
moon-shyern
MÜNCHEN ●

inns-brook
● **INNSBRUCK**

owgs-boorg
AUGSBURG ●

ITALY
ee-tarl-yern
ITALIEN

voorts-boorg
WÜRZBURG ●

FRANKFURT

man-hiym
MANNHEIM ●

high-derl-bairg
HEIDELBERG ●

shtoot-gart
● **STUTTGART**

oolm
● **ULM**

leesh-ten-stiyn
LIECHTENSTEIN

mor-rits
ST. MORITZ ●

mynts
MAINZ ●

karls-roower
KARLSRUHE ●

fry-boorg
FREIBURG ●

zyoor-ish
ZÜRICH ●

loot-sairn
● **LUZERN**

inter-larken
INTERLAKEN ●

zangkt
treer
TRIER ●

bar-den-bar-den
BADEN-BADEN ●

bar-zel
BASEL ●

bairn
BERN ●

SWITZER
LAND

shwightz
SCHWEIZ

FRANCE
frank-riysh
FRANKREICH

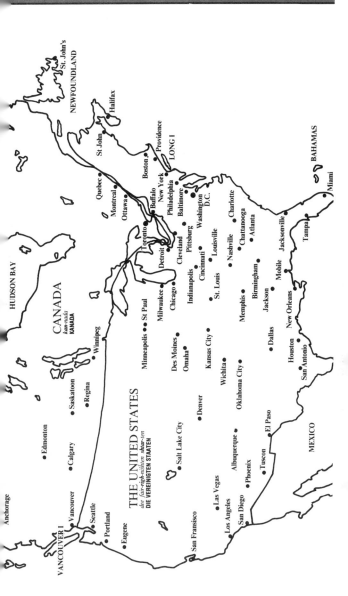

St. John's
NEWFOUNDLAND
Halifax
St. John
Providence
LONG I
Boston
BAHAMAS
Quebec
Montreal
Ottawa
Buffalo
New York
Philadelphia
Baltimore
Washington D.C.
Charlotte
Miami
Toronto
Detroit
Cleveland
Pittsburg
Chattanooga
Atlanta
Cincinnati
Louisville
Nashville
Jacksonville
Tampa
HUDSON BAY
Milwaukee
Chicago
Indianapolis
St. Louis
Memphis
Birmingham
Mobile
CANADA
kan-nada
KANADA
Minneapolis • St Paul
Jackson
New Orleans
Des Moines
Omaha
Kansas City
Winnipeg
Saskatoon
Regina
Wichita
Houston
San Antonio
Dallas
Edmonton
Calgary
Denver
Oklahoma City
THE UNITED STATES
dee fair-righ-nishten shtar-ten
DIE VEREINIGTEN STAATEN
Salt Lake City
Albuquerque
El Paso
MEXICO
Anchorage
Las Vegas
Phoenix
Tuscon
Vancouver
Seattle
Portland
Eugene
Los Angeles
San Diego
San Fransisco
VANCOUVER I

I	*ish* **ICH**	I would like	*ish* **mersh**-ter **ICH MÖCHTE**
we	*veer* **WIR**	we would like	*veer* **mersh**-tern **WIR MÖCHTEN**
you	*zee* **SIE**	do you want	*vol*-ern *zee* **WOLLEN SIE**
it	*ess* **ES**		
		I have	*ish* **har**-ber **ICH HABE**
not	*nisht* **NICHT**	we have	*veer* **har**-bern **WIR HABEN**
no	*kine* **KEIN**	do you have	**har**-bern *zee* **HABEN SIE**
which	**vel**-*shyer* **WELCHER**	can I	*kan ish* **KANN ICH**
where	*voh* **WO**	can we	**ker**-nen *veer* **KÖNNEN WIR**
when	*van* **WANN**	can you	**ker**-nen *zee* **KÖNNEN SIE**
what	*vass* **WAS**		
what time	*uhm* vee-**feel** *ooer* **UM WIEVIEL UHR**	is	*isst* **IST**
		are	*zint* **SIND**
how deep	*vee teef* **WIE TIEF**	is there	*gipt ess* **GIBT ES**
how far	*vee vight* **WIE WEIT**	is it	*ess ist* **ES IST**
how high	*vee hosh* **WIE HOCH**		
how long	*vee* **lang**-er **WIE LANGE**	climb	**klet**-ern **KLETTERN**
how many	vee-**fee**-ler **WIEVIELE**	cross	*oober*-**kvair**-ern **ÜBERQUEREN**
		cycle	**far**-rat-**far**-rern **FAHRRADFAHREN**
nearest	**nex**-ster **NÄCHSTER**	go	**gay**-ern **GEHEN**
near	*in dair* **nay**-er *fon* **IN DER NAHE VON**	have	**har**-bern **HABEN**
		do you know	**viss**-ern *zee* **WISSEN SIE**
and	*oont* **UND**	have lift	**mit**-far-rern **MITFAHREN**
at	*an* **AN**	show me	*tsigh*-gurn *zee meer* **ZEIGEN SIE MIR**
by	*by* **BEI**	stay	**bligh**-bern **BLEIBEN**
for	*foor* **FÜR**	swim	**shvim**-ern **SCHWIMMEN**
from	*fon* **VON**	will take	*nimmt* **NIMMT**
in	*in* **IN**	walk	**lau**-fern **LAUFEN**
on	*owf* **AUF**		
to	*narsh* **NACH**	here	*here* **HIER**
with	*mit* **MIT**	there	*dar* **DA**

name of	*nar-mer fon* **NAME VON**		crossroads	*kroy-tsoong* **KREUZUNG**
this	*dee-zer* **DIESER**		farm	*baoo-wern-horf* **BAUERNHOF**
that	*yay-ner* **JENER**		ferry	*fair-rer* **FÄHRE**
place	*ort* **ORT**		field	*vee-zer* **WIESE**
on map	*owf kar-ter* **AUF KARTE**		forest	*valt* **WALD**
			gate	*tor* **TOR**
somewhere	*eer-goond-voh* **IRGENDWO**		hill	*hoo-gurl* **HÜGEL**
beautiful	*shern* **SCHÖN**		house	*house* **HAUS**
			hut	*hoo-ter* **HÜTTE**
public	*erf-ernt-lee<u>sh</u>* **ÖFFENTLICH**		inn	*gast-horf* **GASTHOF**
private	*pree-vart* **PRIVAT**		lake	*zay* **SEE**
open	*owff* **AUF**		marsh	*moh-ah* **MOOR**
closed	*tsoo* **ZU**		mountain	*bairg* **BERG**
			moorland	*high-der-mo-ah* **HEIDEMOOR**
easy	*liy<u>sht</u>* **LEICHT**		path	*vayg* **WEG**
safe	*oon-gur-fair-li<u>sh</u>* **UNGEFÄHRLICH**		peak	*ghip-fel* **GIPFEL**
dangerous	*gur-fair-li<u>sh</u>* **GEFÄHRLICH**		pond	*viy-er* **WEIHER**
deep	*teef* **TIEF**		railway	*iy-sern-barn* **EISENBAHN**
shallow	*ziy<u>sht</u>* **SEICHT**		river	*flooss* **FLUSS**
			road	*shtrar-ser* **STRASSE**
meters	*may-ter* **METER**		rocks	*fell-zern* **FELSEN**
kilometers	*keelo-may-ter* **KILOMETER**		sea	*mair* **MEER**
compass	*kom-pass* **KOMPASS**		spring	*froo-ling* **FRÜHLING**
			stream	*bar<u>sh</u>* **BACH**
barn	*shoy-ner* **SCHEUNE**		town	*shtat* **STADT**
bridge	*broo-ker* **BRÜCKE**		track	*felt-vaig* **FELDWEG**
building	*gur-boy-der* **GEBÄUDE**		tree	*baoom* **BAUM**
canal	*ka-narl* **KANAL**		valley	*tarl* **TAL**
castle	*shloss* **SCHLOSS**		village	*dorf* **DORF**
church	*keer-<u>sh</u>yer* **KIRCHE**		vineyard	*vine-bairg* **WEINBERG**
cliff	*klip-per* **KLIPPE**		waterfall	*vass-ser-fal* **WASSERFALL**
cottage	*hoyss-<u>sh</u>yern* **HÄUSCHEN**		water tower	*vass-sah-toorm* **WASSERTURM**

icycle hire & rental: 126   hiking equipment: 117   weather: 130

I	*ish* **ICH**		I would like	*ish* **mersh**-ter **ICH MÖCHTE**
me	*mish* **MICH**		he/she would like	*air / zee* **mersh**-ter **ER/SIE MÖCHTE**
my	*mine* **MEIN**		do you want	*vol-ern zee* **WOLLEN SIE**
he	*air* **ER**			
she	*zee* **SIE**		I have	*ish* **har**-ber **ICH HABE**
his	*zine* **SEIN**		he / she has	*air / zee hat* **ER/SIE HAT**
her	*eeyer* **IHR**		do you have	*har-bern zee* **HABEN SIE**
you	*zee* **SIE**			
your	*eeyer* **IHR**		can I	*kan ish* **KANN ICH**
it	*ess* **ES**		can he / she	*kan air / zee* **KANN ER/SIE**
			can you	*ker-nen zee* **KÖNNEN SIE**
not	*nisht* **NICHT**			
no	*kine* **KEIN**		is	*isst* **IST**
			are	*zint* **SIND**
which	*vel-shyer* **WELCHER**		is there	*gipt ess* **GIBT ES**
where	*voh* **WO**		is it	*ist ess* **IST ES**
when	*van* **WANN**			
what time	*uhm vvee-feel ooer* **UM WIEVIEL UHR**		check	*oonter-zoosh-ern* **UNTERSUCHEN**
			come back	*tsoo-rook-kommern* **ZURÜCKKOMMEN**
how long	*vee lang-er* **WIE LANGE**		do	*marsh-ern* **MACHEN**
how much	*vee-feel* **WIEVIEL**		extract	*tsee-ern* **ZIEHEN**
how much will it cost	*vass veert dass koss-tern* **WAS WIRD DAS KOSTEN**		fix	*in ord-noong bring-urn* **IN ORDNUNG BRINGEN**
			have	*har-bern* **HABEN**
			hurts	*toot vay* **TUT WEH**
and	*oont* **UND**		need	*brow-shern* **BRAUCHEN**
at	*an* **AN**		needs	*browsht* **BRAUCHT**
for	*foor* **FÜR**		see	*zay-ern* **SEHEN**
from	*fon* **VON**		will take	*nimmt* **NIMMT**
in	*in* **IN**			
on	*owf* **AUF**		nearest	*nex-ster* **NÄCHSTER**
to	*tsoo* **ZU**		near	*in dair nay-er fon* **IN DER NÄHE VON**
with	*mit* **MIT**		here	*here* **HIER**

appointment	*tair-**meen*** **TERMIN**	crown	*kroh-ner* **KRONE**
now	*yetst* **JETZT**	dentures	*gur-biss* **GEBISS**
soon	*balt* **BALD**	filling	*foo-loong* **FÜLLUNG**
(very)	*zair* **SEHR**	gum	*tsarn-fliysh* **ZAHNFLEISCH**
urgently	*dring-ernt* **DRINGEND**	jaw	*kee-fer* **KIEFER**
		mouth	*moont* **MUND**
earlier	*froo-er* **FRÜHER**	tooth	*tsarn* **ZAHN**
later	*shpay-ter* **SPÄTER**	wisdom tooth	*viyss-heights-tsarn* **WEISHEITSZAHN**
open	*owff* **AUF**	abcess	*aps-tsess* **ABSZESS**
closed	*tsoo* **ZU**	bleeding	*bloo-tert* **BLUTET**
		broken	*gur-brosh-ern* **GEBROCHEN**
name	*nar-mer* **NAME**	come out	*hair-owss-gur-kommern* **HERAUSGEKOMMEN**
address	*ad-dress-ser* **ADRESSE**	decayed	*shlesht* **SCHLECHT**
(here)	*here* **HIER**	hurting	*toot vay* **TUT WEH**
lephone number	*tele-fone noomer* **TELEFONNUMMER**	infected	*infit-see-yert* **INFIZIERT**
		loose	*lock-ker* **LOCKER**
		pain	*shmair—tsern* **SCHMERZEN**
		painful	*shmairts-haft* **SCHMERZHAFT**
necessary	*nur-tig* **NÖTIG**	sensitive	*emp-fint-lish* **EMPFINDLICH**
permanent	*perma-nent* **PERMANENT**	(hot & cold)	*hice oont kalt* **HEISS UND KALT**
temporary	*prov-ee-zor-rish* **PROVISORISCH**	sore	*voont* **WUND**
		throbbing	*klop-fernt* **KLOPFEND**
this (one)	*dee-zer* **DIESER**	toothache	*tsarn-shmairt-sern* **ZAHNSCHMERZEN**
somewhere	*eer-gurnt-voh* **IRGENDWO**		
		allergic	*al-lair-gish* **ALLERGISCH**
very	*zair* **SEHR**	antibiotic	*anti-bee-yot-tickoom* **ANTIBIOTIKUM**
slight	*liysht* **LEICHT**	gas	*gars* **GAS**
severe	*hef-tig* **HEFTIG**	injection	*shprit-ser* **SPRITZE**
still	*nosh* **NOCH**		
constant	*shtay-tig* **STETIG**	extraction	*tsee-yern* **ZIEHEN**
periodic	*inter-mit-teer-ernt* **INTERMITTIEREND**	x-ray	*rernt-gurn* **RÖNTGEN**

amily relations: 74   mehr medizinische Fragen: 42   Verwandte: 74   Zahlung: 47

I	*ish* **ICH**	I want	*ish vil* **ICH WILL**
we	*veer* **WIR**	we want	*veer vol-lern* **WIR WOLLEN**
you	*zee* **SIE**	do you want	*vol-ern zee* **WOLLEN SIE**
it	*ess* **ES**		
not	*nisht* **NICHT**	I have	*ish har-ber* **ICH HABE**
no	*kine* **KEIN**	we have	*veer har-bern* **WIR HABEN**
		do you have	*har-bern zee* **HABEN SIE**
which	***vel**-shyer* **WELCHER**	can I	*kan ish* **KANN ICH**
where	*voh* **WO**	can we	*ker-nen veer* **KÖNNEN WIR**
when	*van* **WANN**	can you	*ker-nen zee* **KÖNNEN SIE**
what	*vass* **WAS**		
what time	*uhm vee-**feel** ooer* **UM WIEVIEL UHR**	is	*isst* **IST**
		is there	*gipt ess* **GIBT ES**
how far	*vee vight* **WIE WEIT**	is this	*ist das* **IST DAS**
how long	*vee **lang**-er* **WIE LANGE**		
how many	*vee-**fee**-ler* **WIEVIELE**	go	*gay-ern* **GEHEN**
		go back	*tsoo-**rook**-gay-ern* **ZURÜCKGEHEN**
nearest	***nex**-ster* **NÄCHSTER**	have lift	*mit-far-rern* **MITFAHREN**
near	*in dair **nay**-er fon* **IN DER NÄHE VON**	do you know	*viss-ern zee* **WISSEN SIE**
here	*here* **HIER**	leads to	*foort narsh* **FÜHRT NACH**
there	*dar* **DA**	show me	*tsigh-gurn zee meer* **ZEIGEN SIE MIR**
		show us	*tsigh-gurn zee oonts* **ZEIGEN SIE UNS**
and	*oont* **UND**	will take	*nimmt* **NIMMT**
at	*an* **AN**	turn	*ap-beegurn* **ABBIEGEN**
by	*by* **BEI**	turn around	*tsoo-**rook**-dray-ern* **ZURÜCKDREHEN**
for	*foor* **FÜR**	write down	*shriy-bern* **SCHREIBEN**
from	*fon* **VON**		
in	*in* **IN**	Where are you going?	*voh **gay**-ern zee hin* **WO GEHEN SIE HIN**
on	*owf* **AUF**	Wrong way!	***fal**-sher **rish**-toong* **FALSCHE RICHTUNG**
then	*dan* **DANN**	Stop here please!	*here bitter **an**-haltern* **HIER BITTE ANHALTEN**
to	*narsh* **NACH**	Wait here please	*here **bit**-ter **var**-tern* **HIER BITTE WARTEN**

this	*dee-zer* **DIESER**		about	*tseer-ka* **CIRCA**
that	*yay-ner* **JENER**			
			meters	*may-ter* **METER**
place	*ort* **ORT**		kilometres	*keelo-may-ter* **KILOMETER**
on map	*owf* **kar**-*ter* **AUF KARTE**		minutes	*min-oo-tern* **MINUTEN**
the) direction	*(dee)* **rish**-*toong* **(DIE) RICHTUNG**		hours	*shtoon-dern* **STUNDEN**
one way	*iyn-gang* **EINGANG**		bridge	*broo-ker* **BRÜCKE**
			canal	*ka-narl* **KANAL**
name	*nar-mer* **NAME**		car park	*park-plats* **PARKPLATZ**
address	*ad-dress-ser* **ADRESSE**		(the) city centre	*(dee)* **shtat**-*mitter* **(DIE) STADTMITTE**
			detour	*oom-vayg* **UMWEG**
next	*nexter* **NÄCHSTE**		junction	*iyn-moon-doong* **EINMÜNDUNG**
first	*air-ster* **ERSTE**		level crossing	*barn-oober-gang* **BAHNÜBERGANG**
second	*tsvo-ter* **ZWOTE**		(the) main road	*(dee)* **howpt**-*shtrar-ser* **(DIE) HAUPTSTRASSE**
third	*drit-ter* **DRITTE**		(the) motorway	*(dee)* **ow**-*toh-barn* **(DIE) AUTOBAHN**
fourth	*fee-yerter* **VIERTE**		(the) path	*(der)* **vayg** **(DER) WEG**
fifth	*foonf-ter* **FÜNFTE**		river	*flooss* **FLUSS**
turning	*ap-bee-goong* **ABBIEGUNG**		(the) road	*(dee)* **shtrar-ser** **(DIE) STRASSE**
			roundabout	*kriyss-fair-care* **KREISVERKEHR**
left	*links* **LINKS**		sign	*shilt* **SCHILD**
right	*reshts* **RECHTS**		(the) square	*(der)* **plats** **(DER) PLATZ**
slight angle	*shraig* **SCHRÄG**		(the) street	*(dee)* **shtrar-ser** **(DIE) STRASSE**
straight ahead	*gur-rar-der-owss* **GERADEAUS**		(one way)	*(iyn-gang)* **(EINGANG)**
again	*vee-der* **WIEDER**		town	*shtat* **STADT**
			traffic lights	*am-pel* **AMPEL**
at	*an* **AN**		village	*dorf* **DORF**
before	*for* **VOR**			
after	*narsh* **NACH**		open	*owff* **AUF**
over	*oo-ber* **ÜBER**		closed	*tsoo* **ZU**
along	*ent-lang* **ENTLANG**			
opposite	*gaygurn-oo-ber* **GEGENÜBER**		toilet	*twal-let-ter* **TOILETTE**

I	*ish* **ICH**	I would like	*ish* **mersh**-*ter* **ICH MÖCHTE**
me	*mish* **MICH**	he/she would like	*air* / *zee* **mersh**-*ter* **ER/SIE MÖCHTE**
my	*mine* **MEIN**	do you want	*vol*-*ern zee* **WOLLEN SIE**
he	*air* **ER**		
she	*zee* **SIE**	I have	*ish* **har**-*ber* **ICH HABE**
his	*zine* **SEIN**	he / she has	*air* / *zee hat* **ER/SIE HAT**
her	*eeyer* **IHR**	do you have	**har**-*bern zee* **HABEN SIE**
you	*zee* **SIE**		
your	*eeyer* **IHR**	can I	*kan ish* **KANN ICH**
it	*ess* **ES**	can he / she	*kan air* / *zee* **KANN ER/SIE**
they	*zee* **SIE**	can you	**ker**-*nern zee* **KÖNNEN SIE**
		I cannot	*ish kan nisht* **ICH KANN NICHT**
not	*nisht* **NICHT**	he / she cannot	*air* / *zee kan nisht* **ER/SIE KANN NICHT**
no	*kine* **KEIN**		
		is	*isst* **IST**
which	**vel**-*shyer* **WELCHER**	are	*zint* **SIND**
where	*voh* **WO**	is there	*gipt ess* **GIBT ES**
when	*van* **WANN**	is it	*ist ess* **IST ES**
what	*vass* **WAS**		
what time	*uhm* **vee-feel** *ooer* **UM WIEVIEL UHR**	I must	*ish moose* **ICH MUSS**
		he / she must	*air* / *zee moose* **ER/SIE MUSS**
how long	*vee* **lang**-*er* **WIE LANGE**	you must	*zee* **moo**-*sern* **SIE MÜSSEN**
how much	**vee**-*feel* **WIEVIEL**		
how often	*vee oft* **WIE OFT**	breathe in	**iyn**-*artmern* **EINATMEN**
		breathe out	**owss**-*artmern* **AUSATMEN**
and	*oont* **UND**	check	**proo**-*fern* **PRÜFEN**
at	*an* **AN**	come back	*tsoo*-**rook**-*kommern* **ZURÜCKKOMMEN**
for	*foor* **FÜR**	cough	**hooss**-*tern* **HUSTEN**
from	*fon* **VON**	drink	**tring**-*kern* **TRINKEN**
in	*in* **IN**	eat	*ess*-*ern* **ESSEN**
on	*owf* **AUF**	feel	*foo*-*lern* **FÜHLEN**
to	*tsoo* **ZU**	feels	*foolt* **FÜHLT**

feel ill	*foo-ler mish krank*	**FÜHLE MICH KRANK**
give	*gay-bern*	**GEBEN**
go	*gay-ern*	**GEHEN**
have	*har-bern*	**HABEN**
hear	*her-rern*	**HÖREN**
hurts	*toot vay*	**TUT WEH**
move	*ber-vay-gurn*	**BEWEGEN**
need	*brow-shern*	**BRAUCHEN**
needs	*browsht*	**BRAUCHT**
rest	*roo-ern*	**RUHEN**
see	*zay-ern*	**SEHEN**
sleep	*shlar-fern*	**SCHLAFEN**
stay	*bliy-bern*	**BLEIBEN**
swallow	*shloo-kern*	**SCHLUCKEN**
take	*nay-mern*	**NEHMEN**
vomit	*zish oober-gay-bern*	**SICH ÜBERGEBEN**

slight	*liysht*	**LEICHT**
severe	*hef-tig*	**HEFTIG**
pain	*shmair-tsern*	**SCHMERZEN**
painful	*shmairts-haft*	**SCHMERZHAFT**

constant	*shten-dig*	**STÄNDIG**
frequent	*hoy-fig*	**HÄUFIG**
sudden	*plurts-lish*	**PLÖTZLICH**
spasmodic	*spaz-moh-dish*	**SPASMODISCH**

every	*al-ler*	**ALLE**
few	*vay-nig*	**WENIG**
minutes	*mee-noo-tern*	**MINUTEN**
hours	*shtoon-dern*	**STUNDEN**
days	*tar-gur*	**TAGE**

started	*an-gur-fang-ern*	**ANGEFANGEN**
stopped	*owf-gur-hurt*	**AUFGEHÖRT**
first time	*air-sters marl*	**ERSTES MAL**
last time	*let-sters marl*	**LETZTES MAL**
long time	*lang-er tsight*	**LANGE ZEIT**
recently	*noy-lish*	**NEULICH**

now	*yetzt*	**JETZT**
later	*shpay-ter*	**SPÄTER**
before	*for-hair*	**VORHER**
after	*narsh-hair*	**NACHHER**

more	*mare*	**MEHR**
less	*vay-nigger*	**WENIGER**

hot	*hice*	**HEISS**
cold	*kalt*	**KALT**

high	*hosh*	**HOCH**
low	*nee-drig*	**NIEDRIG**
temperature	*tempera-toor*	**TEMPERATUR**
blood pressure	*bloot-drook*	**BLUTDRUCK**

suffer from	*liy-dern an*	**LEIDEN AN**
history of	*for-gur-shishter fon*	**VORGESCHICHTE VON**

see above list for following pages ☞

BODY PARTS	*kerp-er-tiyler*		kidney	*nee-rer*
	KÖRPERTEILE			**NIERE**
ankle	*kner-shyerl*		knee	*k-nee*
	KNÖCHEL			**KNIE**
anus	*aff-ter*		leg	*bine*
	AFTER			**BEIN**
appendix	*blint-darm*		ligament	*leega-ment*
	BLINDDARM			**LIGAMENT**
arm	*arm*		lip	*lip-per*
	ARM			**LIPPE**
artery	*ar-tay-reer*		liver	*lay-ber*
	ARTERIE			**LEBER**
baby	*baby*		lung	*loong-er*
	BABY			**LUNGE**
back	*roo-kern*		mouth	*moont*
	RÜCKEN			**MUND**
bladder	*blar-zer*		muscle	*mooss-kerl*
	BLASE			**MUSKEL**
bone	*knoshy-ern*		nail	*nar-gurl*
	KNOCHEN			**NAGEL**
bowels	*darm*		neck	*halss*
	DARM			**HALS**
breast	*broost*		nerve	*nairf*
	BRUST			**NERV**
cheek	*back-er*		nervous system	*nair-vern-sooss-tayn*
	BACKE			**NERVENSYSTEM**
chest	*broost-korp*		nose	*nar-zer*
	BRUSTKORB			**NASE**
chin	*kin*		penis	*pay-nis*
	KINN			**PENIS**
collarbone	*shloos-serl-bine*		rib	*rip-per*
	SCHLÜSSELBEIN			**RIPPE**
ear	*oar*		shoulder	*shool-ter*
	OHR			**SCHULTER**
elbow	*el-boh-gurn*		skin	*howt*
	ELLBOGEN			**HAUT**
eye	*ow-gur*		skull	*shay-derl*
	AUGE			**SCHÄDEL**
face	*gur-zisht*		spine	*veer-berl-zoyler*
	GESICHT			**WIRBELSÄULE**
finger	*fing-er*		stomach	*mar-gurn*
	FINGER			**MAGEN**
foot	*fooss*		testes	*hoad-ern*
	FUSS			**HODEN**
gland	*droo-zer*		tendon	*zay-ner*
	DRÜSE			**SEHNE**
hair	*hair*		thigh	*shen-kerl*
	HAAR			**SCHENKEL**
hand	*hant*		throat	*kay-ler*
	HAND			**KEHLE**
head	*kopf*		thumb	*dow-mern*
	KOPF			**DAUMEN**
heart	*hairts*		toe	*tsay-er*
	HERZ			**ZEHE**
heel	*fair-zer*		tongue	*tsoong-er*
	FERSE			**ZUNGE**
hip	*hoof-ter*		tonsils	*man-derln*
	HÜFTE			**MANDELN**
intestines	*iyn-gur-viy-der*		vagina	*shiy-der*
	EINGEWEIDE			**SCHEIDE**
jaw	*kee-fer*		vein	*vay-ner*
	KIEFER			**VENE**
joint	*gur-lenk*		wrist	*hant-gur-lenk*
	GELENK			**HANDGELENK**

YMPTOMS	*soomp-toh-mer* **SYMPTOME**	pain	*shmair-tsern* **SCHMERZEN**
aching	*shmair-tsern* **SCHMERZEN**	painful	*shairts-haft* **SCHMERZHAFT**
depressed	*daypree-meert* **DEPRIMIERT**	palpitations	*klop-fern* **KLOPFEN**
dizzy	*shvind-lig* **SCHWINDELIG**	paralysed	*para-loo-zeert* **PARALYSIERT**
bleeding	*bloo-toong* **BLUTUNG**	running	*eye-ternt* **EITERND**
blocked	*fair-shtopft* **VERSTOPFT**	shaky	*tsit-trig* **ZITTRIG**
rning feeling	*bren-nern* **BRENNEN**	shivery	*frur-sterlnt* **FRÖSTELND**
(a) cold	*air-kel-toong* **ERKÄLTUNG**	short of breath	*koorts-artmig* **KURZATMIG**
cold	*kallt* **KALT**	sick (nauseous)	*ist oo-berl* **IST ÜBEL**
constipation	*fair-shtop-foong* **VERSTOPFUNG**	sneezing	*nee-zern* **NIESEN**
convulsions	*kremp-fer* **KRÄMPFE**	sore throat	*halss-shmair-tsern* **HALSSCHMERZEN**
(a) cough	*hooss-tern* **HUSTEN**	stiff	*shtiyf* **STEIF**
cramps	*kremp-fer* **KRÄMPFE**	stomach ache	*mar-gurn-shmair-tsern* **MAGENSCHMERZEN**
diarrhoea	*doorsh-fal* **DURCHFALL**	sunburn	*zon-nern-brant* **SONNENBRAND**
ear ache	*or-rern-shmair-tsern* **OHRENSCHMERZEN**	sweating	*shvit-tsern* **SCHWITZEN**
faint	*own-masht* **OHNMACHT**	(a) temperature	*fee-ber* **FIEBER**
feverish	*fee-ber-haft* **FIEBERHAFT**	tired	*moo-der* **MÜDE**
hay fever	*hoy-shnoop-fern* **HEUSCHNUPFEN**	travel sickness	*riy-zer-krank-hite* **REISEKRANKHEIT**
headache	*kopf-shmair-tsern* **KOPFSCHMERZEN**	weak	*shvash* **SCHWACH**
h blood press'	*hoh-er bloot-drook* **HOHER BLUTDRUCK**		
hot	*hice* **HEISS**		
hurting	*toot vay* **TUT WEH**		
ill	*krank* **KRANK**		
indigestion	*mar-gurn-fair-shtim-moong* **MAGENVERSTIMMUNG**	constant	*shten-dig* **STÄNDIG**
infected	*infit-seert* **INFIZIERT**	frequent	*hoy-fig* **HÄUFIG**
itchy	*yookt* **JUCKT**	sudden	*plurts-lish* **PLÖTZLICH**
w blood press'	*nee-drigger bloot-drook* **NIEDRIGER BLUTDRUCK**	spasmodic	*spaz-moh-dish* **SPASMODISCH**
rning sickness	*more-gurnt-lishers air-bresh-ern* **MORGENDLICHES ERBRECHEN**		
migraine	*mee-gray-ner* **MIGRÄNE**	slight	*liysht* **LEICHT**
nausea	*oo-berl-kite* **ÜBELKEIT**	severe	*hef-tig* **HEFTIG**
numb	*emp-fin-doongs-loze* **EMPFINDUNGSLOS**	very	*zair* **SEHR**
oozing	*laoo-fernt* **LAUFEND**	painful	*shmairts-haft* **SCHMERZHAFT**

WOUNDS	*voon-dern*	DAMAGE	*shay-dern*
	WUNDEN		**SCHÄDEN**
bite	*shtish*	burnt	*gur-brant*
	STICH		**GEBRANNT**
blister	*blar-zer*	bruised	*gur-kvetcht*
	BLASE		**GEQUETSCHT**
boil	*foo-roong-kerl*	broken	*gur-brosh-yern*
	FURUNKEL		**GEBROCHEN**
bruise	*kvet-choong*	cracked	*gur-shproong-ern*
	QUETSCHUNG		**GESPRUNGEN**
burn	*brant-voonder*	cut	*gur-shnit-tern*
	BRANDWUNDE		**GESCHNITTEN**
cut	*shnit-voonder*	dislocated	*fair-renkt*
	SCHNITTWUNDE		**VERRENKT**
graze	*ap-shoor-foong*	grazed	*gur-shoorft*
	ABSCHÜRFUNG		**GESCHÜRFT**
infection	*infects-yoan*	ruptured	*gur-riss-sern*
	INFEKTION		**GERISSEN**
insect bite	*in-zeck-tern-shtish*	sprained	*fair-shtowsht*
	INSEKTENSTICH		**VERSTAUCHT**
lump	*boy-ler*	stinging	*brent*
	BEULE		**BRENNT**
rash	*owss-shlarg*	torn	*gur-tsert*
	AUSSCHLAG		**GEZERRT**
sting	*shtish*	twisted	*fair-renkt*
	STICH		**VERRENKT**
sunburn	*zon-nern-brant*		
	SONNENBRAND		
swelling	*shvel-loong*		
	SCHWELLUNG		

slight	*liysht*	
	LEICHT	
severe	*hef-tig*	
	HEFTIG	
very	*zair*	
	SEHR	
painful	*shmairts-haft*	
	SCHMERZHAFT	
constant	*shten-dig*	
	STÄNDIG	
frequent	*hoy-fig*	
	HÄUFIG	
sudden	*plurts-lish*	
	PLÖTZLICH	
spasmodic	*spaz-moh-dish*	
	SPASMODISCH	

BODY FLUIDS	*ker*-per-*floosig*-*kiytern* **KÖRPERFLÜSSIGKEITEN**		
blood	*bloot* **BLUT**		
blood group	*bloot*-*groo*-per **BLUTGRUPPE**	**PAYMENT**	*tsar*-loong **ZAHLUNG**
		how much will it cost?	*ess veert* **vee**-*feel koss*-tern **ES WIRD WIEVIEL KOSTEN?**
A	*ar*	how much is the bill?	**vee**-*feel shool*-der *ish ee*-nern **WIEVIEL SCHULDE ICH IHNEN?**
AB	*ar bay*		
B	*bay*		
O	*oh*	can I	*kan ish* **KANN ICH**
+	*pozz*-ee-teef	can you	*ker*-nern zee **KÖNNEN SIE**
—	*negga*-teef	have	*har*-bern **HABEN**
menses	*moan*-ats-flooss **MONATSFLUSS**	do you have	*har*-bern zee **HABEN SIE**
phlegm	*shlime* **SCHLEIM**		
puss	*iy*-ter **EITER**	pay	*tsar*-lern **ZAHLEN**
saliva	*shpiy*-*shyerl* **SPEICHEL**	pay now	*yetzt* bur-**tsar**-lern **JETZT BEZAHLEN**
stools	*shtool* **STUHL**	pay later	*shpay*-ter bur-*tsar*-lern **SPÄTER BEZAHLEN**
urine	*oo*-reen **URIN**	send bill	*resh*-noong *shick*-ern **RECHNUNG SCHICKEN**
vomit	*air*-**brosh**-ern-ers **ERBROCHENES**		
light	*hell* **HELL**	name	*nar*-mer **NAME**
dark	*doon*-kel **DUNKEL**	address	ad-**dress**-ser **ADRESSE**
		(here)	*here* **HIER**
black	*shvarts* **SCHWARZ**	(home)	*tsoo* **how**-zer **ZU HAUSE**
colourless	*far*-blowss **FARBLOS**	bill	*resh*-noong **RECHNUNG**
green	*groon* **GRÜN**	receipt	*kvit*-toong **QUITTUNG**
red	*roat* **ROT**	insurance	*fair*-**zish**-eroong **VERSICHERUNG**
yellow	*gelp* **GELB**	identification	*owss*-vice **AUSWEIS**
wet	*nass* **NASS**	with	*mit* **MIT**
dry	*trok*-ern **TROCKEN**	cash	*bar* **BAR**
		cheque	*sheck* **CHECK**
		travellers' cheque	*riy*-zer-sheck **REISESCHECK**
		credit card	kray-**deet**-karter **KREDITKARTE**

he	*air* **ER**	**DIAGNOSES & INSTRUCTIONS**	*dee-agg-**no**-zer oont an-viy-zoon-gurn* **DIAGNOSE UND ANWEISUNGEN**	
she	*zee* **SIE**			
his	*zine* **SEIN**	probably	*var-**shine**-li<u>sh</u>* **WAHRSCHEINLICH**	
her	*eeyer* **IHR**	minor	*liy<u>sh</u>t* **LEICHT**	
you	*zee* **SIE**	serious	*airnst* **ERNST**	
your	*eeyer* **IHR**	urgent	*dring-ernd* **DRINGEND**	
it	*ess* **ES**			
		operation	*opper-ratsee-**yown*** **OPERATION**	
not	*ni<u>sh</u>t* **NICHT**	specimen	*pro-ber* **PROBE**	
no	*kine* **KEIN**	test	*proh-ber* **PROBE**	
		X-ray	*rernt-gurn* **RÖNTGEN**	
he / she has	*air / zee hat* **ER / SIE HAT**			
you have	*zee har-bern* **SIE HABEN**	in bed	*im bet* **IM BETT**	
does he / she have	*hat air / zee* **HAT ER / SIE**	clinic	*clinic* **KLINIK**	
do you have	*har-bern zee* **HABEN SIE**	hospital	*krank-ern-house* **KRANKENHAUS**	
is	*isst* **IST**	allergic	*al-**lairg**-ish* **ALLERGISCH**	
are	*zint* **SIND**	prescription	*ray-**tsept*** **REZEPT**	
		.. teaspoonfuls	*tay-ler-ferl* **TEELOFFEL**	
he / she must	*air / zee moose* **ER/SIE MUSS**	..times per day	*marl tay-gli<u>sh</u>* **MAL TÄGLICH**	
you must	*zee moo-sern* **SIE MÜSSEN**	every...hours	*al-ler ... shtoon-dern* **ALLE .... STUNDEN**	
come back	*tsoo-**rook**-kommern* **ZURÜCKKOMMEN**	before	*for* **VOR**	
drink	*tring-kern* **TRINKEN**	after	*nar<u>sh</u>* **NACH**	
eat	*ess-ern* **ESSEN**	between	*tsvish-ern* **ZWISCHEN**	
give	*gay-bern* **GEBEN**	with	*mit* **MIT**	
go (to)	*tsoo gay-ern* **(ZU) GEHEN**			
need	*brow-<u>sh</u>ern* **BRAUCHEN**	meals	*marl-tsight* **MAHLZEIT**	
rest	*roo-ern* **RUHEN**	water	*vass-ser* **WASSER**	
see	*zay-ern* **SEHEN**	in the morning	*more-gurns* **MORGENS**	
stay	*bliy-bern* **BLEIBEN**	at night	*ar-bents* **ABENDS**	
take	*nay-mern* **NEHMEN**	...using toilet	*twal-**let**-ter ber-noot-se* **TOILETTE BENUTZEN**	

AILMENTS *ber-shvair-dern*
BESCHWERDEN

abscess *aps-tsess*
ABSZESS

anaemia *annay-mee*
ANÄMIE

appendicitis *blintdarm-entsoongdoong*
BLINDDARMENTZÜNDUNG

arthritis *art-ree-tiss*
ARTHRITIS

asthma *ast-mar*
ASTHMA

blood clot *bloot-gur-rinnzerl*
BLUTGERINNSEL

bronchitis *bron-shee-tiss*
BRONCHITIS

cancer *kraybs*
KREBS

ardiac cond'n *hairts-liydern*
HERZLEIDEN

(a) cold *air-kel-toong*
ERKÄLTUNG

cold *kallt*
KALT

colitis *dick-darm-cat-tar*
DICKDARMKATARRH

congestion *bloot-andrang*
BLUTANDRANG

diabetes *deeyar-bay-tess*
DIABETES

rug overdose *oo-ber-doh-ziz*
ÜBERDOSIS

dysentery *doo-zern-ter-ree*
DYSENTERIE

epilepsy *eppee-lep-see*
EPILEPSIE

fever *fee-ber*
FIEBER

ood poisoning *lay-bernsmitterl-fairgiftoong*
LEBENSMITTELVERGIFTUNG

gallstones *gal-lern-shtiyner*
GALLENSTEINE

haemorrhoids *hemmor-ro-ee-dern*
HÄMORRHOIDEN

hay fever *hoy-shnoop-fern*
HEUSCHNUPFEN

heart attack *hairts-anfal*
HERZANFALL

hepatitis *lay-ber-ent-soondoong*
LEBERENTZÜNDUNG

herpes *hair-pays*
HERPES

hernia *broosh*
BRUCH

h blood pres' *hoh-er bloot-drook*
HOHER BLUTDRUCK

infection *infekts-yoan*
INFEKTION

lammation of *ent-soondoong fon*
ENTZÜNDUNG VON

influenza *grip-per*
GRIPPE

kidney stones *nee-rern-shtiyner*
NIERENSTEINE

leukemia *loykay-mee*
LEUKÄMIE

low blood press' *nee-drigger bloot-drook*
NIEDRIGER BLUTDRUCK

morn. sickness *morgurntlishers airbreshern*
MORGENDLICHES ERBRECHEN

over-tired *oober-moo-dert*
ÜBERMÜDET

nerv. tension *nair-ver-zer shpan-noong*
NERVÖSE SPANNUNG

parasites *oon-gurtsee-fur*
UNGEZIEFER

pneumonia *loong-ern-ent-soondoong*
LUNGENENTZÜNDUNG

pulled muscle *mooss-kerl-tser-roong*
MUSKELZERRUNG

rheumatism *roy-mar*
RHEUMA

slipped disc *bant-shiybern-shardern*
BANDSCHEIBENSCHADEN

stroke *shlarg-anfal*
SCHLAGANFALL

sunstroke *zon-nern-shtish*
SONNENSTICH

(a) temperature *fee-ber*
FIEBER

tonsillitis *man-derl-ent-soondoong*
MANDELENTZÜNDUNG

ulcer *gur-shvoor*
GESCHWÜR

VD *gur-shleshts-krank-height*
GESCHLECHTSKRANKHEIT

MEDICINES *maydee-kah-men-ter*
MEDIKAMENTE

antibiotic *anti-bee-yot-ikoom*
ANTIBIOTIKUM

cream *kraym*
CRÈME

capsules *kap-zerln*
KAPSELN

drops *trop-fern*
TROPFEN

injection *shprit-ser*
SPRITZE

insulin *inzoo-leen*
INSULIN

lotion *loatsee-yoan*
LOTION

pain reliever *shmairts-stillenders mitterl*
SCHMERZSTILLENDES MITTEL

powder *poo-der*
PUDER

sedative *bee-roo-iggoongs-mitterl*
BERUHIGUNGSMITTEL

sleeping pills *shlarf-tab-lettern*
SCHLAFTABLETTEN

suppositories *tsepf-shyern*
ZÄPFCHEN

tablets *tab-let-tern*
TABLETTEN

tonic *ton-ikoom*
TONIKUM

I	*ish* **ICH**		I would like	*ish* **mersh**-ter **ICH MÖCHTE**
my	*mine* **MEIN**		do you want	*vol-ern* zee **WOLLEN SIE**
me	*mish* **MICH**			
you	*zee* **SIE**		I have	*ish* **har**-ber **ICH HABE**
your	*eeyer* **IHR**		it has	*ess* hat **ES HAT**
it	*ess* **ES**		do you have	*har-bern* zee **HABEN SIE**
not	*nisht* **NICHT**		can I	*kan ish* **KANN ICH**
no	*kine* **KEIN**		can you	*ker-nen* zee **KÖNNEN SIE**
which	*vel-shyer* **WELCHER**		is	*isst* **IST**
where	*voh* **WO**		are	*zint* **SIND**
when	*van* **WANN**		is there	*gipt ess* **GIBT ES**
what	*vass* **WAS**		is it	*ist ess* **IST ES**
what time	*uhm* vee-**feel** *ooer* **UM WIEVIEL UHR**			
			change	*owss-veck-seln* **AUSWECHSELN**
how long	vee **lang**-er **WIE LANGE**		check	*proo-fern* **PRÜFEN**
how many	*vee-fee*-ler **WIEVIELE**		clean	*riy-niggern* **REINIGEN**
how much is (that)	*vass* **koss**-tert (das) **WAS KOSTET (DAS)**		fill up	*foll-tankern* **VOLLTANKEN**
			get	*ber-**kom**-ern* **BEKOMMEN**
nearest	**nex**-ster **NÄCHSTER**		go	*far-rern* **FAHREN**
near	*in dair* **nay**-er *fon* **IN DER NÄHE VON**		have	**har**-bern **HABEN**
here	*here* **HIER**		not know	*nisht* **viss**-ern **NICHT WISSEN**
there	*dar* **DA**		need	*brow-shern* **BRAUCHEN**
			park	**par**-kern **PARKEN**
and	*oont* **UND**		pay	*tsar-lern* **ZAHLEN**
at	*an* **AN**		not possible	*nisht* **mer**-glish **NICHT MÖGLICH**
for	*foor* **FÜR**		will be ready	*veert* **fair**-tig **WIRD FERTIG**
from	*fon* **VON**		repair	*reppar-**ree**-rern* **REPARIEREN**
in	*in* **IN**		see	*zay-ern* **SEHEN**
to	*narsh* **NACH**		I'm sorry	*ess toot meer light* **ES TUT MIR LEID**
with	*mit* **MIT**		stop	*an-hal-turn* **ANHALTEN**

BORDER	*gren-tser*	FILLING STATION	*tank-shtel-ler*
	GRENZE		**TANKSTELLE**
green card	*groo-ner kar-ter*	open	*owff*
	GRÜNE KARTE		**AUF**
thing to declare	*nishts tsoo fair-tsol-lern*	closed	*tsoo*
	NICHTS ZU VERZOLLEN		**ZU**
passport	*pas*	receipt	*kvit-toong*
	PASS		**QUITTUNG**
POLICE	*polit-tsigh*	car	*ow-toh*
	POLIZEI		**AUTO**
driver	*far-rer*	lorry / truck	*ell-car-vay*
	FAHRER		**LKW**
driving license	*foo-rer-shine*	moped	*moh-far*
	FÜHRERSCHEIN		**MOFA**
fine	*shtrar-fer*	motorcycle	*moh-tor-rard*
	STRAFE		**MOTORRAD**
insurance	*fair-zish-eroong*	van	*lee-fer-vargurn*
	VERSICHERUNG		**LIEFERWAGEN**
interpreter	*dol-metcher*		
	DOLMETSCHER	petrol/gas	*ben-tseen*
km/hr	*shtoon-dern-kilo-mayter*		**BENZIN**
	STUNDENKILOMETER	(regular)	*nor-marl*
passport	*pas*		**NORMAL**
	PASS	(super)	*zoo-per*
police station	*polit-tsigh-reveer*		**SUPER**
	POLIZEIREVIER	(unleaded)	*bligh-fry*
registration book	*kraft-fartsoyg-breef*		**BLEIFREI**
	KRAFTFAHRZEUGBRIEF	diesel	*diesel-erl*
sign	*shilt*		**DIESELÖL**
	SCHILD	oil	*erl*
			ÖL
now	*yetst*	litres	*lee-ter*
	JETZT		**LITER**
later	*shpay-ter*		
	SPÄTER	air	*looft*
too fast	*tsoo shnell*		**LUFT**
	ZU SCHNELL	(pressure)	*drook*
not permitted	*fair-boat-ern*		**DRUCK**
	VERBOTEN	battery	*batter-ree*
wrong way	*fal-sher rish-toong*		**BATTERIE**
	FALSCHE RICHTUNG	car wash	*ow-toe-vesher*
			AUTOWÄSCHE
name	*nar-mer*	de-icer *(spray)*	*ent-iy-zer*
	NAME		**ENTEISER**
address	*ad-dress-ser*	distilled water	*desstil-leer-ters vass-er*
	ADRESSE		**DESTILLIERTES WASSER**
		puncture	*plat-tern*
			PLATTEN
PARKING	*par-kern*	tyre / tire	*rye-fern*
	PARKEN		**REIFEN**
car park	*park-plats*	water	*vass-ser*
	PARKPLATZ		**WASSER**
parking disc	*park-shiyber*	washers	*shy-bern-vash-anlargur*
	PARKSCHEIBE		**SCHEIBENWASCHANLAGE**
parking lights	*shtant-lisht*	windscreen / windshield	*vint-shoots-shighber*
	STANDLICHT		**WINDSCHUTZSCHEIBE**
parking meter	*park-oor*		
	PARKUHR		
small change	*kline-ghelt*	toilet	*twal-let-ter*
	KLEINGELD		**TOILETTE**

I	*ish* **ICH**		I would like	*ish mersh-ter* **ICH MÖCHT**
my	*mine* **MEIN**		do you want	*vol-ern zee* **WOLLEN SIE**
you	*zee* **SIE**			
your	*eeyer* **IHR**		I have	*ish har-ber* **ICH HABE**
it	*ess* **ES**		it has	*ess hat* **ES HAT**
			do you have	*har-bern zee* **HABEN SIE**
not	*nisht* **NICHT**			
no	*kine* **KEIN**		can I	*kan ish* **KANN ICH**
			can you	*ker-nen zee* **KÖNNEN SIE**
which	*vel-shyer* **WELCHER**			
where	*voh* **WO**		is	*isst* **IST**
what	*vass* **WAS**		are	*zint* **SIND**
what time	*uhm vee-feel ooer* **UM WIEVIEL UHR**		is there	*gipt ess* **GIBT ES**
			is it	*ist ess* **IST ES**
how far	*vee vight* **WIE WEIT**			
how long	*vee lang-er* **WIE LANGE**		adjust	*narsh-shtel-lern* **NACHSTELLEN**
how much is (that)	*vass koss-tert (das)* **WAS KOSTET (DAS)**		broken down	*hat iyn-er pan-ner* **HAT EINE PANNE**
how much will it cost	*ess veert vee-feel koss-tern* **ES WIRD WIEVIEL KOSTEN**		check	*proo-fern* **PRÜFEN**
			come	*kom-mern* **KOMMEN**
			do	*mash-ern* **MACHEN**
nearest	*nex-ster* **NÄCHSTER**		get	*ber-kom-mern* **BEKOMMEN**
near	*in dair nay-er fon* **IN DER NÄHE VON**		give lift	*mit-nay-mern* **MITNEHMEN**
here	*here* **HIER**		give tow	*shlep-ern* **SCHLEPPEN**
there	*dar* **DA**		have	*har-bern* **HABEN**
			help me	*hel-fern zee meer* **HELFEN SIE MIR**
and	*oont* **UND**		leave (vehicle)	*lass-ern* **LASSEN**
at	*an* **AN**		needs	*browsht* **BRAUCHT**
by	*by* **BEI**		not possible	*nisht mer-glish* **NICHT MÖGLICH**
for	*foor* **FÜR**		will be ready	*veert fair-tig* **WIRD FERTIG**
from	*fon* **VON**		repair	*reppar-ree-rern* **REPARIEREN**
in	*in* **IN**		replace	*air-zet-sern* **ERSETZEN**
to	*narsh* **NACH**		will take	*nimmt* **NIMMT**

garage	*vairk-shtat*	**SYMPTOMS**	*soomp-toh-mer*
	WERKSTATT		**SYMPTOME**
haust centre	*owss-poof-deenst*	broken	*ka-poot*
	AUSPUFFDIENST		**KAPUTT**
tyre centre	*riy-fern-deenst*	dirty	*shmoot-sig*
	REIFENDIENST		**SCHMUTZIG**
		dry	*trock-ern*
			TROCKEN
car	*ow-toh*	fallen off	*ap-gur-fal-lern*
	AUTO		**ABGEFALLEN**
motorcycle	*moh-**tor**-rard*	faulty	*day-feckt*
	MOTORRAD		**DEFEKT**
vehicle	*var-gurn*	frozen	*iyn-gur-**fror**-rern*
	WAGEN		**EINGEFROREN**
		jammed	*block-keert*
the work	*dee **ar**-biy-tern*		**BLOCKIERT**
	DIE ARBEITEN	leaking	*oon-disht*
:) mechanic	*dair mesh-**ar**-neeker*		**UNDICHT**
	(DER) MECHANIKER	locked	*fair-**klemmt***
			VERKLEMMT
		loose	*lock-er*
			LOCKER
something	*et-vars*	misfiring	*gibt fayl-tsoon-doong-gurn*
	ETWAS		**GIBT FEHLZÜNDUNGEN**
necessary	*ner-tig*	(part) missing	*fay-lernd*
	NÖTIG		**FEHLEND**
temporary	*provee-**zor**-rish*	noisy	*tsoo lowt*
	PROVISORISCH		**ZU LAUT**
very bad	*zair shlim*	overheating	*oo-ber-**hit**-soong*
	SEHR SCHLIMM		**ÜBERHITZUNG**
new	*noy*	poor connection	*vack-erl-kontact*
	NEU		**WACKELKONTAKT**
		puncture	*plat-ern*
			PLATTEN
now	*yetst*	slipping	*rotcht*
	JETZT		**RUTSCHT**
quickly	*shnell*	won't start	*shpringt nisht an*
	SCHNELL		**SPRINGT NICHT AN**
soon	*balt*	vibrating	*vib-**reert***
	BALD		**VIBRIERT**
sooner	*froo-er*	not working	*foonk-tseeyo-neert nisht*
	FRÜHER		**FUNKTIONIERT NICHT**
maybe	*fee-**liysht***	worn	*fair-**shliss**-ern*
	VIELLEICHT		**VERSCHLISSEN**
hours	*shtoon-dern*	the charge	*dee **koss**-tern*
	STUNDEN		**DIE KOSTEN**
days	*tar-gur*	itemised	*owf-gur-**shloo**-selter*
	TAGE		**AUFGESCHLÜSSELTE**
		bill	*resh-noong*
open	*owff*		**RECHNUNG**
	AUF	receipt	*kvit-toong*
closed	*tsoo*		**QUITTUNG**
	ZU	credit card	*kre-**deet**-karter*
			KREDITKARTE
		insurance	*fair-**zish**-eroong*
			VERSICHERUNG
lubrication	*shmee-roong*		
	SCHMIERUNG		
fuel can	*ben-**tseen**-kanister*	name	*nar-mer*
	BENZINKANISTER		**NAME**
spare part	*air-**zats**-tiyl*	address	*ad-**dress**-ser*
	ERSATZTEIL		**ADRESSE**

vehicle parts: overleaf

PARTS	*tie-ler*	diesel	*dee-zerl-erl*
	TEILE		**DIESELÖL**
accelerator	*garss-paydarl*	dip switch	*ap-blent-shall-ter*
	GASPEDAL		**ABBLENDSCHALTER**
air conditioner	*kleematee-zattsee-own*	disc brake	*shigh-bern-bremzer*
	KLIMATISATION		**SCHEIBENBREMSE**
air filter	*looft-filter*	distributor	*fair-tiy-ler*
	LUFTFILTER		**VERTEILER**
air pump	*looft-poom-per*	dynamo	*lisht-masheener*
	LUFTPUMPE		**LICHTMASCHINE**
alternator	*lisht-masheener*	electrical system	*el-leck-trisher an-lar*
	LICHTMASCHINE		**ELEKTRISCHE ANLAGE**
axle	*ax-er*	engine	*moh-tor*
	ACHSE		**MOTOR**
battery	*batta-ree*	exhaust pipe	*owss-poof-ror*
	BATTERIE		**AUSPUFFROHR**
bearing	*lar-gur*	fan	*ventil-la-tor*
	LAGER		**VENTILATOR**
bolt	*bol-tsern*	fan belt	*kiyl-reemern*
	BOLZEN		**KEILRIEMEN**
bonnet	*how-ber*	filter	*filter*
	HAUBE		**FILTER**
boot	*kof-fer-raoom*	footbrake	*brems-paydarl*
	KOFFERRAUM		**BREMSPEDAL**
brakes	*brem-zern*	fuel cap	*tank-vair-shlooss*
	BREMSEN		**TANKVERSCHLUSS**
brake drum	*brems-trommerl*	fuel pump	*ben-tseen-poomper*
	BREMSTROMMEL		**BENZINPUMPE**
brake fluid	*bremz-floo-sigkite*	fuel tank	*ben-tseen-tank*
	BREMSFLÜSSIGKEIT		**BENZINTANK**
brake light	*brems-loysh-ter*	fuse	*zish-eroong*
	BREMSLEUCHTE		**SICHERUNG**
brake shoe	*brems-backer*	gasket	*deesh-toong*
	BREMSBACKE		**DICHTUNG**
bulb	*gloo-beer-ner*	gear box	*gur-tree-ber*
	GLÜHBIRNE		**GETRIEBE**
cable	*liy-toong*	gears	*shall-toong*
	LEITUNG		**SCHALTUNG**
camshaft	*nock-ern-veller*	gear lever	*shalt-hayberl*
	NOCKENWELLE		**SCHALTHEBEL**
carburettor	*fair-gar-zer*	handbrake	*hant-bremzer*
	VERGASER		**HANDBREMSE**
choke	*shoke*	handle	*koor-berl*
	CHOKE		**KURBEL**
clutch	*koop-ploong*	hazard warning light	*varn-blink-lisht*
	KUPPLUNG		**WARNBLINKLICHT**
clutch plate	*koop-loongs-shiy-ber*	headlight	*shine-verfer*
	KUPPLUNGSSCHEIBE		**SCHEINWERFER**
condenser	*kon-denzator*	heater	*high-tsoong*
	KONDENSATOR		**HEIZUNG**
contact	*kon-tact*	horn	*hoo-per*
	KONTAKT		**HUPE**
cooling system	*koo-loong*	hose	*shlowsh*
	KÜHLUNG		**SCHLAUCH**
crankcase	*koor-berl-gur-hoy-zer*	hub cap	*rard-capper*
	KURBELGEHÄUSE		**RADKAPPE**
crankshaft	*koor-berl-veller*	ignition coil	*tsoont-shpooler*
	KURBELWELLE		**ZÜNDSPULE**
cylinder	*tsoo-lin-der*	ignition system	*tsoon-doong*
	ZYLINDER		**ZÜNDUNG**
cylinder head	*tsoo-lin-der-kopf*	indicator	*blin-ker*
	ZYLINDERKOPF		**BLINKER**
diaphragm	*mem-bran*	indicator light	*blink-lisht*
	MEMBRAN		**BLINKLICHT**

inner tube	*looft-shlaoosh* **LUFTSCHLAUCH**	spare wheel	*ray-zair-ver-rard* **RESERVERAD**
jack	*hay-ber* **HEBER**	spark plug	*tsoont-kairt-zer* **ZÜNDKERZE**
joint	*gur-lenk* **GELENK**	speedometer	*tacko-may-ter* **TACHOMETER**
leads	*liy-toong-ern* **LEITUNGEN**	spring	*fay-der* **FEDER**
levers	*hay-berl* **HEBEL**	starter	*an-lasser* **ANLASSER**
lights	*ber-loysh-koong* **BELEUCHTUNG**	steering	*len-koong* **LENKUNG**
lock	*shloss* **SCHLOSS**	steering column	*lenk-zoy-ler* **LENKSÄULE**
rication system	*shmeer-soostaym* **SCHMIERSYSTEM**	steering wheel	*lenk-rard* **LENKRAD**
mudguard	*coat-floogurl* **KOTFLÜGEL**	stop light	*bremz-loyshter* **BREMSLEUCHTE**
nut	*moo-ter* **MUTTER**	suspension	*fay-deroong* **FEDERUNG**
oil	*erl* **ÖL**	tappets	*shter-serl* **STÖSSEL**
oil filter	*erl-filter* **ÖLFILTER**	teeth	*tsay-ner* **ZÄHNE**
pressure gauge	*erl-drook-antsigh-gur* **ÖLDRUCKANZEIGE**	thermostat	*tair-mor-stat* **THERMOSTAT**
oil pump	*erl-poom-per* **ÖLPUMPE**	transmission	*gur-tree-ber* **GETRIEBE**
petrol	*ben-tseen* **BENZIN**	(automatic)	*owtoh-mar-teek* **AUTOMATIK**
petrol filter	*ben-tseen-filter* **BENZINFILTER**	(manual)	*hant-shall-toong* **HANDSCHALTUNG**
piston	*kol-bern* **KOLBEN**	turn indicator	*rish-toongs-antsigh-gur* **RICHTUNGSANZEIGER**
piston rings	*kol-bern-ringer* **KOLBENRINGE**	tyre	*riy-fern* **REIFEN**
radiator	*koo-ler* **KÜHLER**	(tubeless)	*shlaush-low-zer* **SCHLAUCHLOSE**
points	*oon-ter-bresher-kontack-ter* **UNTERBRECHERKONTAKTE**	valve	*ven-teel* **VENTIL**
rear light	*shlooss-loyshter* **SCHLUSSLEUCHTE**	washer	*oonter-layg-shiy-ber* **UNTERLEGSCHEIBE**
ear view mirror	*rook-shpee-gurl* **RÜCKSPIEGEL**	water pump	*vass-er-poom-per* **WASSERPUMPE**
reflectors	*rayfleck-tor-rern* **REFLEKTOREN**	wheel	*rard* **RAD**
reversing light	*rook-far-loysh-tern* **RÜCHFAHRLEUCHTEN**	windscreen	*vint-shoots-shighber* **WINDSCHUTZSCHEIBE**
screw	*shrau-ber* **SCHRAUBE**	windscreen wipers	*shy-bern-visher* **SCHEIBENWISCHER**
seat	*zits* **SITZ**	windscreen washers	*shy-bern-vash-anlargur* **SCHEIBENWASCHANLAGE**
seat belt	*zish-er-heights-goorterl* **SICHERHEITSGÜRTEL**		
shaft	*vel-ler* **WELLE**	left	*links* **LINKS**
shock absorber	*shtows-dempfer* **STOSSDÄMPFER**	right	*reshts* **RECHTS**
side light	*shtant-lisht* **STANDLICHT**	front	*for-ner* **VORNE**
silencer	*shall-dempfer* **SCHALLDÄMPFER**	rear	*hin-tern* **HINTEN**
spare part	*air-zats-tiyl* **ERSATZTEIL**	inside	*in-nern-zights* **INNENSEITS**

German to English section for mechanic - overleaf: ☞

SPARE PARTS — ERSATZTEILE

dip switch	ABBLENDSCHALTER
axle	ACHSE
starter motor	ANLASSER
connection	ANSCHLUSS
exhaust pipe	AUSPUFFROHR
battery	BATTERIE
light	BELEUCHTUNG
petrol	BENZIN
petrol filter	BENZINFILTER
fuel pump	BENZINPUMPE
fuel tank	BENZINTANK
indicator	BLINKER
brake shoes	BREMSBACKEN
brakes	BREMSEN
brake fluid	BREMSFLÜSSIGKEIT
brake light	BREMSLEUCHTE
brake drum	BREMSTROMMEL
brushes	BÜRSTEN
choke	CHOKE
injection pump	EINSPRITZPUMPE
electrical system	ELEKTRISCHE ANLAGE
spare part	ERSATZTEIL
springs	FEDERN
suspension	FEDERUNG
accelerator	GASPEDAL
joint	GELENK
gear box / transmission	GETRIEBE
bulb	GLÜHBIRNE
handbrake	HANDBREMSE
levers	HEBEL
jack	HEBER
heating	HEIZUNG
horn	HUPE
cable	KABEL
universal joint	KARDANGELENK
fan belt	KEILRIEMEN
piston	KOLBEN
piston rings	KOLBENRINGE
condenser	KONDENSATOR
contact	KONTAKT
mudguard	KOTFLÜGEL
radiator	KÜHLER
cooling system	KÜHLUNG
clutch	KUPPLUNG
clutch plate	KUPPLUNGSSCHEIBE
crankcase	KURBELGEHÄUSE
crankshaft	KURBELWELLE
bearings	LAGER
leads	LEITUNGEN
steering box	LENKGEHÄUSE
steering column	LENKSÄULE
steering	LENKUNG
generator	LICHTMASCHINE
air filter	LUFTFILTER
inner tube	LUFTSCHLAUCH
diaphragm	MEMBRAN
engine	MOTOR
engine block	MOTORBLOCK
camshaft	NOCKENWELLE
oil	ÖL
oil pressure gauge	ÖLDRUCKANZEIGE
oil filter	ÖLFILTER
oil pump	ÖLPUMPE
wheels	RÄDER
reflectors	REFLEKTOREN
tyre	REIFEN
(tubeless)	SCHLAUCHLOSE
turn indicator	RICHTUNGSANZEIGER
reversing light	RÜCKFAHRLEUCHTEN
rear-view mirror	RÜCKSPIEGEL
silencer	SCHALLDÄMPFER
gears	SCHALTUNG
gear lever	SCHALTHEBEL
disc brake	SCHEIBENBREMSE
headlights	SCHEINWERFER
hose	SCHLAUCH
rear light	SCHLUSSLEUCHTE
lubrication system	SCHMIERSYSTEM
seat belt	SICHERHEITSGÜRTEL
fuse	SICHERUNG
track rod ends	SPURSTANGENENDEN
side light	STANDLICHT
shock absorber	STOSSDÄMPFER
tappets	STÖSSEL
speedometer	TACHOMETER
thermostat	THERMOSTAT
points	UNTERBRECHERKONTA
valve	VENTIL
fan	VENTILATOR
carburettor	VERGASER
distributor	VERTEILER
hazard warning light	WARNBLINKLICHT
water pump	WASSERPUMPE
shaft	WELLE
teeth	ZÄHNE
spark plugs	ZÜNDKERZEN
ignition coil	ZÜNDSPULE
ignition system	ZÜNDUNG
cylinder	ZYLINDER
cylinder head	ZYLINDERKOPF
cylinder head gasket	ZYLINDERKOPFDICHTU

SYMPTOMS — SYMPTOME

jammed	BLOCKIERT
defective	DEFEKT
blown	DURCHGEBRANNT
frozen	EINGEFROREN
misfiring	FEHLZÜNDUNGEN
broken	KAPUTT
loose	LOCKER
slipping	RUTSCHT
dry	TROCKEN
overheating	ÜBERHITZT
leaking	UNDICHT
worn	VERSCHLISSEN
poor connection	WACKELKONTAKT

ACTIONS — MASSNAHMEN

charge	AUFLADEN
strip down	AUSBAUEN
change	AUSWECHSELN
balance	AUSWUCHTEN
bleed	ENTLÜFTEN
replace	ERSETZEN
adjust	NACHSTELLEN
clean	REINIGEN
repair	REPARIEREN

keep your distance	**ABSTAND HALTEN**
take care	**ACHTUNG**
Swiss automobile assoc	**ACS**
German automobile assoc	**ADAC**
access only	**ANLIEGER FREI**
Sundays & Bank Hols free	**AN SONN- UND FEIERTAGEN**
for (5km)	**AUF (5KM)**
loading & unlaoding only	**AUF- UND ABLADEN**
exit	**AUSFAHRT**
motorway	**AUTOBAHN**
motorways merge	**AUTOBAHNKREUZ**
road works	**BAUSTELLE**
construction traffic	**BAUSTELLENVERKEHR**
ue parking zone (disc reqd)	**BLAUE ZONE**
through traffic	**DURCHGANGSVERKEHR**
one-way street	**EINBAHNSTRASSE**
do not obstruct entrance	**EINFAHRT FREIHALTEN**
entrance	**EINGANG**
get in lane	**EINORDNEN**
single file traffic	**EINSPURIGER VERKEHR**
end of no-parking zone	**ENDE DES PARKVERBOTS**
...permitted	**...ERLAUBT**
lane closed	**FAHRSPUR GESPERRT**
keep clear	**FREI HALTEN**
frost damage	**FROSTSCHÄDEN**
pedestrians	**FUSSGÄNGER**
danger	**GEFAHR**
two-way traffic	**GEGENVERKEHR**
stop, police	**HALT, POLIZEI**
maximum stay parking	**HÖCHSTPARKDAUER**
headroom	**HÖHE**
hooting forbidden	**HUPEN VERBOTEN**
hairpin bend	**KEHRE**
no exit	**KEIN AUSGANG**
no thoroughfare	**KEINE DURCHFAHRT**
no entry	**KEIN EINGANG**
no access	**KEINE EINFAHRT**
limited parking zone	**KURZPARKZONE**
slow	**LANGSAM**
reduce speed now	**LANGSAM FAHREN**
avalanche area	**LAWINENGEFAHR**
danger	**LEBENSGEFAHR**
keep left	**LINKS FAHREN/GEHEN**
heavy vehicle route	**LKW**
except for access	**NUR FÜR ANLIEGER**
Austrian automobile assoc	**ÖAMTC**
no parking	**PARKEN VERBOTEN**
parking limited to.....mins	**PARKZEIT......MINUTEN**
maximum parking....hrs	**PARKZEIT MAX....STUNDEN**
lay-by	**RASTPLATZ**
keep right	**RECHTS FAHREN/GEHEN**
poor road surface	**SCHLECHTE FAHRBAHN**
school	**SCHULE**
dead slow	**SEHR LANGSAM**
falling rocks	**STEINSCHLAG**
road works ahead	**STRASSENARBEITEN**
road clear	**STRASSE FREI**
ring road	**UMGEHUNGSSTRASSE**
diversion	**UMLEITUNG**
accident	**UNFALL**
detour	**UNWEG**
...prohibited	**...VERBOTEN**
caution	**VORSICHT**
customs	**ZOLL**

AUSTRIA

U-turn compulsory

Tram turn

GERMANY

Umleitung

Diversion

Transit Praha

Transit Route

Parking Disc
Reqd (2hr max)

Danger of
sudden fog patches

Slow Lane
(below 15km/hr)

Tram or Bus Stop

70-110
km

Street lights
not on all night

Recommended
speed range

SWITZERLAND

Semi-motorway

Parking disc
compulsory

Postal vehicles
have priority

Tunnel
(lights compulsory)

(Flashing red light)
level/railroad crossing

(Flashing lights)
level/railroad crossing

I	*ish*		I would like	*ish mersh-ter*
	ICH			**ICH MÖCHTE**
my	*mine*		we would like	*veer mersh-tern*
	MEIN			**WIR MÖCHTEN**
he	*air*		do you want	*vol-ern zee*
	ER			**WOLLEN SIE**
she	*zee*			
	SIE			
we	*veer*		I have	*ish har-ber*
	WIR			**ICH HABE**
our	*oon-ser*		we have	*veer har-bern*
	UNSER			**WIR HABEN**
us	*unts*		do you have	*har-bern zee*
	UNS			**HABEN SIE**
you	*zee*			
	SIE			
your	*eeyer*		can I	*kan ish*
	IHR			**KANN ICH**
it	*ess*		can we	*ker-nen veer*
	ES			**KÖNNEN WIR**
			can you	*ker-nen zee*
				KÖNNEN SIE
not	*nisht*			
	NICHT			
no	*kine*		is	*isst*
	KEIN			**IST**
			are	*zint*
				SIND
which	*vel-shyer*		is there	*gipt ess*
	WELCHER			**GIBT ES**
where	*voh*		is it	*ist ess*
	WO			**IST ES**
when	*van*			
	WANN			
what	*vass*		change	*en-dern*
	WAS			**ÄNDERN**
what time	*uhm vee-feel ooer*		cook	*kosh-ern*
	UM WIEVIEL UHR			**KOCHEN**
			eat	*ess-ern*
				ESSEN
how long	*vee lang-er*		have	*har-bern*
	WIE LANGE			**HABEN**
how many	*vee-fee-ler*		order	*ber-shtel-ern*
	WIEVIELE			**BESTELLEN**
how much	*vee-feel*		recommend	*emp-fay-lern*
	WIEVIEL			**EMPFEHLEN**
			reserve	*rezzair-vee-rern*
				RESERVIEREN
and	*oont*		see	*zay-ern*
	UND			**SEHEN**
at	*an*		sit	*zit-sern*
	AN			**SITZEN**
for	*foor*		wait	*var-tern*
	FÜR			**WARTEN**
in	*in*			
	IN			
of	*fon*		nearest	*nex-ster*
	VON			**NÄCHSTER**
on	*owf*		near	*in dair nay-er fon*
	AUF			**IN DER NÄHE VON**
too	*tsoo*		here	*here*
	ZU			**HIER**
with	*mit*		there	*dar*
	MIT			**DA**

(a) snack	*iyn im-biss* **(EIN) IMBISS**		hot	*varm* **WARM**
breakfast	*froo-shtook* **FRÜHSTÜCK**		cold	*kalt* **KALT**
lunch	*mit-targ-essern* **MITTAGESSEN**			
dinner	*ar-bent-essern* **ABENDESSEN**		large	*gross* **GROSS**
			small	*kline* **KLEIN**
(a) table	*iyn tish* **(EIN) TISCH**		a little	*iyn biss-shyern* **EIN BISSCHEN**
person	*pair-zone* **PERSON**		more	*mair* **MEHR**
people	*loy-ter* **LEUTE**		another	*nosh iy-ner* **NOCH EINE**
			portion	*portsee-yown* **PORTION**
y window	*am fen-ster* **AM FENSTER**			
outside	*drow-sern* **DRAUSSEN**		open	*owff* **AUF**
chair	*shtool* **STUHL**		closed	*tsoo* **ZU**
high chair	*baby-shtool* **BABYSTUHL**			

EATING PLACES

	beer-hal-ler **BIERHALLE**	Beer hall, but also serves food.
now	*yetst* **JETZT**	
earlier	*froo-er* **FRÜHER**	*caf-fay* / *kondi-tor-eye* **CAFE / KONDITOREI** — Cafe serving coffee cakes (home-made cake at latter)
later	*shpay-ter* **SPÄTER**	*gast-horf* / *gast-shetter* **GASTHOF / GASTSTÄTTE** — Restaurant with traditional German food.
some	*et-vars* **ETWAS**	*im-biss (shtoober)* **IMBISS (STUBE)** — Snack bar, especially for sausages & hamburgers.
something	*et-vars* **ETWAS**	*restau-rang* **RESTAURANT** — Restaurant for full meals, often international.
this	*dee-zer* **DIESER**	*ine-shtoober hoy-rigger* **WEINSTUBE / HEURIGER** — Restaurant, with emphasis on local wine
that	*yay-ner* **JENER**	*balkan-shpetsi-ali-tay-tern* **BALKANSPEZIALITÄTEN** — Greek and Yugoslav food

		alcoholic drinks	68	alkoholische Getränke
		appetisers	61	Vorspeisen
hot *(spicy)*	*sharf* **SCHARF**	breakfast	60	Frühstück
		cheese	65	Käse
fresh	*frish* **FRISCH**	condiments etc	60	Gewürze usw
		desserts	66	Dessert
ght *(food)*	*liysh-ters ess-sern* **LEICHTES (ESSEN)**	eggs	64	Eier
		fish	62	Fisch
local dish	*shpetzeealee-tayt dair gay-gunt* **SPEZIALITÄT DER GEGEND**	fruit	66	Obst
		meat	63	Fleisch
vegetarian	*vairgay-tar-rish* **VEGETARISCH**	potatoes	64	Kartoffeln
		poultry & game	62	Geflügel und Wild
		rice & noodles	64	Reis und Nudeln
		salads	64	Salat
menu	*shpiy-zer-karter* **SPEISEKARTE**	sausages	62	Würstchen
		snacks	67	Imbiße
set menu	*mee-noo tar-gurs-karter* **MENU / TAGESKARTE**	soft drinks	67	alkoholfreie Getränke
		soups & stews	65	Suppen und Eintopf
wine list	*vine-karter* **WEINKARTE**	tea & coffee	67	Tee und Kaffee
		vegetables	64	Gemüse

CONDIMENTS ETC	*gur-voor-tser* GEWÜRZE USW.	BREAKFAST	*froo-shtook* FRÜHSTÜCK
bread	*broat* BROT	fruit juice	*zaft* SAFT
butter	*boo-ter* BUTTER	cereal	*gur-try-der-flockern* GETREIDEFLOCKEN
dressing	*zo-ser* SOSSE	muesli	*muesli* MÜSLI
honey	*hoh-nig* HONIG	yogurt	*yoh-goort* JOGHURT
jam	*kon-fee-too-rer* KONFITÜRE		
lemon	*tsee-troh-ner* ZITRONE	boiled egg	*gur-kosh-ters-eye* GEKOCHTES EI
lemon juice	*tsee-troh-nern-zaft* ZITRONENSAFT	(soft)	*viysh* WEICH
margarine	*mar-ga-ree-ner* MARGARINE	(hard)	*hart* HART
milk	*meelsh* MILCH	fried egg	*shpee-gurl-eye* SPIEGELEI
mustard	*zenf* SENF	(done both sides)	*by-der zy-tern gur-brar-ter* BEIDE SEITEN GEBRATEN
oil	*za-lart-erl* SALATÖL	scrambled egg	*roor-eye-yer* RÜHREIER
roll	*brurt-shyern* BRÖTCHEN	omelet	*om-let* OMELETT
rolls	*brurt-shyern* BRÖTCHEN	bacon & egg	*shpeck oont eye* SPECK UND EI
salt & pepper	*zalts oont pfef-fer* SALZ UND PFEFFER		
sauce	*ket-choop* KETCHUP	(spreading) cheese	*shtriysh kay-zer* (STREICH-) KÄSE
(tomato sauce)	*tom-ar-tern ket-choop* TOMATENKETCHUP	lunch meat	*frish-voorst* FRISCHWURST
sugar	*tsoo-ker* ZUCKER	salami-type sausage	*dow-er-voorst* DAUERWURST
syrup	*zee-roop* SIRUP	toast	*toast* TOAST
vinegar	*ess-sig* ESSIG	black bread	*foll-korn-broat* VOLLKORNBROT
water	*vass-ser* WASSER	roll	*brurt-shyern* BRÖTCHEN
		jam	*kon-fee-too-rer* KONFITÜRE
EQUIPMENT	*owss-roo-stoong* AUSRÜSTUNG	marmalade	*or-ran-jern-marma-larder* ORANGENMARMELADE
knife	*mess-ser* MESSER		
fork	*gar-berl* GABEL	tea	*tay* TEE
spoon	*ler-ferl* LÖFFEL	(lemon)	*tsee-troh-ner* ZITRONE
ashtray	*ash-ern-becker* ASCHENBECKER	coffee	*kaf-fay* KAFFEE
cup	*tass-ser* TASSE		
glass	*glass* GLAS	cream	*zar-ner* SAHNE
napkin	*sairv-yet-ter* SERVIETTE	milk	*milsh* MILCH
plate	*tel-ler* TELLER	(skimmed milk)	*mar-gur-meelsh* MAGERMILCH
serviette	*sairv-yet-ter* SERVIETTE	sugar	*tsoo-ker* ZUCKER

cheeses: 65   eggs: 64   fruit: 66   paying: 69

APPETISERS	*for-shpiy-zern*	home made paté	*ter-ree-ner*
	VORSPEISEN		**TERRINE**
eel	*arl*	tuna	*toon-fish*
	AAL		**THUNFISCH**
artichokes	*artee-shock-ern*	sausage (sliced)	*voorst*
	ARTISCHOCKEN		**WURST**
oysters	*owss-tern*	sausages (whole)	*voorst-shyern*
	AUSTERN		**WÜRSTCHEN**
avocado pear	*avo-car-doh*		
	AVOCADO	**APPETISER TYPES**	*for-shpiyzer-toopern*
herring	*hay-ring*		**VORSPEISETYPEN**
	HERING	cheese	*kay-zer*
lobster	*hoo-mer*		**KÄSE**
	HUMMER	egg	*eye*
caviar	*caviar*		**EI**
	KAVIAR	fish	*fish*
rawns / shrimps	*crab-ern*		**FISCH**
	KRABBEN	fruit	*ohbst*
salmon	*lax*		**OBST**
	LACHS	fruit juice	*zaft*
meat loaf	*lay-ber-kayzer*		**SAFT**
	LEBERKÄSE	meat	*fliysh*
mackerel	*mah-kray-ler*		**FLEISCH**
	MAKRELE	salad	*zah-lart*
salted herring	*mat-yayss-hay-ring*		**SALAT**
	MATJESHERING	vegetables	*gur-moo-zer*
sea food	*mair-rers-froosh-ter*		**GEMÜSE**
	MEERESFRÜCHTE		
melon	*mer-lo-ner*		
	MELONE		
mussels	*moosh-erln*	a	*iyn*
	MUSCHELN		**EIN**
olives	*oh-lee-vern*	a little	*iyn biss-shyern*
	OLIVEN		**EIN BISSCHEN**
mushrooms	*pil-tser*	some	*et-vars*
	PILZE		**ETWAS**
radishes	*rah-dees-shern*		
	RADIESCHEN		
smoked herring	*roy-shyer-hay-ring*	hot	*varm*
	RÄUCHERHERING		**WARM**
smoked salmon	*roy-shyer-lax*	cold	*kalt*
	RÄUCHERLACHS		**KALT**
smoked ham	*roy-shyer-shinkern*		
	RÄUCHERSCHINKEN		
cured ham	*ro-shinkern*		
	ROHSCHINKEN	large	*gross*
rollmop herring	*rol-mops*		**GROSS**
	ROLLMOPS	small	*kline*
scrambled egg	*roor-eye-yer*		**KLEIN**
	RÜHREIER	more	*mair*
egg mayonnaise	*roo-sisher eye-yer*		**MEHR**
	RUSSISCHE EIER	extra	*ex-tra*
anchovies	*zar-del-lern*		**EXTRA**
	SARDELLEN	another	*nosh iyner*
sardines	*zar-dee-nern*		**NOCH EINE**
	SARDINEN	portion	*portsee-yown*
ham	*shin-kern*		**PORTION**
	SCHINKEN		
snails	*shneck-ern*		
	SCHNECKEN	with	*mit*
asparagus	*shpar-gurl*		**MIT**
	SPARGEL	without	*oh-ner*
m, egg & onions	*shtram-mer max*		**OHNE**
	STRAMMER MAX		

POULTRY	*gur-floo-gurl*
	GEFLÜGEL
duck	*en-ter*
	ENTE
pheasant	*fah-zarn*
	FASAN
goose	*ganss*
	GANS
chicken	*hairn-shyern*
	HÄHNCHEN
guinea fowl	*pairl-hoon*
	PERLHUHN
turkey	*poo-ter*
	PUTE
partridge	*rape-hoon*
	REBHUHN
plover	*ray-gurn-pfiy-fer*
	REGENPFEIFER
pigeon	*taoo-ber*
	TAUBE
turkey	*troot-harn*
	TRUTHAHN
quail	*vash-terl*
	WACHTEL
grouse	*valt-hoon*
	WALDHUHN
woodcock	*valt-shnep-fer*
	WALDSCHNEPFE

GAME	*vilt*
	WILD
hare	*har-zer*
	HASE
deer	*heersh*
	HIRSCH
rabbit	*kah-neen-shyern*
	KANINCHEN
roebuck	*ray-bock*
	REHBOCK
venison	*vilt*
	WILD
wild boar	*vilt-shvine*
	WILDSCHWEIN
kid goat	*tsick-line*
	ZICKLEIN

SAUSAGES	*voorst-shyern*
	WÜRSTCHEN
beer sausages	*beer-voorst*
	BIERWURST
black pudding	*bloot-voorst*
	BLUTWURST
large frankfurter	*bock-voorst*
	BOCKWURST
fried sausage	*brart-voorst*
	BRATWURST
Bologna sausage	*fliysh-kayzer*
	FLEISCHKÄSE
black pudding	*roat-voorst*
	ROTWURST
assorted sausages	*shlasht-platter*
	SCHLACHTPLATTE

FISH	*fish*
	FISCH
eel	*arl*
	AAL
oysters	*owss-tern*
	AUSTERN
perch	*barsh*
	BARSCH
bream	*bras-sern*
	BRASSEN
codfish	*dorsh*
	DORSCH
fish croquettes	*fish-frickar-dell*
	FISCHFRIKADELLEN
flounder	*floon-der*
	FLUNDER
trout	*foh-rel-ler*
	FORELLE
prawns	*gar-nay-lern*
	GARNELEN
pike	*hesht*
	HECHT
halibut	*hiyl-boot*
	HEILBUTT
herring	*hay-ring*
	HERING
lobster	*hoo-mer*
	HUMMER
cod	*kar-berl-yow*
	KABELJAU
scallops	*kam-moo-sherln*
	KAMMUSCHELN
crab	*krayps*
	KREBS
salmon	*lax*
	LACHS
lobster	*lan-goo-ster*
	LANGUSTE
mackerel	*mah-kray-ler*
	MAKRELE
mussels	*moo-sherln*
	MUSCHELN
lamprey	*noyn-owgur*
	NEUNAUGE
red sea bass	*roat-barsh*
	ROTBARSCH
salmon	*zalm*
	SALM
sardines	*zar-dee-nern*
	SARDINEN
haddock	*shell-fish*
	SCHELLFISCH
plaice	*sholl-er*
	SCHOLLE
brill	*zay-boot*
	SEEBUTT
sole	*zay-tsoong-er*
	SEEZUNGE
sprat	*shprot-ter*
	SPROTTER
sturgeon	*shtoor*
	STÖR
tuna	*toon-fish*
	THUNFISCH

MEAT	*fliysh*	**COOKING METHODS**	*kosh-met-taoodern*	
	FLEISCH		**KOCHMETHODEN**	
hamburger	*ham-**boor**-gur*	baked	*gur-**back**-ern*	
	HAMBURGER		**GEBACKEN**	
cured beef	*boond-ner-fliysh*	steamed	*gur-**dempft***	
	BÜNDNERFLEISCH		**GEDÄMPFT**	
pig's trotter	*ice-bine*	stuffed	*gur-**foolt***	
	EISBEIN		**GEFÜLLT**	
chopped veal	*gur-**shnet**-tserl-ters*	grilled	*gur-**grillt***	
	GESCHNETZELTES		**GEGRILLT**	
mutton	*ham-merl*	boiled	*gur-**kosht***	
	HAMMEL		**GEKOCHT**	
veal	*kalps-fliysh*	smoked	*gur-**roy**-shyert*	
	KALBSFLEISCH		**GERÄUCHERT**	
lamb	*lam-fliysh*	braised	*gur-**shmort***	
	LAMMFLEISCH		**GESCHMORT**	
beef	*rint-fliysh*	fried	*in dair **pfan**-ner gur-**brar**-tern*	
	RINDFLEISCH		**IN DER PFANNE GEBRATEN**	
ham	*shin-kern*	roasted	*im **oh**-fern gur-**brar**-tern*	
	SCHINKEN		**IM OFEN GEBRATEN**	
pork	*shviy-ner-fliysh*	casseroled	*im topf gur-**shmort***	
	SCHWEINEFLEISCH		**IM TOPF GESCHMORT**	
bacon	*shpeck*	poached	*posh-**eert***	
	SPECK		**POCHIERT**	
		barbecued	*fom grill*	
			VOM GRILL	
		broiled	*fom roast*	
FORM OF	*lay-berns-mitterl-artern*		**VOM ROST**	
FOOD	**LEBENSMITTELARTEN**			
mince	*far-**sheer**-ters*			
	FASCHIERTES	rare	*eng-lish **bloo**-tig*	
fillet	*fee-lay*		**ENGLISCH / BLUTIG**	
	FILET	medium	*mit-terl*	
meatballs	*fliysh-klops*		**MITTEL**	
	FLEISCHKLOPS	well-done	*goot **doorsh**-gur-brartern*	
goulash	*goo-lash*		**GUT DURCHGEBRATEN**	
	GULASCH			
meatloaf	*hack-brartern*			
	HACKBRATEN			
cutlet	*kot-let*			
	KOTELETT	with	*mit*	
tripe	*koot-erln*		**MIT**	
	KUTTELN	without	*oh-ner*	
liver	*lay-ber*		**OHNE**	
	LEBER	a little	*iyn **biss**-shyern*	
meatloaf	*lay-ber-kayzer*		**EIN BISSCHEN**	
	LEBERKÄSE	some	*et-vars*	
kidneys	*nee-rern*		**ETWAS**	
	NIEREN			
rib	*rip-per*			
	RIPPE	garlic	*knoh-**blaoosh***	
scallop	*shnit-serl*		**KNOBLAUCH**	
	SCHNITZEL	herbs	*kroy-ter*	
steak	*shtayk*		**KRÄUTER**	
	STEAK	pepper	*pfef-fer*	
tongue	*tsoong-er*		**PFEFFER**	
	ZUNGE	sauce	*zaw-ser*	
			SOSSE	
		hot	*varm*	
			WARM	
		cold	*kalt*	
			KALT	

vegetables: 64   Käse: 65   Kräuter: 81   Gemüse: 64

EGGS	*eye*-yer	**VEGETABLES**	*gur-moo*-zer oont za-
	EIER	**& SALADS**	**GEMÜSE UND SAL**
boiled egg	*gur-kosh*-ters eye	mixed vegetables	*al-gur-moozer*
	GEKOCHTES EI		**ALLGEMÜSE**
fried egg	*shpee*-gurl-eye	artichoke	*arti-shock*-ker
	SPIEGELEI		**ARTISCHOCKE**
poached egg	*posh-eer*-ters eye	aubergine	*oh-ber-jee*-ner
	POCHIERTES EI		**AUBERGINE**
scrambled egg	*roor*-eye-yer	avocado	*avo-car-doh*
	RÜHREIER		**AVOCADO**
omelet	*om-let*	cauliflower	*bloo-mern-coal*
	OMELETT		**BLUMENKOHL**
		beans	*bo-nern*
			BOHNEN
		broad beans	*dick-er-boh-nern*
			DICKEBOHNEN
POTATOES	*kar-tof-ferln*	button mushrooms	*sham-peen-yons*
	KARTOFFELN		**CHAMPIGNONS**
hash-browns	*gur-rers-terl*	chicory	*en-dee-vyern*
	GERÖSTEL		**ENDIVIEN**
roast potatoes	*brart-kar-tofferln*	peas	*airb-zern*
	BRATKARTOFFELN		**ERBSEN**
mashed potato	*kar-tof-ferl-poo-ray*	gherkins	*ess-sig-goorkern*
	KARTOFFELPUREE		**ESSIGGURKEN**
potato dumplings	*kar-tof-ferl-klurser*	fresh vegetables	*frish-ers gur-moo-zer*
(N Germany)	**KARTOFFELKLÖSSE**		**FRISCHES GEMÜSE**
potato dumplings	*kar-tof-ferl-knurderl*	mixed salad	*gur-mish-ter za-lart*
(S Germany)	**KARTOFFELKNÖDEL**		**GEMISCHTER SALAT**
potato fritters	*kar-tof-ferl-poofer*	green beans	*groo-ner bo-nern*
	KARTOFFELPUFFER		**GRÜNE BOHNEN**
croquette potatoes	*kar-tof-ferl-krokettern*	green salad	*groo-ner za-lart*
	KARTOFFELKROKETTEN		**GRÜNER SALAT**
potato salad	*kar-tof-ferl-zalart*	green vegetables	*groo-ners gur-moo-ze*
	KARTOFFELSALAT		**GRÜNES GEMÜSE**
potatoes boiled	*pel-kar-tofferln*	cucumber	*goor-ker*
in skins	**PELLKARTOFFELN**		**GURKE**
chips	*pom frit*	carrots	*kar-rot-tern*
	POMMES FRITES		**KAROTTEN**
boiled potatoes	*zalts-kar-tofferln*	potatoes	*kar-tof-ferln*
	SALZKARTOFFELN		**KARTOFFELN**
		cabbage	*coal*
			KOHL
		lettuce	*kopf-zalart*
			KOPFSALAT
RICE	*rice*	pumpkin	*koor-bis*
	REIS		**KÜRBIS**
buttered rice	*boo-ter-rice*	lentils	*lin-zern*
	BUTTERREIS		**LINSEN**
curried rice	*koo-ree-rice*	sweetcorn	*mice*
	CURRYREIS		**MAIS**
		carrots	*mur-rern*
			MÖHREN
		peppers	*pap-reeka*
NOODLES	*noo-derln*	parsnips	*pastee-nar-ker*
	NUDELN		**PASTINAKE**
macaroni	*macka-ro-nee*	flat mushrooms	*pilt-tser*
	MAKKARONI		**PILZE**
spaghetti	*shpah-get-tee*	leeks	*por-rays*
	SPAGHETTI		**PORREES**
thick noodles	*spayt-slee*	radishes	*ra-dees-shyern*
	SPÄTZLI		**RADIESCHEN**
		rice	*rice*
			REIS

Brussels sprouts	*ro-zern-coal* **ROSENKOHL**	**MILD CHEESE**	*mil-der kay-zer* **MILDER KÄSE**	
beetroot	*ro-ter bayter* **ROTE BEETE**	hard cheese with fruity flavour	*ap-pern-tseller* **APPENZELLER**	
turnips	*roo-bern* **RÜBEN**	mild cheese with red rind	*ay-dammer* **EDAMER**	
salad	*za-lart* **SALAT**			
(sliced & salted cabbage)	*zow-wer-krowt* **SAUERKRAUT**	nutty hard cheese with large holes	*em-men-tarler* **EMMENTALER**	
asparagus	*shpar-gurl* **SPARGEL**	nutty hard cheese with small holes	*groo-yair* **GRUYERE**	
spinach	*shpee-nart* **SPINAT**			
celery	*shtang-ern-zellery* **STANGENSELLERIE**	cheese with caraway seeds	*koo-merl-kayzer* **KÜMMELKÄSE**	
tomatoes	*tom-mar-tern* **TOMATEN**	smooth low-fat cheese	*kvark* **QUARK**	
truffles	*troo-ferl* **TRÜFFEL**			
‹argettes / zucchini	*tsoo-kee-nee* **ZUCCHINI**	smoked cheese	*roy-shyer-kayzer* **RÄUCHERKÄSE**	
onions	*tsvee-berln* **ZWIEBELN**	sour cheese with small holes	*til-zitter* **TILSITER**	
)UPS & STEWS	*zoo-pern oont iyn-topf* **SUPPEN UND EINTOPF**	smooth low-fat cheese	*vice-kayzer* **WEISSKÄSE**	
g. soup & sausage	*baoo-ern-zooper* **BAUERSUPPE**			
bean soup	*bo-nern-zooper* **BOHNENSUPPE**	**STRONG CHEESE**	*shar-fer kay-zer* **SCHARFER KÄSE**	
consomme	*bwee-yon* **BOUILLON**	sour-milk cheese often served with onions	*hant-kayzer* **HANDKÄSE**	
stew	*iyn-topf* **EINTOPF**			
pea soup	*airb-zern-zooper* **ERBSENSUPPE**	strong sour-milk cheese	*hart-zer kay-zer* **HARZER KÄSE**	
fish soup	*fish-zooper* **FISCHSUPPE**	strong cheese with herbs	*sharp-tseegur* **SCHABZIGER**	
dumpling soup	*grees-nockerl-zooper* **GRIESSNOCKELSUPPE**			
goulash soup	*goo-lash-zooper* **GULASCHSUPPE**			
chicken broth	*hoo-ner-brewer* **HÜHNERBRÜHE**			
‹er dumpling soup	*lay-ber-knur-derl-zooper* **LEBERKNÖDELSUPPE**	a little	*iyn biss-shyern* **EIN BISSCHEN**	
lentil soup	*lin-zern-zooper* **LINSENSUPPE**	a (small) piece of	*iyn shtook (-shyern)* **EIN STÜCK (-CHEN)**	
noodle soup	*noo-derl-zooper* **NUDELSUPPE**	some	*et-vars* **ETWAS**	
ox-tail soup	*ox-ern-shvants-zooper* **OCHSENSCHWANZSUPPE**	large	*gross* **GROSS**	
turtle soup	*shilt-krur-tern-zooper* **SCHILDKRÖTENSUPPE**	small	*kline* **KLINE**	
hot bean soup	*zair-bisher bo-ner-zooper* **SERBISCHE BOHNENSUPPE**	portion	*portsee-yown* **PORTION**	
tomato soup	*tom-mar-tern-zooper* **TOMATENSUPPE**			
onion soup	*tsvee-berl-zooper* **ZWIEBELSUPPE**	with	*mit* **MIT**	
(with sausage)	*mit voorst-shyern* **MIT WÜRSTCHEN**	without	*oh-ner* **OHNE**	

DESSERT	narsh-shpiy-zer day-sair	FRUIT	ohbst
	NACHSPEISE/DESSERT		**OBST**
apple strudel	ap-ferl-shtroo-derl	pineapple	an-annass
	APFELSTRUDEL		**ANANAS**
ice cream	ice	apple	ap-ferl
	EIS		**APFEL**
pancake	pfan-koosh-ern	orange	apferl-zee-ner
	PFANNKUCHEN		**APFELSINE**
pancake strips	kiy-zer-shmar-rern	apricots	appree-koh-zern
	KAISERSCHMARREN		**APRIKOSEN**
potato cakes	riy-ber-koosh-ern	bananas	ba-nar-nern
	REIBEKUCHEN		**BANANEN**
pudding	pud-ding	pears	beer-nern
	PUDDING		**BIRNEN**
rice pudding	milsh-rice	prunes	dur-pflowmern
	MILCHREIS		**DÖRRPFLAUMEN**
sago-type fruit pudding	ro-ter groot-tser	strawberries	airt-bair-rern
	ROTE GRÜTZE		**ERDBEEREN**
stewed apple	ap-ferl-mooss	figs	fiy-gurn
	APFELMUS		**FEIGEN**
water-ice sorbet	vass-ser-ice	pomegranates	gra-nart-epferl
	WASSEREIS		**GRANATÄPFEL**
		blueberries	hiy-derl-bair-rern
			HEIDELBEEREN
CAKES	koosh-ern	raspberries	him-bair-rern
	KUCHEN		**HIMBEEREN**
apple cake	ap-ferl-koosh-ern	redcurrants	yo-han-niss-bair-r
	APFELKUCHEN		**JOHANNISBEEREN**
chocolate layer cake	hair-rern-torter	cherries	keer-shern
	HERRENTORTE		**KIRSCHEN**
cheese cake	kay-zer-koosh-ern	limes	lee-met-tern
	KÄSEKUCHEN		**LIMETTEN**
Vienna chocolate cake	zash-er-torter	tangerines	manda-ree-ner
	SACHERTORTE		**MANDARINE**
Black Forest cherry cake	shvarts-velder	melon	mel-lo-ner
	-keersh-torter		**MELONE**
	SCHWARZWÄLDER	nuts	noo-ser
	-**KIRSCHTORTE**		**NÜSSE**
plum tart/cake	tsvetch-gurn-koosh-ern	olives	oh-lee-vern
	ZWETSCHGENKUCHEN		**OLIVEN**
		grapefruit	pam-perl-moozer
			PAMPELMUSE
		peaches	pfeer-zisher
a (small) piece of	iyn shtook -shyern		**PFIRSICHE**
	EIN STÜCK(–CHEN)	plums	pflow-mern
a little	iyn biss-shyern		**PFLAUMEN**
	EIN BISSCHEN	raisins	ro-zee-nern
some / something	et-vars		**ROSINEN**
	ETWAS	grapes	traoo-bern
not too sweet	nisht tsoo zoosss		**TRAUBEN**
	NICHT ZU SÜSS	water melon	vass-ser-mello-ner
with	mit		**WASSERMELONE**
	MIT	lemon	tsee-troh-ner
without	oh-ner		**ZITRONE**
	OHNE		
sauce	zor-ser		
	SOSSE		
sugar	tsoo-ker		
	ZUCKER		
cream	zar-ner		
	SAHNE		
whipped cream	shlarg-zarner		
	SCHLAGSAHNE		

(fruit in English alphabetical order: 78)

SOFT DRINKS	*gur-**tren**-ker*		**SNACKS**	*im-bisser*
	GETRÄNKE			**IMBISSE**
a	*iyn*		biscuits	*cake-ser*
	EIN			**KEKSE**
cup of	*tass-er*		bread	*broat*
	TASSE			**BROT**
glass of	*glass*		cake	*koosh-ern*
	GLAS			**KUCHEN**
			(bar of)	*tar-ferl*
				TAFEL
chocolate	*shocko-**lar**-der*		chocolate	*shocko-**lar**-der*
	SCHOKOLADE			**SCHOKOLADE**
coffee	*kaf-**fay***		hamburger	*ham-**boor**-gur*
	KAFFEE			**HAMBURGER**
(decaffeinated coffee)	*kof-**feen**-fryer kaf-**fay***		hot-dog	*hot dog*
	KOFFEINFREIER KAFFEE			**HOT DOG**
(espresso coffee)	*ess-**press**-so-kaf-fay*		ice cream	*ice*
	ESPRESSOKAFFEE			**EIS**
(ice coffee)	*ice-kaffay*		open sandwich	*ber-**layg**-ters broat*
	EISKAFFEE			**BELEGTES BROT**
fruit juice	*zaft*		pizza slice	*shtook pizza*
	SAFT			**STÜCK PIZZA**
lemonade	*tsee-**troh**-nern-leemonarder*		pastry	*turt-shern*
	ZITRONENLIMONADE			**TÖRTCHEN**
lime	*leemon-**nel**-lern-zaft*		potato fritter	*riy-ber-koosh-ern*
	LIMONELLENSAFT			**REIBEKUCHEN**
milk	*milsh*		roll	***brurt**-shyern*
	MILCH			**BRÖTCHEN**
milk shake	***milsh**-mix*		roll with cheese	*kaizer-brurt-shyern*
	MILCHMIX			**KÄSEBRÖTCHEN**
mineral water	*minnair-**rarl**-vasser*		roll with fish	*fish-brurt-shyern*
	MINERALWASSER			**FISCHBRÖTCHEN**
orangeade	*orran-**jar**-der*		roll with sausage	*voorst-brurt-shyern*
	ORANGEADE			**WURSTBRÖTCHEN**
soda water	*zoh-da-vasser*		salad	*za-**lart***
	SODAWASSER			**SALAT**
squash	***froosht**-gur-trenk*		sandwich	*sen-vitch*
	FRUCHTGETRÄNK			**SANDWICH**
			sweets	***bon**-bons*
				BONBONS
tea	*tay*		sausage	*voorst-shyern*
	TEE			**WÜRSTCHEN**
(iced tea)	*ice-tay*		toast	*toast*
	EISTEE			**TOAST**
with:	*mit*		waffle	*vaf-ferl*
	MIT			**WAFFEL**
(milk)	*milsh*			
	MILCH		with	*mit*
(sugar)	*tsoo-ker*			**MIT**
	ZUCKER		butter	***boo**-ter*
(lemon)	*tsee-**troh**-ner*			**BUTTER**
	ZITRONE		margarine	*margar-**ree**-ner*
(camomile tea)	*ka-**mill**-lern-tay*			**MARGARINE**
	KAMILLENTEE		syrup	*zee-roop*
(rosehip tea)	***har**-gur-bootern-tay*			**SIRUP**
	HAGEBUTTENTEE			
(peppermint tea)	***pfef**-fer-mints-tay*			
	PFEFFERMINZTEE		one	*iyns*
				EINS
tonic water	***ton**-nic*		two	*tsvigh*
	TONIC			**ZWEI**
water	***vass**-ser*		three	*drigh*
	WASSER			**DREI**

alcoholic drinks: 68   paying: 69

ALCOHOLIC DRINKS	*alko-hol-lisher gur-tren-ker* **ALKOHOLISCHE GETRÄNKE**		a	*iyner* **EINE**
aperitif	*appairra-tif* **APERITIF**	carafe of	*ka-raf-fer* **KARAFFE**
beer	*beer* **BIER**	bottle of	*flash-er* **FLASCHE**
(dark beer)	*doon-klers beer* **DUNKLES BIER**	half-bottle of	*hal-ber flash-er* **HALBE FLASCHE**
(light beer)	*hel-lers beer* **HELLES BIER**	litre of	*lee-ter* **LITER**
brandy	*vine-brant* **WEINBRAND**			
(fruit brandy)	*ohb-stler* **OBSTLER**	a	*iyn* **EIN**
cider	*appferl-vine* **APFELWEIN**	glass of	*glahs* **GLAS**
cocktail	*cock-tail* **COCKTAIL**	(quarter pint) glass of	*arsh-terl* **ACHTEL**
cognac	*cognac* **KOGNAK**	(half pint) glass of	*feer-terl* **VIERTEL**
gin	*gin* **GIN**	(pint) glass of	*hal-bers lee-ter* **HALBES LITER**
liqueur	*lee-kur* **LIKÖR**	(quart) mug of	*mars* **MASS**
mulled wine	*glew-vine* **GLÜHWEIN**			
port	*port-vine* **PORTWEIN**	red	*roat* **ROT**
rum	*room* **RUM**	rosé	*ro-zay* **ROSE**
rye liqueur	*korn* **KORN**	white	*vice* **WEISS**
sherry	*shair-ree* **SHERRY**			
schnapps	*shnaps* **SCHNAPS**	dry	*trock-kern* **TROCKEN**
vermouth	*vair-moot* **WERMUT**	full-bodied	*foll-moondig* **VOLLMÜNDIG**
vodka	*vod-kah* **WODKA**	light-bodied	*liysht* **LEICHT**
wine	*vine* **WEIN**	medium	*mit-terl* **MITTEL**
whisky	*veess-kee* **WHISKY**	sparkling	*shaoom-vine* **SCHAUMWEIN**
		sweet	*zooss* **SÜSS**
and:	*mit* **MIT:**			
coke	*coca cola* **COCA COLA**	chilled	*geh-koolt* **GEKÜHLT**
dry ginger	*dry gin-ger* **DRY GINGER**	at room temperature	*by tsim-mer-tempera-too...* **BEI ZIMMERTEMPERATUR**
ice	*ice* **EIS**	double	*iyn gross-sers* **EIN GROSSES**
lemonade	*tsee-troh-nern-lee-monnarder* **ZITRONENLIMONADE**	straight	*poor* **PUR**
lime	*leemon-nel-lern-zaft* **LIMONELLENSAFT**			
soda	*zo-dah* **SODA**			
tonic	*ton-nic* **TONIC**			
water	*vass-ser* **WASSER**	CHEERS!	*proast tsoom vole* **PROST / ZUM WOHL!**

soft drinks: 67

PAYING	*tsar*-lern **ZAHLEN**		I would like	*ish* **mersh**-ter **ICH MÖCHTE**
I	*ish* **ICH**		we would like	*veer* **mersh**-tern **WIR MÖCHTEN**
my	*mine* **MEIN**		do you want	*vol-ern zee* **WOLLEN SIE**
we	*veer* **WIR**			
our	*oon-ser* **UNSER**		can I have	*kan ish* **har**-bern **KANN ICH HABEN**
you	*zee* **SIE**		can we have	*kan veer* **har**-bern **KANN WIR HABEN**
your	*eeyer* **IHR**			
it	*ess* **ES**		is	*isst* **IST**
			are	*zint* **SIND**
not	*nisht* **NICHT**		is there	*gipt ess* **GIBT ES**
no	*kine* **KEIN**			
			go	*gay-urn* **GEHEN**
which	*vel-shyer* **WELCHER**		pay	*tsar-lern* **ZAHLEN**
where	*voh* **WO**			
when	*van* **WANN**		(the) bill	*(dee)* **resh**-noong **(DIE) RECHNUNG**
what	*vass* **WAS**		receipt	*kvit-oong* **QUITTUNG**
			service charge	*ber-dee-noong* **BEDIENUNG**
what is this for	*voh-tsoo ist dass* **WOZU IST DAS**		taxes	*shtoy-ern* **STEUERN**
w much is (that)	*vass koss-tert (das)* **WAS KOSTET (DAS)**		included	*in-ber-griffern* **INBEGRIFFEN**
this	*dee-zer* **DIESER**		together	*tsoo-zam-mern* **ZUSAMMEN**
these	*dee-zer* **DIESER**		separately	*gur-trent* **GETRENNT**
here	*here* **HIER**			
			credit card	*kray-deet-karter* **KREDITKARTE**
and	*oont* **UND**		travellers' cheque	*riy-zer-sheck* **REISESCHECK**
for	*foor* **FÜR**		small change	*kline-gelt* **KLEINGELD**
in	*in* **IN**			
now	*yetst* **JETZT**		I think there may be a mistake here	*stimmt das* **STIMMT DAS?**
on	*owf* **AUF**			
of	*fon* **VON**			
to	*tsoo* **ZU**		That was very good	*dass var zair goot* **DAS WAR SEHR GUT**
with	*mit* **MIT**		I / we enjoyed it very much	*ess hat gur-shmeckt* **ES HAT GESCHMECKT**

I	*ish* **ICH**	I would like	*ish* **mersh**-ter **ICH MÖCHTE**	
my	*mine* **MEIN**	we would like	*veer* **mersh**-tern **WIR MÖCHTEN**	
we	*veer* **WIR**	do you want	*vol*-ern *zee* **WOLLEN SIE**	
our	**oon**-ser **UNSER**			
you	*zee* **SIE**	I have	*ish* **har**-ber **ICH HABE**	
it	*ess* **ES**	we have	*veer* **har**-bern **WIR HABEN**	
		do you have	**har**-bern *zee* **HABEN SIE**	
not	*nisht* **NICHT**			
no	*kine* **KEIN**	can I	*kan ish* **KANN ICH**	
		can we	**ker**-nen *veer* **KÖNNEN WIR**	
which	**vel**-shyer **WELCHER**	can you	**ker**-nen *zee* **KÖNNEN SIE**	
where	*voh* **WO**			
when	*van* **WANN**	is	*isst* **IST**	
what	*vass* **WAS**	are	*zint* **SIND**	
what time	*uhm* vee-**feel** *ooer* **UM WIEVIEL UHR**	is there	*gipt ess* **GIBT ES**	
		is it	*ist ess* **IST ES**	
how long	*vee* **lang**-er **WIE LANGE**			
how many	vee-**fee**-ler **WIEVIELE**	get	ber-**kom**-ern **BEKOMMEN**	
how much is (that)	*vass* **koss**-tert *(das)* **WAS KOSTET (DAS)**	have	**har**-bern **HABEN**	
		listen to	**her**-rern **HÖREN**	
nearest	**nex**-ster **NÄCHSTER**	*will be* ready	*veert* **fair**-tig **WIRD FERTIG**	
near	*in dair* **nay**-er *fon* **IN DER NÄHE VON**	recommend	emp-**fay**-lern **EMPFEHLEN**	
here	*here* **HIER**	repair	reppar-**ree**-rern **REPARIEREN**	
		see	**zay**-ern **SEHEN**	
and	*oont* **UND**	show me	**tsigh**-gurn *zee* mee **ZEIGEN SIE MIR**	
at	*an* **AN**	*will* take	*nimmt* **NIMMT**	
by	*by* **BEI**	how does..work	*vee* foonk-tseo-**neer** **WIE FUNKTIONIERT....**	
for	*foor* **FÜR**			
from	*fon* **VON**	receipt	**kvit**-toong **QUITTUNG**	
of	*fon* **VON**	deposit	**an**-tsar-loong **ANZAHLUNG**	
on	*owf* **AUF**	taxes	**shtoy**-ern **STEUERN**	
to	*tsoo* **ZU**	included	**in**-ber-griffen **INBEGRIFFEN**	

good	*goot* **GUT**	**ELECTRICAL GOODS**	*elec*-trisher gur-**ray**-ter **ELEKTRISCHE GERÄTE**
inexpensive	*price*-goonstig **PREISGÜNSTIG**	spare part for	*air*-zats-tiyl foor **ERSATZTEIL FÜR**
cheaper	*bil*-ligger **BILLIGER**		
better	*bess*-er **BESSER**	adaptor	*tsvish*-ern-shtecker **ZWISCHENSTECKER**
alternative	*al*-tairna-*tee*-ver **ALTERNATIVE**	alarm clock	*veck*-er **WECKER**
latest	*noy*-ster **NEUSTE**	amplifier	fair-**shtair**-ker **VERSTÄRKER**
		battery	*batta*-**ree** **BATTERIE**
MUSIC	*moo*-**zeek** **MUSIK**	cassette recorder	kass-**set**-tern-ray-corder **KASSETTENREKORDER**
lank) cassette	*(oon*-bur-shpeelter) *kass*-**set**-er **(UNBESPIELTE) KASSETTE**	clock	*oor* **UHR**
tape			
compact disc	*com*-pact disc **COMPACT DISC**	compact disc player	*com*-pact disc-gur-**rayt** **COMPACT DISC-GERÄT**
record	*plat*-ter **PLATTE**	hair drier	*har*-trockner **HAARTROCKNER**
single	*single* **SINGLE**	iron	*boo*-gurl-iyzern **BÜGELEISEN**
LP	*lang*-shpeel-platter **LANGSPIELPLATTE**	(travelling iron)	*riy*-zer-boo-gur-ligh-zern **REISEBÜGELEISEN**
stylus	*nar*-derl **NADEL**	kettle	*vass*-ser-topf **WASSERTOPF**
		light bulb	*gloo*-beer-ner **GLÜHBIRNE**
classical music	*klass*-isher *moo*-**zeek** **KLASSISCHE MUSIK**	percolator	*kaf*-fay-masheener **KAFFEEMASCHINE**
jazz	*jazz* **JAZZ**	plug	*shteck*-er **STECKER**
folk music	*folks*-moozeek **VOLKSMUSIK**	record player	*plat*-tern-shpeeler **PLATTENSPIELER**
light music	*oon*-ter-haltoongs-moozeek **UNTERHALTUNGSMUSIK**	radio	*rar*-dyo **RADIO**
pop music	*pop*-moozeek **POP-MUSIK**	shaver	ra-**zeer**-apparrat **RASIERAPPARAT**
opera	*oh*-per **OPER**	tape recorder	*tone*-bant-gur-rait **TONBANDGERÄT**
		television	*fairn*-zay-apparrat **FERNSEHAPPARAT**
regional	ray-gheeyo-**narl** **REGIONAL**	transformer	*trar*-foh **TRAFO**
national	natseeyo-**narl** **NATIONAL**		
		for car	foor dass **ow**-toh **FÜR DAS AUTO**
choral	*core*-moozeek **CHORMUSIK**	for travelling	tsoom **riy**-zern **ZUM REISEN**
group	*groo*-per **GRUPPE**	portable	*trarg*-bar **TRAGBAR**
instrumental	*instrument*-**tarl**-moozeek **INSTRUMENTALMUSIK**	voltage	*shpan*-noong **SPANNUNG**
male	*men*-ner **MÄNNER**		
female	*frow*-ern **FRAUEN**	broken	gur-**brosh**-ern **GEBROCHEN**
orchestral	or-**kess**-ter-moozeek **ORCHESTERMUSIK**	jammed	*block*-**keert** **BLOCKIERT**
singer	*zeng*-er **SÄNGER**	not working	funktseeyo-**neert** *nisht* **FUNKTIONIERT NICHT**

video equipment: 106

I	*ish* **ICH**	I would like	*ish* ***mersh***-ter **ICH MÖCHTE**
my	*mine* **MEIN**	we would like	*veer* ***mersh***-tern **WIR MÖCHTEN**
we	*veer* **WIR**	do you want	*vol*-ern *zee* **WOLLEN SIE**
our	***oon***-ser **UNSER**		
you	*zee* **SIE**	I have	*ish* ***har***-ber **ICH HABE**
who	*vair* **WER**	we have	*veer* ***har***-bern **WIR HABEN**
it	*ess* **ES**	do you have	***har***-bern *zee* **HABEN SIE**
not	*nisht* **NICHT**	can I	*kan* *ish* **KANN ICH**
no	*kine* **KEIN**	can we	*ker*-nen *veer* **KÖNNEN WIR**
		can you	*ker*-nen *zee* **KÖNNEN SIE**
which	***vel***-shyer **WELCHER**		
where	*voh* **WO**	is	*isst* **IST**
when	*van* **WANN**	are	*zint* **SIND**
what	*vass* **WAS**	is there	*gipt* *ess* **GIBT ES**
what's on	*vass* *gibt* *ess* **WAS GIBT ES**	is it	*ist* *ess* **IST ES**
what time	*uhm* *vvee-***feel** *ooer* **UM WIEVIEL UHR**		
how long	*vee* ***lang***-er **WIE LANG**	dance	*tan*-tsern **TANZEN**
how much is (that)	*vass* ***koss***-tert *(das)* **WAS KOSTET (DAS)**	get	*ber*-***kom***-ern **BEKOMMEN**
		go	*gay*-ern **GEHEN**
nearest	***nex***-ster **NÄCHSTER**	have	***har***-bern **HABEN**
near	*in* *dair* ***nay***-er *fon* **IN DER NÄHE VON**	hear	***her***-rern **HÖREN**
here	*here* **HIER**	like	***mer***-gurn **MÖGEN**
		reserve	*rezzair*-***vee***-rern **RESERVIEREN**
and	*oont* **UND**	see	***zay***-ern **SEHEN**
at	*an* **AN**	watch	***tsoo***-zayern **ZUSEHEN**
by	*by* **BEI**		
for	*foor* **FÜR**	box office	***lor***-jer **LOGE**
from	*fon* **VON**	queue	***shlang***-er **SCHLANGE**
of	*fon* **VON**	entrance fee	*iyn*-*trits*-*gur*-*boor* **EINTRITTSGEBÜHR**
at	*tsoo* **ZU**	ticket	***kar***-ter **KARTE**
		deposit	*an*-*tsarloong* **ANZAHLUNG**

reduction	*air-**may**-sigoong* **ERMÄSSIGUNG**	performance	*for-shtelloong* **VORSTELLUNG**
group	*groo-per* **GRUPPE**	programme	*pro-**gram*** **PROGRAMM**
child	*kint* **KIND**	singing	*zing-ern* **SINGEN**
student	*shtoo-**dent*** **STUDENT**	dancing	*tant-sern* **TANZEN**
or citizen	*zay-nyor* **SENIOR**	music	*moo-**zeek*** **MUSIK**

seat	*plats* **PLATZ**	classical	*klass-sish* **KLASSISCH**
table	*tish* **TISCH**	modern	*moh-**dairn*** **MODERN**
		traditional	*traditseeyo-**nel*** **TRADITIONELL**

balcony	*rang* **RANG**	ballet	*bal-**let*** **BALLETT**
stalls	*shpair-zits* **SPERRSITZ**	cabaret	*lo-**karl** mit **owff**-trit* **LOKAL MIT AUFTRITT**
front	*for-ner* **VORNE**	concert	*con-**tsairt*** **KONZERT**
middle	*mit-ter* **MITTE**	a dance	*iyn tants* **EIN TANZ**
back	*hin-tern* **HINTEN**	film	*film* **FILM**
cheaper	*goon-stigger* **GÜNSTIGER**	(subtitles)	*oon-ter-tit-terln* **UNTERTITELN**
better	*bess-ser* **BESSER**	(dubbed)	*zoon-kroni-**zeert*** **SYNCHRONISIERT**
alternative	*al-tairna-**tee**-ver* **ALTERNATIVE**	(in English)	*owf **eng**-glish* **AUF ENGLISCH**
		musical	*moo-zee-karl* **MUSICAL**
now	*yetst* **JETZT**	opera	*oh-per* **OPER**
later	*shpay-ter* **SPÄTER**	play	*shaoo-shpeel* **SCHAUSPIEL**
starts	*ber-**gint*** **BEGINNT**	revue	*rer-**voo*** **REVUE**
finishes	*ist tsoo **en**-der* **IST ZU ENDE**		
		cinema	*kee-noh* **KINO**
today	*hoy-ter* **HEUTE**	concert hall	*con-**tsairt**-hal-ler* **KONZERTHALLE**
tomorrow	*more-gurn* **MORGEN**	dance hall	*tants-lo-karl* **TANZLOKAL**
matinee	*mattee-**nay*** **MATINEE**	discotheque	*disko-**tayk*** **DISKOTHEK**
evening	*ar-bent* **ABEND**	folk club	*kloob mit **folks**-moozeek* **KLUB MIT VOLKSMUSIK**
		jazz club	*kloob mit **jazz**-moozeek* **KLUB MIT JAZZMUSIK**
sual dress	*ts**vang**-loh-zer **kliy**-doong* **ZWANGLOSE KLEIDUNG**	night club	*nar**sht**-kloob* **NACHTKLUB**
ning dress	*ar-bent-garder-ohber* **ABENDGARDEROBE**	opera house	*oh-pern-house* **OPERNHAUS**
cloakroom	*garder-**roh**-ber* **GARDEROBE**	theatre	*tay-**ar**-ter* **THEATER**

ore types of music: 71

I	*ish* **ICH**	I would like	*ish* **mersh**-ter **ICH MÖCHTE**
my	*mine* **MEIN**	we would like	*veer* **mersh**-tern **WIR MÖCHTEN**
he	*air* **ER**	do you want	*vol*-ern zee **WOLLEN SIE**
she	*zee* **SIE**		
his	*eeyer* **IHR**	I have	*ish* **har**-ber **ICH HABE**
her	*zine* **SEIN**	we have	*veer* **har**-bern **WIR HABEN**
we	*veer* **WIR**	do you have	**har**-bern zee **HABEN SIE**
our	**oon**-ser **UNSER**		
you	*zee* **SIE**	can I	*kan* **ish** **KANN ICH**
your	*eeyer* **IHR**	can we	**ker**-nen veer **KÖNNEN WIR**
		can you	**ker**-nen zee **KÖNNEN SIE**
not	**nisht** **NICHT**		
no	*kine* **KEIN**	is	*isst* **IST**
		are	*zint* **SIND**
which	**vel**-*shyer* **WELCHER**	is there	*gipt ess* **GIBT ES**
where	*voh* **WO**		
when	*van* **WANN**	change (*baby*)	**trock**-ern-lay-gurn **TROCKENLEGEN**
what	*vass* **WAS**	come back	*tsoo*-**rook**-kommern **ZURÜCKKOMMEN**
what time	*uhm* vee-**feel** ooer **UM WIEVIEL UHR**	feed	**foo**-tern **FÜTTERN**
		go	**gay**-ern **GEHEN**
how long	*vee* **lang**-er **WIE LANGE**	have	**har**-bern **HABEN**
how many	*vee*-**fee**-ler **WIEVIELE**	play	**shpee**-lern **SPIELEN**
how old	*vee alt* **WIE ALT**	warm (*bottle*)	**owf**-vair-men **AUFWÄRMEN**
and	*oont* **UND**	nearest	**nex**-ster **NÄCHSTER**
at	*an* **AN**	near	*in dair* **nay**-er fon **IN DER NÄHE VON**
by	*by* **BEI**	here	*here* **HIER**
for	*foor* **FÜR**	there	*dar* **DA**
from	*fon* **VON**	somewhere	**eer**-goon-dvoh **IRGENDWO**
in	*in* **IN**	open	*owf* **AUF**
to	*tsoo* **ZU**		
with	*mit* **MIT**	this / these	**dee**-zer **DIESE**

name	*nar-mer*	aunt	*tan-ter*
	NAME		**TANTE**
address	*ad-dress-ser*	baby	*baby*
	ADRESSE		**BABY**
phone no.	*tel-lay-phone-noo-mer*	boy	*yoong-er*
	TELEFONNUMMER		**JUNGE**
		boyfriend	*froynt*
			FREUND
single	*lay-dig*	brother	*broo-der*
	LEDIG		**BRUDER**
married	*fair-high-rar-tert*	child	*kint*
	VERHEIRATET		**KIND**
divorced	*gur-shee-dern*	children	*kin-der*
	GESCHIEDEN		**KINDER**
		cousin	*koo-san*
			KUSIN
older	*el-ter*	colleague	*kol-lay-gur*
	ÄLTER		**KOLLEGE**
younger	*yoong-er*	daughter	*tosh-ter*
	JÜNGER		**TOCHTER**
same age	*gliysh-altrig*	father	*far-ter*
	GLEICHALTRIG		**VATER**
		fiancé	*fer-loab-ter*
			VERLOBTE(R)
born	*gur-bor-rern*	friend	*froynt*
	GEBOREN		**FREUND**
died	*gur-shtor-bern*	girl	*maid-shyern*
	GESTORBEN		**MÄDCHEN**
age	*al-ter*	girlfriend	*froyn-din*
	ALTER		**FREUNDIN**
		grand-daughter	*en-ker-leen*

	19		
0	0	grandfather	*gross-farter*
1	1		**GROSSVATER**
2	2	grandmother	*gross-mooter*
3	3		**GROSSMUTTER**
4	4	grandson	*en-kerl*
5	5		**ENKEL**
6	6	husband	*man*
7	7		**MANN**
8	8	man	*man*
9	9		**MANN**

grand-daughter *en-ker-leen*
ENKELIN

		mother	*moo-ter*
			MUTTER
creche	*kin-der-kripper*	nephew	*nef-fer*
	KINDERKRIPPE		**NEFFE**
ddling pool	*platch-beckern*	niece	*nish-ter*
	PLATSCHBECKEN		**NICHTE**
playground	*shpeel-plats*	sister	*shvess-ter*
	SPIELPLATZ		**SCHWESTER**
		son	*zone*
			SOHN
babysitter	*babysitter*	uncle	*on-kerl*
	BABYSITTER		**ONKEL**
bedtime	*shlar-ferns-tsight*	wife	*frow*
	SCHLAFENSZEIT		**FRAU**
bottle	*flash-er*	woman	*frow*
	FLASCH		**FRAU**
cot	*kin-der-bet-shyern*		
	KINDERBETTCHEN		
nappy	*vin-derl*	anything for	*et-vars vass dee kin-der*
	WINDEL	children to do	*mash-ern kur-nern*
high chair	*baby-shtool*		**ETWAS WAS DIE KINDER**
	BABYSTUHL		**MACHEN KÖNNEN**

I	*ish* **ICH**		I would like	*ish* **mersh**-*ter* **ICH MÖCHTE**
we	*veer* **WIR**		we would like	*veer* **mersh**-*tern* **WIR MÖCHTEN**
you	*zee* **SIE**		do you want	*vol*-*ern zee* **WOLLEN SIE**
your	*eeyer* **IHR**			
not	*nisht* **NICHT**		I have	*ish* **har**-*ber* **ICH HABE**
no	*kine* **KEIN**		we have	*veer* **har**-*bern* **WIR HABEN**
			do you have	**har**-*bern zee* **HABEN SIE**
which	**vel**-*shyer* **WELCHER**		can I	*kan ish* **KANN ICH**
where	*voh* **WO**		can we	**ker**-*nen veer* **KÖNNEN WIR**
when	*van* **WANN**		can you	**ker**-*nen zee* **KÖNNEN SIE**
what	*vass* **WAS**			
what time	*uhm* vvee-**feel** *ooer* **UM WIEVIEL UHR**		is	*isst* **IST**
			are	*zint* **SIND**
how many	*vee-fee-ler* **WIEVIELE**		is there	*gipt ess* **GIBT ES**
how much	*vee-feel* **WIEVIEL**		is it	*ist ess* **IST ES**
how much is (that)	*vass* **koss**-*tert (das)* **WAS KOSTET (DAS)**			
			buy	**kow**-*fern* **KAUFEN**
nearest	**nex**-*ster* **NÄCHSTER**		cut	**shniy**-*dern* **SCHNEIDEN**
near	*in dair* **nay**-*er fon* **IN DER NÄHE VON**		fill	**foo**-*lern* **FÜLLEN**
here	*here* **HIER**		have	**har**-*bern* **HABEN**
there	*dar* **DA**		show me	**tsigh**-*gurn-zee-mee* **ZEIGEN SIE MIR**
			see	**zay**-*ern* **SEHEN**
and	*oont* **UND**		wrap	**iyn**-*vickerln* **EINWICKELN**
any	**iyn**-*nigger* **EINIGE**		write down	**shriy**-*bern* **SCHREIBEN**
by	*by* **BEI**			
for	*foor* **FÜR**		that's fine	*in* **ord**-*noong* **IN ORDNUNG**
from	*fon* **VON**			
in	*in* **IN**		this	**dee**-*zer* **DIESER**
of	*fon* **VON**		these	**dee**-*zer* **DIESER**
to	*tsoo* **ZU**		that	**yay**-*ner* **JENER**
with	*mit* **MIT**		those	**jay**-*ner* **JENE**

receipt	*kvit-toong*		open	*owff*
	QUITTUNG			**AUF**
each	*yay*		closed	*tsoo*
	JE			**ZU**
per	*pro*			
	PRO		fresh	*frish*
				FRISCH
100gm	**hoon**-*dert gram*		frozen	*teef-gur-froh-rern*
125gm	**hoon**-*dert-foonf-oont-tsvantsig gram*			**TIEFGEFROREN**
250gm	*tsvoh-hoondert-foonftsig gram*			
			food	*lay-berns-mitterl*
½	**hal**-*bers*			**LEBENSMITTEL**
1	*iynts*		drinks	*gur-**tren**-ker*
2	*tsvigh*			**GETRÄNKE**
3	*dry*			
4	*fear*			
5	*foonf*		bag	*too-ter*
6	*zex*			**TÜTE**
7	**zee**-*bern*		bottle	**flash**-*er*
8	*asht*			**FLASCHE**
9	*noyn*		box	*shash-terl*
10	*tsayn*			**SCHACHTEL**
			can	**door**-*zer*
grams	*gram*			**DOSE**
	GRAMM		carrier bag	*trar-gur-tasher*
kilo	*kee-lo*			**TRAGETASCHE**
	KILO		jar	*glass*
litre	*lee-ter*			**GLAS**
	LITER		packet	*pack-**ayt***
				PAKET
a	*iyn*		tin	**door**-*zer*
	EIN			**DOSE**
a little	*iyn biss-shyern*		tube	*too-ber*
	EIN BISSCHEN			**TUBE**
some	*et-vars*			
	ETWAS			
something	*et-vars*		baker	*becker-**rye***
	ETWAS			**BÄCKEREI**
piece	*shtook*		butcher	*mets-gur-**rye***
	STÜCK			**METZGEREI**
slice	**shigh**-*ber*		dairy	**milsh**-*hant-loong*
	SCHEIBE			**MILCHHANDLUNG**
			delicatessen	*delikat-**ess**-sern-gursheft*
more	*mair*			**DELIKATESSENGESCHÄFT**
	MEHR		fishmonger	**fish**-*hant-loong*
less	*vay-nigger*			**FISCHHANDLUNG**
	WENIGER		greengrocer	*gur-**moo**-zer-hant-loong*
bigger	*grur-ser*			**GEMÜSEHANDLUNG**
	GRÖSSER		grocer	*lay-berns-mitterl-gursheft*
smaller	*kliy-ner*			**LEBENSMITTELGESCHÄFT**
	KLEINER		health food shop	*rair-**form**-house*
better	*bess-ser*			**REFORMHAUS**
	BESSER		market	*markt*
cheaper	*bil-ligger*			**MARKT**
	BILLIGER		pastry shop	*condi-tor-**riy***
				KONDITOREI
			supermarket	*zoo-per-markt*
with	*mit*			**SUPERMARKT**
	MIT		sweetshop	*zooss-varrern-lardern*
without	*oh-ner*			**SÜSSWARENLADEN**
	OHNE		wine merchant	**vine**-*hant-loong*
				WEINHANDLUNG

roceries vegetables & herbs: 80-81   fruit meat sausages & fish: overleaf

FRUIT	*ohbst*		MEAT	*fliysh*
	OBST			**FLEISCH**
apples	*ep-ferl*		bacon	*shpeck*
	ÄPFEL			**SPECK**
apricots	*appree-koh-zern*		beef	*rint-fliysh*
	APRIKOSEN			**RINDFLEISCH**
bananas	*ba-nar-nern*		chicken	*hairn-shyern*
	BANANEN			**HÄHNCHEN**
cherries	*keer-shern*		ham	*shin-kern*
	KIRSCHEN			**SCHINKEN**
figs	*fiy-gurn*		game	*vilt*
	FEIGEN			**WILD**
grapefruit	*pam-perl-moozer*		lamb	*lam-fliysh*
	PAMPELMUSE			**LAMMFLEISCH**
grapes	*traoo-bern*		pork	*shviy-ner-fliysh*
	TRAUBEN			**SCHWEINEFLEISCH**
lemons	*tsee-troh-nern*		turkey	*poo-ter*
	ZITRONEN			**PUTE**
limes	*lee-met-tern*		veal	*kalp-fliysh*
	LIMETTEN			**KALBFLEISCH**
melon	*mel-lo-ner*			
	MELONE			
nuts	*noo-ser*		bone	*knosh-ern*
	NÜSSE			**KNOCHEN**
olives	*oh-lee-vern*		chop	*kot-let*
	OLIVEN			**KOTELETT**
oranges	*or-ran-jern*		cutlet	*kot-let*
	ORANGEN			**KOTELETT**
peaches	*pfeer-zisher*		fat	*fet*
	PFIRSICHE			**FETT**
pears	*beer-nern*		hamburgers	*ham-boor-gur*
	BIRNEN			**HAMBURGER**
pineapple	*an-annass*		joint	*brar-tern*
	ANANAS			**BRATEN**
plums	*pflow-mern*		kidneys	*near-ren*
	PFLAUMEN			**NIEREN**
pomegranates	*gra-nart-epferl*		liver	*lay-ber*
	GRANATÄPFEL			**LEBER**
raisins	*ro-zee-nern*		mince	*hack-fliysh*
	ROSINEN			**HACKFLEISCH**
raspberries	*him-bair-rern*		ribs	*rip-pern*
	HIMBEEREN			**RIPPEN**
strawberries	*airt-bair-rern*		scallop	*shnit-serl*
	ERDBEEREN			**SCHNITZEL**
tangerines	*manda-ree-nern*		steak	*shtayk*
	MANDARINEN			**STEAK**
			tongue	*tsoong-er*
				ZUNGE
fresh	*frish*			
	FRISCH			
dried	*der*		SAUSAGES	*voorst-shyern*
	DÖRR			**WÜRSTCHEN**
			beer sausage	*beer-voorst*
				BIERWURST
			black pudding	*bloot-voorst*
				BLUTWURST
			large frankfurter	*bock-voorst*
				BOCKWURST
			fried sausage	*brart-voorst*
				BRATWURST
			Bologna sausage	*fliysh-kayzer*
				FLEISCHKÄSE
			liver sausage	*lay-ber-voorst*
				LEBWEWURST

FISH	*fish*		squid	*tin-tern-fish*
	FISCH			**TINTENFISCH**
anchovies	*zar-del-lern*		sturgeon	*shtoor*
	SARDELLEN			**STÖR**
bass	*roat-barsh*		swordfish	*shvairt-fish*
	ROTBARSCH			**SCHWERTFISCH**
carp	*karp-fern*		tench	*shliy-er*
	KARPFEN			**SCHLEIE**
caviar	*caviar*		trout	*for-rel-ler*
	KAVIAR			**FORELLE**
clams	*vay-nooss-moo-sherln*		tuna	*toon-fish*
	VENUSMUSCHELN			**THUNFISCH**
cod	*kar-berl-yow*		whitebait	*bright-linger*
	KABELJAU			**BREITLINGE**
crab	*krayps*		whiting	*vice-fish*
	KREBS			**WEISSFISCH**
crayfish	*flooss-krayps*			
	FLUSSKREBS			
cuttlefish	*tin-ternfish*		fillet	*fee-lay*
	TINTENFISCH			**FILET**
eel	*arl*		fingers	*shtayb-shyern*
	AAL			**STÄBCHEN**
hake	*zay-hesht*			
	SEEHECHT			
halibut	*hiyl-boot*		fresh	*frish*
	HEILBUTT			**FRISCH**
herring	*hay-ring*		frozen	*teef-gur-froh-rern*
	HERING			**TIEFGEFROREN**
John Dory	*hay-rings-kurnig*		dried	*der*
	HERINGSKÖNIG			**DÖRR**
lamprey	*noyn-owgur*		smoked	*gur-roysh-yert*
	NEUNAUGE			**GERÄUCHERT**
lobster	*hoo-mer*			
	HUMMER			
mackerel	*mah-kray-ler*			
	MAKRELE			
mullet	*mair-esher*		do you have	*har-bern zee*
	MEERÄSCHE			**HABEN SIE**
mussels	*moo-sherln*		can I have	*kan ish har-bern*
	MUSCHELN			**KANN ICH HABEN**
octopus	*krar-ker*			
	KRAKE			
oysters	*ow-stern*		a little	*iyn biss-shyern*
	AUSTERN			**EIN BISSCHEN**
perch	*barsh*		some	*et-vars*
	BARSCH			**ETWAS**
pike	*hesht*		more	*mair*
	HECHT			**MEHR**
plaice	*shol-ler*		less	*vay-nigger*
	SCHOLLE			**WENIGER**
prawns	*gar-nay-lern*			
	GARNELEN			
salmon	*lax*		bigger	*grur-ser*
	LACHS			**GRÖSSER**
sardines	*zar-dee-nern*		smaller	*kliy-ner*
	SARDINEN			**KLEINER**
scallops	*ya-kops-moo-sherln*			
	JAKOBSMUSCHELN			
scampi	*kur-nigs-krabbern*		fresher	*frish-er*
	KÖNIGSKRABBEN			**FRISCHER**
shrimps	*krab-bern*		leaner	*mar-gur-rer*
	KRABBEN			**MAGERER**
sole	*zay-tsoong-er*		riper	*riy-fer*
	SEEZUNGE			**REIFER**

soft drinks: 67   alcoholic drinks: 68   groceries vegetables & herbs: overleaf ☞

GROCERIES	*lay-berns-mitterl*	orange juice	*apfel-zee-nern-zarft*
	LEBENSMITTEL		**APFELSINENSAFT**
apple juice	*ap-ferl-zarft*	olive oil	*ol-lee-vern-erl*
	APFELSAFT		**OLIVENÖL**
baby food	*baby-naroong*	pepper	*pfef-fer*
	BABYNAHRUNG		**PFEFFER**
beer	*beer*	pickles	*mixed pickles*
	BIER		**MIXED PICKLES**
biscuits	*cake-ser*	pie	*pass-tay-ter*
	KEKSE		**PASTETE**
bread	*broat*	rice	*rice*
	BROT		**REIS**
(rolls)	*brurt-shyern*	rolls	*brurt-shyern*
	BRÖTCHEN		**BRÖTCHEN**
butter	*boo-ter*	salt	*zalts*
	BUTTER		**ZALZ**
cake	*koosh-ern*	salt & pepper	*zalts oont pfef-fer*
	KUCHEN		**SALZ UND PFEFFER**
cereal	*gur-try-der-flockern*	sandwiches	*sen-vitches*
	GETREIDEFLOCKEN		**SANDWICHES**
cheese	*kay-zer*	sausages	*voorst-shyern*
	KÄSE		**WÜRSTCHEN**
chocolate	*shocko-lar-der*	spaghetti	*shpah-get-tee*
	SCHOKOLADE		**SPAGHETTI**
coffee	*kaf-fay*	soft drinks	*alko-hoal-friyer gur-tren-k*
	KAFFEE		**ALKOHOLFREIE GETRÄNKE**
cold cuts	*owf-shnit*	soup	*zoo-per*
	AUFSCHNITT		**SUPPE**
cooking oil	*shpiy-zer-erl*	sugar	*tsoo-ker*
	SPEISEÖL		**ZUCKER**
cooking fat	*kosh-fet*	sweets	*bon-bons*
	KOCHFETT		**BONBONS**
crackers	*krair-kers*	syrup	*zee-roop*
	CRACKERS		**SIRUP**
cream	*zar-ner*	tea	*tay*
	SAHNE		**TEE**
crisps	*kar-toff-erl-chips*	tomato juice	*tom-mar-tern-zarft*
	KARTOFFELCHIPS		**TOMATENSAFT**
dried herbs	*trock-ern-kroy-ter*	vinegar	*ess-sig*
	TROCKENKRÄUTER		**ESSIG**
eggs	*eye-yer*	wine	*vine*
	EIER		**WEIN**
flour	*mayl*	yogurt	*yoh-goort*
	MEHL		**JOGHURT**
fruit juice	*ohbst-zaft*		
	OBSTSAFT		
grapefruit juice	*parm-perl-moo-zern-zarft*	a	*iyn*
	PAMPELMUSENSAFT		**EIN**
honey	*hoh-nig*	bag	*too-ter*
	HONIG		**TÜTE**
ice cream	*ice*	bottle	*flash-er*
	EIS		**FLASCHE**
jam	*konfee-too-rer*	box	*shash-terl*
	KONFITÜRE		**SCHACHTEL**
margarine	*mar-gar-ree-ner*	can	*door-zer*
	MARGARINE		**DOSE**
marmalade	*or-ran-jern-marmar-larder*	jar	*glars*
	ORANGENMARMELADE		**GLAS**
milk	*milsh*	packet	*pack-ayt*
	MILCH		**PAKET**
(skimmed milk)	*mar-gur-meelsh*	tube	*too-ber*
	MAGERMILCH		**TUBE**
mustard	*zenf*	of	*fon*
	SENF		**VON**

overleaf : fruit meat sausages & fish: 78   soft drinks: 67

VEGETABLES	*gur-moo-zer*	tomatoes	*tom-mar-tern*
	GEMÜSE		**TOMATEN**
artichokes	*arti-shock-ern*	turnips	*roo-bern*
	ARTISCHOCKEN		**RÜBEN**
asparagus	*shpar-gurl*	truffles	*troo-ferl*
	SPARGEL		**TRÜFFEL**
aubergines	*oh-ber-jee-nern*	zucchini	*tsoo-kee-nee*
	AUBERGINEN		**ZUCCHINI**
avocado	*avo-car-doh*		
	AVOCADO		
beetroot	*ro-ter-bay-ter*	**HERBS**	*kroy-ter*
	ROTE BEETE		**KRÄUTER**
broad beans	*dick-er bo-nern*	basil	*bah-zeel-yern-krowt*
	DICKE BOHNEN		**BASILIENKRAUT**
cabbage	*coal*	bay leaf	*lor-bair-blat*
	KOHL		**LORBEERBLATT**
carrots	*kar-rot-tern / mer-rern*	garlic	*knoh-blaoosh*
	KAROTTEN / MÖHREN		**KNOBLAUCH**
cauliflower	*bloo-mern-coal*	ginger	*ing-ver*
	BLUMENKOHL		**INGWER**
celery	*shtang-ern-zellery*	mint	*min-tser*
	STANGENSELLERIE		**MINZE**
courgettes	*tsoo-kee-nee*	rosemary	*rose-mar-rin*
	ZUCCHINI		**ROSMARIN**
cucumber	*goor-ker*	sage	*zal-by*
	GURKE		**SALBEI**
gherkins	*ess-sig-goorkern*	tarragon	*ess-trargon*
	ESSIGGURKEN		**ESTRAGON**
green beans	*groo-ner bo-nern*	thyme	*too-mee-yarn*
	GRÜNE BOHNEN		**THYMIAN**
leaks	*por-rays*		
	PORREES		
lentils	*lin-zern*		
	LINSEN		
lettuce	*kopf-zalart*	do you have	*har-bern zee*
	KOPFSALAT		**HABEN SIE**
marrow	*mark-koorbiss*	can I have	*kan ish har-bern*
	MARKKÜRBIS		**KANN ICH HABEN**
mushrooms	*pilt-tser*		
	PILZE		
onions	*tsvee-berln*	a	*iyn*
	ZWIEBELN		**EIN**
parsley	*payter-zeel-yer*	a little	*iyn biss-shyern*
	PETERSILIE		**EIN BISSCHEN**
parsnip	*pastee-nar-ker*	some	*et-vars*
	PASTINAKE		**ETWAS**
peas	*airb-zern*	piece	*shtook*
	ERBSEN		**STÜCK**
peppers	*pap-reeka*	slice	*shigh-ber*
	PAPRIKA		**SCHEIBE**
potatoes	*kar-tof-ferln*	of	*fon*
	KARTOFFELN		**VON**
pumpkin	*koor-biss*		
	KÜRBIS		
radishes	*ra-dees-shyern*	more	*mair*
	RADIESCHEN		**MEHR**
shallots	*shal-lot-tern*	less	*vay-nigger*
	SCHALLOTTEN		**WENIGER**
spinach	*shpee-nart*	bigger	*grur-ser*
	SPINAT		**GRÖSSER**
Brussels sprouts	*ro-zern-coal*	smaller	*kliy-ner*
	ROSENKOHL		**KLEINER**
sweetcorn	*mice*	fresher	*frish-er*
	MAIS		**FRISCHER**

alcoholic drinks: 68

I	*ish* **ICH**		I would like	*ish mersh-ter* **ICH MÖCHTE**
my	*mine* **MEIN**		do you want	*vol-ern* zee **WOLLEN SIE**
you	*zee* **SIE**			
your	*eeyer* **IHR**		I have	*ish har-ber* **ICH HABE**
it	*ess* **ES**		do you have	*har-bern* zee **HABEN SIE**
not	*nisht* **NICHT**		can I	*kan ish* **KANN ICH**
no	*kine* **KEIN**		can you	*ker-nen* zee **KÖNNEN SIE**
which	*vel-shyer* **WELCHER**		is	*isst* **IST**
where	*voh* **WO**		are	*zint* **SIND**
when	*van* **WANN**		is there	*gipt ess* **GIBT ES**
what	*vass* **WAS**		is it	*ist ess* **IST ES**
what time	*uhm vvee-feel ooer* **UM WIEVIEL UHR**			
how	*vee* **WIE**		brush	*boor-stern* **BÜRSTEN**
how much	*vee-feel* **WIEVIEL**		comb	*kem-mern* **KÄMMEN**
how much is (it)	*vass koss-tert* **WAS KOSTET**		cut	*shniy-dern* **SCHNEIDEN**
how much is (that)	*vass koss-tert das* **WAS KOSTET DAS**		do	*mash-ern* **MACHEN**
			have	*har-bern* **HABEN**
			leave it	*ess lass-ern* **ES LASSEN**
nearest	*nex-ster* **NÄCHSTER**		like it	*ess mur-gurn* **ES MÖGEN**
near	*in dair nay-er fon* **IN DER NAHE VON**		make it	*ess mash-ern* **ES MACHEN**
here	*here* **HIER**			
			hairdresser	*free-zer* **FRISEUR**
and	*oont* **UND**		beauty salon	*koz-may-teek-zalon* **KOSMETIKSALON**
at	*an* **AN**		mens'	*hair-ern* **HERREN-**
from	*fon* **VON**		womens'	*dar-mern* **DAMEN-**
for	*foor* **FÜR**			
off	*fon* **VON**		appointment	*tair-meen* **TERMIN**
on	*owff* **AUF**		name	*nar-mer* **NAME**
to	*tsoo* **ZU**		open	*owff* **AUF**
too	*tsoo* **ZU**		closed	*tsoo* **ZU**

same	*gliysh*		beard	*bart*
	GLEICH			**BART**
different	*an-ders*		hair	*har*
	ANDERS			**HAAR**
style	*shteel*		moustache	*shnoor-bart*
	STIL			**SCHNURRBART**
colour	*far-ber*		sideboards	*kot-let-tern*
	FARBE			**KOTELETTEN**

a little	*iyn **biss**-shyern*		blowdry	*fur-nern*
	EIN BISSCHEN			**FÖNEN**
plenty	*feel*		haircut	*har-shnit*
	VIEL			**HAARSCHNITT**
enough	*gur-noog*		manicure	*mannee-koo-rer*
	GENUG			**MANIKÜRE**
more	*mair*		pedicure	*peddee-koo-rer*
	MEHR			**PEDIKÜRE**
less	*vay-nigger*		perm	*dow-er-veller*
	WENIGER			**DAUERWELLE**
			rinse	*farp-shpoo-loong*
				FARBSPÜLUNG
front	*for-ner*		set	*lay-gurn*
	VORNE			**LEGEN**
back	*hin-tern*		shampoo	*vash-ern*
	HINTEN			**WASCHEN**
top	*oh-bern*		shave	*ra-zee-rern*
	OBEN			**RASIEREN**
sides	*zigh-tern*		tint	*tur-noong*
	SEITEN			**TÖNUNG**
			touch-up	*owff-rish-loong*
long	*lang*			**AUFFRISCHUNG**
	LANG		trim	*tsoo-resht-shniy-dern*
short	*koorts*			**ZURECHTSCHNEIDEN**
	KURZ			
longer	*leng-er*		layered	*shtoo-fig gur-shnit-ern*
	LÄNGER			**STUFIG GESCHNITTEN**
shorter	*koort-ser*		shaped	*noy gur-formt*
	KÜRZER			**NEU GEFORMT**
			streaked	*shtray-nern-fair-boong*
light	*hell*			**STRÄHNENFÄRBUNG**
	HELL		curly	*lock-ig*
dark	*doonk-el*			**LOCKIG**
	DUNKEL		fluffy	*viysh*
				WEICH
			fringe	*po-nee*
				PONY
lighter	*hel-ler*		ringlets	*lurk-shyern*
	HELLER			**LÖCKCHEN**
darker	*doonk-ler*		wavy	*gur-velt*
	DUNKLER			**GEWELLT**

auburn	*kass-tarn-yern-brown*		conditioner	*har-koor*
	KASTANIENBRAUN			**HAARKUR**
black	*shvarts*		cream	*kraym*
	SCHWARZ			**CREME**
blond	*blont*		lacquer	*shpray*
	BLOND			**SPRAY**
brunette	*brown*		oil	*erl*
	BRAUN			**ÖL**
colour chart	*farp-tabeller*		tonic	*har-vasser*
	FARBTABELLE			**HAARWASSER**

I	*ish* **ICH**	I would like	*ish* **mersh**-ter **ICH MÖCHTE**
my	*mine* **MEIN**	we would like	*veer* **mersh**-tern **WIR MÖCHTEN**
we	*veer* **WIR**	do you want	*vol*-ern zee **WOLLEN SIE**
our	*oon*-ser **UNSER**		
you	*zee* **SIE**	I have	*ish* **har**-ber **ICH HABE**
your	*eeyer* **IHR**	we have	*veer* **har**-bern **WIR HABEN**
who	*vair* **WER**	do you have	**har**-bern zee **HABEN SIE**
it	*ess* **ES**		
		can I	*kan ish* **KANN ICH**
not	*nisht* **NICHT**	can we	*ker*-nen veer **KÖNNEN WIR**
no	*kine* **KEIN**	can you	*ker*-nen zee **KÖNNEN SIE**
where	*voh* **WO**	is	*isst* **IST**
when	*van* **WANN**	are	*zint* **SIND**
what	*vass* **WAS**	is there	*gipt ess* **GIBT ES**
what time	*uhm* vvee-**feel** ooer **UM WIEVIEL UHR**	is it	*ist ess* **IST ES**
how	*vee* **WIE**	buy	*cow*-fern **KAUFEN**
how often	*vee oft* **WIE OFT**	go	*gay*-urn **GEHEN**
how long	*vee* **lang**-er **WIE LANGE**	do	*mash*-ern **MACHEN**
how many	*vee-fee*-ler **WIEVIEL**	have	*har*-bern **HABEN**
		hire	*mee*-tern **MIETEN**
near	*in dair* **nay**-er fon **IN DER NÄHE VON**	learn	*ler*-nern **LERNEN**
here	*here* **HIE**	interested in	*an* ..... interess-**seert** **AN ...... INTERESSIERT**
		do you know	*viss*-ern zee **WISSEN SIE**
and	*oont* **UND**	like	*mur*-gurn **MÖGEN**
at	*an* **AN**	meet	*tref*-ern **TREFFEN**
for	*foor* **FÜR**	play	*shpee*-lern **SPIELEN**
in	*in* **IN**	show me	*tsigh*-gurn zee meer **ZEIGEN SIE MIR**
on	*owf* **AUF**	studying	*shtoo*-dyum **STUDIUM**
to	*tsoo* **ZU**	take part	*tile*-naymern **TEILNEHMEN**
with	*mit* **MIT**	watch	*tsoo*-zayurn **ZUSEHEN**

anyone	*yay-mant* **JEMAND**	**CHESS**	*sharsh* **SCHACH**
people	*loy-ter* **LEUTE**	chess board	*sharsh-bret* **SCHACHBRETT**
club	*cloob* **KLUB**	bishop	*loy-fer* **LÄUFER**
		castle	*toorm* **TURM**
beginner	*an-feng-er* **ANFÄNGER**	king	*kur-nig* **KÖNIG**
average	*mit-terl-maysig* **MITTELMÄSSIG**	knight	*shpring-er* **SPRINGER**
experienced	*air-far-rern* **ERFAHREN**	pawn	*baoo-er* **BAUER**
		queen	*dar-mer* **DAME**
partner	*part-ner* **PARTNER**	**CHECK!**	*shash* **SCHACH**
player	*shpee-ler* **SPIELER**	**MATE!**	*mat* **MAT**
team	*man-shaft* **MANNSCHAFT**		
		CARDS	*kar-tern-shpeel* **KARTENSPIEL**
game	*shpeel* **SPIEL**	ace	*ars* **AS**
match	*shpeel* **SPIEL**	jack	*boo-ber* **BUBE**
tournament	*vet-kampf* **WETTKAMPF**	joker	*joker* **JOKER**
		king	*kur-nig* **KÖNIG**
very	*zair* **SEHR**	queen	*dar-mer* **DAME**
fairly	*tseem-lish* **ZIEMLICH**		
easy	*liysht* **LEICHT**	hearts	*hairts* **HERZ**
difficult	*shveer-rig* **SCHWIERIG**	diamonds	*kar-roh* **KARO**
		clubs	*kroyts* **KREUZ**
place	*ort* **ORT**	spades	*peek* **PIK**
shop	*lar-dern* **LADEN**		
		Bridge	*bridge* **BRIDGE**
equipment	*owss-roostoong* **AUSRÜSTUNG**	(a rubber)	*rob-er* **ROBBER**
instruction	*oon-ter-risht* **UNTERRICHT**	Canasta	*ka-nass-ta* **KANASTA**
lesson	*lair-shtoonder* **LEHRSTUNDE**	Gin Rummy	*rom-may* **ROMMÉ**
permit	*owss-vice* **AUSWEIS**	Whist	*whist* **WHIST**
		Pontoon	*zeeb-tsayn oont feer* **SIEBZEHN UND VIER**
open	*owff* **AUF**	Poker	*poker* **POKER**
closed	*tsoo* **ZU**		
		I'M OUT!	*fair-tig* **FERTIG!**

HOBBIES	*hob-ees*	computers	*com-pyou-ter*
	HOBBYS		**COMPUTER**
acting	*shpee-lern*	cooking	*kosh-ern*
	SPIELEN		**KOCHEN**
amateur dramatics	*ama-ter-tay-arter*	crafts	*hant-vair-ker*
	AMATEURTHEATER		**HANDWERKE**
antiques	*an-tick-vee-tay-tern*	croquet	*kroh-ket*
	ANTIQUITÄTEN		**KROCKET**
archeology	*al-ter-tooms-koonder*	crosswords	*kroyts-vort-ray-tserln*
	ALTERTUMSKUNDE		**KREUZWORTRÄTSELN**
architecture	*arshee-teck-toor*	current affairs	*tar-gurz-air-riyg-nisse*
	ARCHITEKTUR		**TAGESEREIGNISSE**
aircraft	*floog-stoy-gur*	cycling	*rard-far-rern*
	FLUGZEUGE		**RADFAHREN**
art	*koonst*	dancing	*tants*
	KUNST		**TANZ**
astronomy	*astronno-mee*	(ballroom dancing)	*gur-zel-shafts-tants*
	ASTRONOMIE		**GESELLSCHAFTSTANZ**
backgammon	*poof-shpeel*	(aerobics)	*air-roh-bick*
	PUFFSPIEL		**AEROBIK**
ballet	*bal-let*	(folk dancing)	*folks-tants*
	BALLETT		**VOLKSTANZ**
billiards	*bill-yard-shpeel*	(pop dancing)	*disco-tants*
	BILLÁRDSPIEL		**DISKOTANZ**
bird watching	*foh-gurl-ber-oh-barsh-toong*	darts	*pfile-vair-fern*
	VOGELBEOBACHTUNG		**PFEILWERFEN**
biology	*bee-ohlo-ghee*	debating	*day-bar-tee-rern*
	BIOLOGIE		**DEBATTIEREN**
board games	*bret-shpee-ler*	design	*design*
	BRETTSPIELE		**DESIGN**
boating	*bort-far-rern*	dominoes	*dom-mee-noh*
	BOOTFAHREN		**DOMINO**
boats	*bort-er*	draughts	*dar-mer-shpeel*
	BOOTE		**DAMESPIEL**
botany	*boh-tan-neek*	drawing	*tsiysh-nern*
	BOTANIK		**ZEICHNEN**
butterflies	*shmet-ter-linger*	driving	*far-rern*
	SCHMETTERLINGE		**FAHREN**
calligraphy	*kal-lee-graf-fee*	electronics	*ellek-troh-neek*
	KALLIGRAPHIE		**ELEKTRONIK**
camping	*tsel-tern*	environment	*oom-velt*
	ZELTEN		**UMWELT**
canals	*bin-nern-vasser-fart*	fashion	*mor-der*
	BINNENWASSERFAHRT		**MODE**
cards	*kar-tern-shpee-lern*	fish	*fish-er*
	KARTEN SPIELEN		**FISCHE**
carpentry	*tsim-mer-hant-vairk*	fishing	*ang-gurln*
	ZIMMERHANDWERK		**ANGELN**
cars	*var-gurn*	flower arranging	*bloo-mern-shteck-ern*
	WAGEN		**BLUMENSTECKEN**
(old cars)	*al-ter var-gurn*	gardens	*gair-tern*
	ALTE WAGEN		**GÄRTEN**
chemistry	*shem-mee*	gardening	*gairt-nern*
	CHEMIE		**GÄRTNERN**
chess	*sharsh*	geography	*aird-koon-der*
	SCHACH		**ERDKUNDE**
cinema	*kee-no*	geology	*gay-ohlo-ghee*
	KINO		**GEOLOGIE**
collecting	*zam-erln*	handicrafts	*koonst-hant-vair-ker*
	SAMMELN		**KUNSTHANDWERKE**
concerts	*con-tsair-ter*	hiking	*van-dern*
	KONZERTE		**WANDERN**
conservation	*oom-velt-shoots*	history	*gur-shish-ter*
	UMWELTSCHUTZ		**GESCHICHTE**

arts & antiques: 11   sports: 116-117

industrial	*in-dooss-tree-el-ler*	photography	*photo-graph-fee*
	INDUSTRIELLE		**PHOTOGRAPHIE**
rcheology	*arshay-ohlo-ghee*	physics	*foo-zeek*
	ARCHÄOLOGIE		**PHYSIK**
insects	*in-zeck-tern*	politics	*pol-lee-tick*
	INSEKTEN		**POLITIK**
w puzzles	*zets-shpee-ler*	(communist)	*commoo-niss-tish*
	SETZSPIELE		**KOMMUNISTISCH**
knitting	*shtrick-kern*	(social democrat)	*zoh-tsee-yarl-demo-krar-tish*
	STRICKEN		**SOZIALDEMOKRATISCH**
languages	*shprar-shern*	(centre)	*fon der mit-ter*
	SPRACHEN		**VON DER MITTEE**
literature	*li-ter-rar-toor*	(right)	*reshts*
	LITERATUR		**RECHTS**
ne biology	*mair-rerz-bee-ohlo-ghee*	(far right)	*ex-traym-reshts*
	MEERESBIOLOGIE		**EXTREM RECHTS**
athematics	*matter-mar-teek*	pool	*art bill-yard-shpeel*
	MATHEMATIK		**art BILLARDSPIEL**
mechanics	*ma-shee-nern-lair-rer*	pottery	*terp-fer-righ*
	MASCHINENLEHRE		**TÖPFEREI**
metalwork	*met-tarl-bay-ar-bigh-toong*	radio	*roont-foonk*
	METALLBEARBEITUNG		**RUNDFUNK**
del making	*moh-del-baoo*	reading	*lay-zern*
	MODELLBAU		**LESEN**
models	*moh-del-ler*	roulette	*roo-let*
	MODELLE		**ROULETT**
eroplanes)	*floog-tsoy-gur*	science	*nar-toor-vissern-sharf-tern*
	FLUGZEUGE		**NATURWISSENSCHAFTEN**
(boats)	*bor-ter*	sculpture	*bilt-how-wer-righ*
	BOOTE		**BILDHAUEREI**
(buses)	*boo-ser*	singing	*zing-ern*
	BUSSE		**SINGEN**
(trams)	*shtrar-sern-bar-nern*	sketching	*shkit-tseer-rern*
	STRASSENBAHNEN		**SKIZZIEREN**
(railways)	*iy-zern-bar-nern*	skittles	*kay-gurln*
	EISENBAHNEN		**KEGELN**
Monopoly	*mono-pol-lee*	snooker	*art bill-yard-shpeel*
	MONOPOLY		**art BILLARDSPIEL**
notorcycles	*moh-tor-ray-der*	social sciences	*so-tsee-yarl-vissern-sharf-tern*
	MOTORRÄDER		**SOZIALWISSENSCHAFTEN**
otorcycling	*moh-tor-rard-far-rern*	speleology	*shpay-lay-ohlo-ghee*
	MOTORRADFAHREN		**SPELÄOLOGIE**
music	*moo-zeek*	sports	*shport*
	MUSIK		**SPORT**
(classical)	*klass-see-sher*	stamp collecting	*breef-markern zam-erln*
	KLASSISCHE		**BRIEFMARKEN SAMMELN**
folk music)	*folks-moo-zeek*	theatre	*tay-ar-ter*
	VOLKSMUSIK		**THEATER**
(jazz)	*jazz*	transport	*trans-port-vay-zern*
	JAZZ		**TRANSPORTWESEN**
pop music)	*pop-moo-zeek*	(see models)	*zee-er moh-dell-er*
	POPMUSIK		**(siehe Modelle)**
ural history	*nah-toor-gur-shish-ter*	travelling	*riy-zern*
	NATURGESCHICHTE		**REISEN**
needlework	*nay-yer-riy*	TV	*fairn-zay*
	NÄHEREI		**FERNSEH**
opera	*oh-per*	walking	*van-dern*
	OPER		**WANDERN**
painting	*mar-lern*	weaving	*vay-bern*
	MALEN		**WEBEN**
pets	*house-teer-rer*	woodwork	*holts-bay-ar-bigh-toong*
	HAUSTIERE		**HOLZBEARBEITUNG**
picnicking	*pick-nick-kern*	writing	*shriy-bern*
	PICKNICKEN		**SCHREIBEN**

types of music: 71

I	*ish* **ICH**	I would like	*ish* **mersh**-ter **ICH MÖCHTE**
my	*mine* **MEIN**	he/she would like	*air / zee* mersh-**ter** **ER/SIE MÖCHTE**
me	*mish* **MICH**	do you want	*vol-ern zee* **WOLLEN SIE**
he	*air* **ER**		
she	*zee* **SIE**	I have	*ish* **har**-ber **ICH HABE**
you	*zee* **SIE**	he / she has	*air / zee hat* **ER/SIE HAT**
it	*ess* **ES**	do you have	**har**-bern *zee* **HABEN SIE**
		does he/she have	*hat air / zee* **HAT ER/SIE**
not	*nisht* **NICHT**		
no	*kine* **KEIN**	can I	*kan ish* **KANN ICH**
		can he / she	*kan air / zee* **KANN ER/SIE**
which	**vel**-shyer **WELCHER**	can you	**ker**-nen *zee* **KÖNNEN SIE**
where	*voh* **WO**	I cannot	*ish can nisht* **ICH KANN NICHT**
when	*van* **WANN**	he / she cannot	*air / zee kan nish* **ER/SIE KANN NICHT**
what	*vass* **WAS**		
what time	*uhm* vee-**feel** *ooer* **UM WIEVIEL UHR**	is	*isst* **IST**
		are	*zint* **SIND**
how	*vee* **WIE**	is there	*gipt ess* **GIBT ES**
how long	*vee* **lang**-er **WIE LANGE**	is it	*ist ess* **IST ES**
how many	vee-**fee**-ler **WIEVIELE**		
how much	vee-**feel** **WIEVIEL**	check	oonter-**zoo**-shern **UNTERSUCHEN**
how often	*vee oft* **WIE OFT**	drink	*trin-kern* **TRINKEN**
		eat	*ess-ern* **ESSEN**
and	*oont* **UND**	feel	*foo-lern* **FÜHLEN**
at	*an* **AN**	have	*har-bern* **HABEN**
for	*foor* **FÜR**	help	*hel-fern zee* **HELFEN SIE**
from	*fon* **VON**	give	*gay-bern zee* **GEBEN SIE**
in	*in* **IN**	go	*gay-ern* **GEHEN**
on	*owf* **AUF**	see	*zay-ern* **SEHEN**
to	*tsoo* **ZU**	need	*brow-shern* **BRAUCHEN**
too	*tsoo* **ZU**	stay	*bligh-bern* **BLEIBEN**
with	*mit* **MIT**	take	*nay-mern* **NEHMEN**

a little	*iyn **biss**-shyern* **EIN BISSCHEN**	**EQUIPMENT**	*gur-**ray**-ter* **GERÄTE**
very	*zair* **SEHR**	bed	*bet* **BETT**
pain	*shmairts* **SCHMERZ**	bed pan	*shtesh-beckern* **STECHBECKEN**
painful	*shmairts-haft* **SCHMERZHAFT**	headphones	*kopf-hur-rer* **KOPFHÖRER**
faint	*dair **own**-masht **nah**-er* **DER OHNMACHT NAHE**	meal tray	*ess-sern-tablet* **ESSENTABLETT**
sick	*oo-berl* **ÜBEL**	pyjamas	*shlarf-antsoog* **SCHLAFANZUG**
shaky	*tsit-ter-rig* **ZITTERIG**	respirator	*ar-term-gur-rayt* **ATEMGERÄT**
hot	*hice* **HEISS**	telephone	*taylay-phone* **TELEFON**
cold	*kalt* **KALT**	urine bottle	*oo-reen-flasher* **URINFLASCHE**
		TREATMENTS	*ber-hant-loongurn* **BEHANDLUNGEN**
SAMPLES	*pro-bern* **PROBEN**	allergy	*al-lair-gish* **ALLERGISCH**
blood	*bloot* **BLUT**	a bath	*iyn bart* **EIN BAD**
blood group	*bloot-groo-per* **BLUTGRUPPE**	examination	*oonter-zoo-shoong* **UNTERSUCHUNG**
saliva	*shpiy-shyerl* **SPEICHEL**	exercise	*oo-boong* **ÜBUNG**
stools	*shtool* **STUHL**	general anaesthetic	*foll-narko-zer* **VOLLNARKOSE**
urine	*oo-reen* **URIN**	injection	*shprit-ser* **SPRITZE**
		intensive care	*inten-seef-shtatsee-yone* **INTENSIVSTATION**
PEOPLE	*loy-ter* **LEUTE**	intravenous	*intra-vay-nurse* **INTRAVENÖS**
doctor	*artst* **ARZT**	local anaesthetic	*urt-lisher ber-toy-boong* **ÖRTLICHE BETÄUBUNG**
nurse	*kran-kern-shvester* **KRANKENSCHWESTER**	medicine	*may-deeka-ment* **MEDIKAMENT**
visitor	*ber-zoo-sher* **BESUCHER**	operation	*operratsee-yone* **OPERATION**
physiotherapist	*foo-zeeyo-tairra-poyt* **PHYSIOTHERAPEUT**	oxygen	*zower-shtof* **SAUERSTOFF**
specialist	*fash-artst* **FACHARZT**	pain reliever	*shmairts-shtill-enders mit-erl* **SCHMERZSTILLENDES MITTEL**
		physiotherapy	*foo-zeeyo-tair-rappee* **PHYSIOTHERAPIE**
ROOMS	*roy-mer* **RÄUME**	plaster cast	*gips-fairbant* **GIPSVERBAND**
bathroom	*bar-der-tsimmer* **BADEZIMMER**	sedative	*ber-roo-igoongs-mitterl* **BERUHIGUNGSMITTEL**
day room	*tar-gurs-rowm* **TAGESRAUM**	stitches	*gur-nayt vair-dern* **GENÄHT WERDEN**
dining room	*shpiy-zer-zarl* **SPEISESAAL**	temperature	*temper-toor* **TEMPERATUR**
operating theatre	*operratsee-yones-zarl* **OPERATIONSAAL**	transfusion	*trans-foozee-yone* **TRANSFUSION**
toilet	*twal-let-ter* **TOILETTE**	X-ray	*rernt-gurn* **RÖNTGEN**
ward	*shtatsee-yone* **STATION**	a wash	*mish vash-ern* **MICH WASCHEN**

I	*ish* **ICH**	I would like	*ish mersh-ter* **ICH MÖCHTE**
my	*mine* **MEIN**	we would like	*veer mersh-tern* **WIR MÖCHTEN**
we	*veer* **WIR**	do you want	*vol-ern zee* **WOLLEN SIE**
our	*oon-ser* **UNSER**		
you	*zee* **SIE**	I have	*ish har-ber* **ICH HABE**
your	*eeyer* **IHR**	does it have	*hat ess* **HAT ES**
it	*ess* **ES**	do you have	*har-bern zee* **HABEN SIE**
not	*nisht* **NICHT**	can I	*kan ish* **KANN ICH**
no	*kine* **KEIN**	can we	*ker-nen veer* **KÖNNEN WIR**
		can you	*ker-nen zee* **KÖNNEN SIE**
which	*vel-shyer* **WELCHER**		
where	*voh* **WO**	is	*isst* **IST**
when	*van* **WANN**	are	*zint* **SIND**
what	*vass* **WAS**	is there	*gipt ess* **GIBT ES**
what time	*uhm vvee-feel ooer* **UM WIEVIEL UHR**	is it	*ist ess* **IST ES**
how long	*vee lang-er* **WIE LANGE**	carry	*trar-gurn* **TRAGEN**
how many	*vee-fee-ler* **WIEVIELE**	depart	*ap-far-rern* **ABFAHREN**
how much is (that)	*vass koss-tert (das)* **WAS KOSTET (DAS)**	have	*har-bern* **HABEN**
		pay	*tsar-lern* **ZAHLEN**
near	*in dair nay-er fon* **IN DER NÄHE VON**	reserve	*rezzair-vee-rern* **RESERVIEREN**
here	*here* **HIER**	show me	*tsigh-gurn zee meer* **ZEIGEN SIE MIR**
there	*dar* **DA**	stay	*bligh-bern* **BLEIBEN**
		take	*nay-mern* **NEHMEN**
and	*oont* **UND**	write	*shriy-bern* **SCHREIBEN**
at	*an* **AN**		
for	*foor* **FÜR**	per	*pro* **PRO**
from	*fon* **VON**	night	*nasht* **NACHT**
in	*in* **IN**	week	*vosh-er* **WOCHE**
of	*fon* **VON**	person	*pair-zone* **PERSON**
until	*biss* **BIS**	people	*loy-ter* **LEUTE**

rvice charge	*ber-dee-noong* **BEDIENUNG**		front	*for-ner* **VORNE**
taxes	*shtoy-ern* **STEUERN**		back	*hin-tern* **HINTEN**
included	*in-ber-griffern* **INBEGRIFFEN**		high up	*oh-bern* **OBEN**
bill	*resh-noong* **RECHNUNG**		quiet	*roo-wig* **RUHIG**
receipt	*kvit-toong* **QUITTUNG**		quieter	*roo-wigger* **RUHIGER**
deposit	*an-tsarloong* **ANZAHLUNG**			
credit card	*kre-deet-karter* **KREDITKARTE**		with	*mit* **MIT**
ellers cheque	*riy-zer-sheck* **REISECHECK**		(private)	*iy-gurn* **EIGEN**
			(shared)	*gur-tiylt* **GETEILT**
name	*nar-mer* **NAME**		bathroom	*bar-der-tsimmer* **BADEZIMMER**
address	*ad-dress-ser* **ADRESSE**		shower	*doo-sher* **DUSCHE**
passport	*pas* **PASS**		balcony	*bal-kon* **BALKON**
			air conditioning	*klee-mattee-sattsee-yown* **KLIMATISATION**
husband	*man* **MANN**		view	*mit owss-zisht* **MIT AUSSICHT**
wife	*frow* **FRAU**			
child	*kint* **KIND**		bed & breakfast	*tsim-mer mit froo-shtook* **ZIMMER MIT FRÜHSTÜCK**
children	*kin-der* **KINDER**		half-board	*halp-penzee-yown* **HALBPENSION**
baby	*baby* **BABY**		full-board	*foll-penzee-yown* **VOLLPENSION**
inexpensive	*price-goonstig* **PREISGÜNSTIG**		guest house	*penzee-yown* **PENSION**
good	*goot* **GUT**		hotel	*ho-tel* **HOTEL**
cheaper	*bil-ligger* **BILLIGER**		inn	*gast-house* **GASTHAUS**
better	*bess-er* **BESSER**		motel	*rast-house* **RASTHAUS**
single room	*iyn-tsell-tsimmer* **EINZELZIMMER**		probably	*var-shine-lish* **WAHRSCHEINLICH**
double room	*doh-perl-tsimmer* **DOPPELZIMMER**		now	*yetst* **JETZT**
-bedded room	*tsimm-mer mit tsvigh bet-tern* **ZIMMER MIT ZWEI BETTEN**		later	*shpay-ter* **SPÄTER**
extra	*tsoo-zets-lish* **ZUSÄTZLICH**		open	*owff* **AUF**
bed	*bet* **BETT**		closed	*tsoo* **ZU**
cot	*vee-gur* **WIEGE**		checkout time	*ap-fart-tsight* **ABFAHRTZEIT**

tel problems: 94 ☞   hotel enquiries & services: overleaf ☞

I	*ish* **ICH**	I would like	*ish* **mersh**-ter **ICH MÖCHTE**
my	*mine* **MEIN**	we would like	*veer* **mersh**-tern **WIR MÖCHTEN**
we	*veer* **WIR**	do you want	*vol*-ern *zee* **WOLLEN SIE**
our	**oon**-ser **UNSER**		
you	*zee* **SIE**	I have	*ish* **har**-ber **ICH HABE**
your	*eeyer* **IHR**	do you have	**har**-bern *zee* **HABEN SIE**
it	*ess* **ES**		
		can I	*kan ish* **KANN ICH**
not	*nisht* **NICHT**	can we	**ker**-nen *veer* **KÖNNEN WIR**
no	*kine* **KEIN**	can you	**ker**-nen *zee* **KÖNNEN SIE**
which	**vel**-shyer **WELCHER**	is	*isst* **IST**
where	*voh* **WO**	are	*zint* **SIND**
when	*van* **WANN**	is there	*gipt ess* **GIBT ES**
what	*vass* **WAS**	is it	*ist ess* **IST ES**
what time	*uhm vee-**feel** ooer* **UM WIEVIEL UHR**		
		carry	**trar**-gurn **TRAGEN**
how long	*vee **lang**-er* **WIE LANGE**	call me	**roo**-fern *zee mish* **RUFEN SIE MICH**
how many	*vee-**fee**-ler* **WIEVIELE**	change *(money)*	**eck**-serln **WECHSELN**
how much is (that)	*vass **koss**-tert (das)* **WAS KOSTET (DAS)**	go	**far**-rern **FAHREN**
		have	**har**-bern **HABEN**
near	*in dair **nay**-er fon* **IN DER NÄHE VON**	leave *(things)*	**lass**-ern **LASSEN**
here	*here* **HIER**	order	*ber-**shtel**-ern* **BESTELLEN**
		pay	**tsar**-lern **ZAHLEN**
and	*oont* **UND**	post	*tsoor posst **bring**-e* **ZUR POST BRINGEN**
at	*an* **AN**	*will be* ready	*veert **fair**-tig* **WIRD FERTIG**
by	*by* **BEI**	show me	*tsigh-gurn zee mee* **ZEIGEN SIE MIR**
for	*foor* **FÜR**	*will* take	*nimmt* **NIMMT**
from	*fon* **VON**	telephone	**an**-roofern **ANRUFEN**
in	*in* **IN**		
on	*owf* **AUF**	JUST A MOMENT!	*kline mo-**ment*** **KLEIN MOMENT!**
to	*tsoo* **ZU**	COME IN!	*hair-**rine*** **HEREIN**

room	*tsim-mer* **ZIMMER**	morning call	*veck-anroof* **WECKANRUF**
number	*noo-mer* **NUMMER**	room service	*house-deener* **HAUSDIENER**
name	*nar-mer* **NAME**		
		bar	*bar* **BAR**
now	*yetst* **JETZT**	car park	*park-plats* **PARKPLATZ**
later	*shpay-ter* **SPÄTER**	cloakroom	*gar-der-roh-ber* **GARDEROBE**
soon	*balt* **BALD**	creche	*kin-der-kripper* **KINDERKRIPPE**
sooner	*froo-er* **FRÜHER**	dining room	*shpiy-zer-zarl* **SPEISESAAL**
		hairdressing salon	*free-zeer-zal-lon* **FRISIERSALON**
today	*hoy-ter* **HEUTE**	left luggage office	*gur-peck-owf-ber-var-roong* **GEPÄCKAUFBEWAHRUNG**
tomorrow	*more-gurn* **MORGEN**	lounge	*owff-ent-halts-rowm* **AUFENTHALTSRAUM**
morning	*for-mittarg* **VORMITTAG**	reception	*emp-fang* **EMPFANG**
midday	*mit-targ* **MITTAG**	sauna	*zow-ner* **SAUNA**
afternoon	*narsh-mittarg* **NACHMITTAG**	toilet	*twal-let-ter* **TOILETTE**
evening	*ar-bent* **ABEND**		
		car	*ow-toh* **AUTO**
minutes	*mee-noo-tern* **MINUTEN**	front door	*house-toor* **HAUSTÜR**
hours	*shtoon-dern* **STUNDEN**	key	*shloo-serl* **SCHLÜSSEL**
days	*tar-gur* **TAGE**	luggage	*gur-peck* **GEPÄCK**
		mail	*posst* **POST**
open	*owff* **AUF**	message	*narsh-risht* **NACHRICHT**
closed	*tsoo* **ZU**	money	*gelt* **GELD**
		security safe	*tray-zore* **TRESOR**
breakfast	*froo-shtook* **FRÜHSTÜCK**	taxi	*tax-ee* **TAXI**
lunch	*mit-tar-guessern* **MITTAGESSEN**	telephone	*taylay-phone* **TELEFON**
dinner	*ar-ben-tessern* **ABENDESSEN**	valuables	*vairt-sashern* **WERTSACHEN**
snack	*im-biss* **IMBISS**		
drink	*gur-trenk* **GETRÄNK**	clothes	*kliy-doong* **KLEIDUNG**
		drycleaned	*shay-mish gur-riy-nigt* **CHEMISCH GEREINIGT**
manager	*light-er* **LEITER**	ironed	*gur-boo-gelt* **GEBÜGELT**
chambermaid	*tsim-mer-mayd-shyern* **ZIMMERMÄDCHEN**	laundered	*gur-vash-ern* **GEWASCHEN**
porter	*por-tyay* **PORTIER**	shoes cleaned	*shoo-er gur-pootst* **SCHUHE GEPUTZT**

alcoholic drinks: 68   telephone: 120   hotel problems: overleaf ☞

I	*ish* **ICH**	I would like	*ish mersh-ter* **ICH MÖCHTE**	
my	*mine* **MEIN**	we would like	*veer mersh-tern* **WIR MÖCHTEN**	
we	*veer* **WIR**	do you want	*vol-ern zee* **WOLLEN SIE**	
our	*oon-ser* **UNSER**			
you	*zee* **SIE**	I have	*ish har-ber* **ICH HABE**	
your	*eeyer* **IHR**	we have	*veer har-bern* **WIR HABEN**	
it	*ess* **ES**	do you have	*har-bern zee* **HABEN SIE**	
not	*nisht* **NICHT**	can I	*kan ish* **KANN ICH**	
no	*kine* **KEIN**	can we	*ker-nen veer* **KÖNNEN WIR**	
		can you	*ker-nen zee* **KÖNNEN SIE**	
which	*vel-shyer* **WELCHER**			
where	*voh* **WO**	is	*isst* **IST**	
when	*van* **WANN**	are	*zint* **SIND**	
what	*vass* **WAS**	is there	*gipt ess* **GIBT ES**	
what time	*uhm vee-feel ooer* **UM WIEVIEL UHR**	is it	*ist ess* **IST ES**	
how many	*vee-fee-ler* **WIEVIELE**	clean	*zau-ber mash-ern* **SAUBERMACHEN**	
how much is (that)	*vas koss-tert (das)* **WAS KOSTET (DAS)**	change	*owss-veck-serln* **AUSWECHSELN**	
here	*here* **HIER**	come	*kom-mern* **KOMMEN**	
there	*dar* **DA**	fix	*reppar-ree-rern* **REPARIEREN**	
		have	*har-bern* **HABEN**	
		leave *(things)*	*lass-ern* **LASSEN**	
and	*oont* **UND**	lost	*fair-lor-rern* **VERLOREN**	
by	*by* **BEI**	make up *(bed)*	*mash-ern* **MACHEN**	
for	*foor* **FÜR**	need	*brow-shern* **BRAUCHEN**	
from	*fon* **VON**	how does..work	*vee foonk-tseo-neert ..* **WIE FUNKTIONIERT ....**	
in	*in* **IN**	show me	*tsigh-gurn zee meer* **ZEIGEN SIE MIR**	
on	*owf* **AUF**	will be ready	*veert fair-tig* **WIRD FERTIG**	
to	*tsoo* **ZU**			
too	*owsh* **AUCH**	JUST A MOMENT!	*kline mo-ment* **KLEIN MOMENT!**	
with	*mit* **MIT**	COME IN!	*hair-rine* **HEREIN**	

room	*tsim-mer* **ZIMMER**	chair	*shtool* **STUHL**
number	*noo-mer* **NUMMER**	curtains	*for-henger* **VORHÄNGE**
name	*nar-mer* **NAME**	coat hangers	*kliy-der-boogurl* **KLEIDERBÜGEL**
		drinking water	*trink-vasser* **TRINKWASSER**
ambermaid	*tsim-mer-mayd-shyern* **ZIMMERMÄDCHEN**	duvet	*fay-der-bet* **FEDERBETT**
porter	*por-tyay* **PORTIER**	electricity	*shtrome* **STROM**
reception	*emp-fang* **EMPFANG**	heating	*high-tsoong* **HEIZUNG**
om service	*house-deener* **HAUSDIENER**	key	*shloo-serl* **SCHLÜSSEL**
		laundry	*vesh-er* **WÄSCHE**
dirty	*shmoot-zig* **SCHMUTZIG**	lift	*owf-tsoog* **AUFZUG**
noisy	*tsoo lowt* **ZU LAUT**	light bulb	*gloo-beerner* **GLÜHBIRNE**
ot working	*foonk-tseeyo-neert nisht* **FUNKTIONIERT NICHT**	lock	*shloss* **SCHLOSS**
blocked	*block-keert* **BLOCKIERT**	note paper	*shriyp-papeer* **SCHREIBPAPIER**
broken	*kah-poot* **KAPUTT**	pillow	*kopf-kissern* **KOPFKISSEN**
		pillowcase	*kopf-kissern-bertsoog* **KOPFKISSENBEZUG**
some	*et-vars* **ETWAS**	plug *(basin)*	*shtop-fern* **STOPFEN**
extra	*ex-trar* **EXTRA**	plug *(electrical)*	*shteck-dozer* **STECKDOSE**
fresh	*frish* **FRISCH**	radio	*rar-dyoh* **RADIO**
		razor socket	*ra-zeer-apparrart-shteck-dozer* **RASIERAPPARATSTECKDOSE**
hot	*varm* **WARM**	sheet	*lar-kern* **LAKEN**
cold	*kalt* **KALT**	soap	*zigh-fer* **SEIFE**
		shower	*doo-sher* **DUSCHE**
on	*iyn* **EIN**	toilet	*twar-let-ter* **TOILETTE**
off	*owss* **AUS**	toilet paper	*twar-let-tern-papeer* **TOILETTENPAPIER**
open	*owff* **AUF**	towel	*hant-toosh* **HANDTUCH**
closed	*tsoo* **ZU**	television set	*fairn-zay-appar-rart* **FERNSEHAPPARAT**
		ventilator	*loof-ter* **LÜFTER**
conditioning	*klee-mattee-sattsee-yown* **KLIMATISATION**	voltage	*shpan-noong* **SPANNUNG**
ashtray	*ash-ern-becker* **ASCHENBECKER**	wash basin	*vash-beckern* **WASCHBECKEN**
bath	*bard* **BAD**	water	*vass-ser* **WASSER**
bed	*bet* **BETT**	wardrobe	*kliy-der-shrank* **KLEIDERSCHRANK**
blanket	*deck-er* **DECKE**	window	*fen-ster* **FENSTER**

I	*ish* **ICH**		I would like	*ish **mersh**-ter* **ICH MÖCHTE**
my	*mine* **MEIN**		we would like	*veer **mersh**-tern* **WIR MÖCHTEN**
we	*veer* **WIR**		do you want	*vol-ern zee* **WOLLEN SIE**
our	***oon**-ser* **UNSER**			
you	*zee* **SIE**		I have	*ish **har**-ber* **ICH HABE**
your	*eeyer* **IHR**		we have	*veer **har**-bern* **WIR HABEN**
who	*vair* **WER**		do you have	***har**-bern zee* **HABEN SIE**
it	*ess* **ES**			
			can I	*kan ish* **KANN ICH**
not	*nisht* **NICHT**		can we	***ker**-nen veer* **KÖNNEN WIR**
no	*kine* **KEIN**		can you	***ker**-nen zee* **KÖNNEN SIE**
where	*voh* **WO**		is	*isst* **IST**
when	*van* **WANN**		are	*zint* **SIND**
what	*vass* **WAS**		is there	*gipt ess* **GIBT ES**
what time	*uhm vee-**feel** ooer* **UM WIEVIEL UHR**		is it	*ist ess* **IST ES**
how long	*vee **lang**-er* **WIE LANGE**		get	*ber-**kom**-mern* **BEKOMMEN**
how many	*vee-**fee**-ler* **WIEVIELE**		have	***har**-bern* **HABEN**
how much is (that)	*vass **koss**-tert (das)* **WAS KOSTET (DAS)**		repair	*reppar-**ree**-rern* **REPARIEREN**
			will be ready	*veert **fair**-tig* **WIRD FERTIG**
near	*in dair **nay**-er fon* **IN DER NÄHE VON**		see	***zay**-ern* **SEHEN**
here	*here* **HIER**		send	***shick**-ern* **SCHICKEN**
			show me	***tsigh**-gurn zee mee* **ZEIGEN SIE MIR**
about	***tseer**-ker* **CIRCA**		how does..work	*vee **foonk-tseo-neer*** **WIE FUNKTIONIERT..**
and	*oont* **UND**		wrap	***iyn**-packern* **EINPACKEN**
at	*an* **AN**			
by	*by* **BEI**		name	***nar**-mer* **NAME**
for	*foor* **FÜR**		receipt	***kvit**-toong* **QUITTUNG**
in	*in* **IN**		deposit	***an**-tsar-loong* **ANZAHLUNG**
of	*fon* **VON**		taxes	***shtoy**-ern* **STEUERN**
to	*tsoo* **ZU**		included	*ent-**hal**-tern* **ENTHALTEN**

open	*owff* **AUF**	**JEWELLERY** *shmook* **SCHMUCK**	
closed	*tsoo* **ZU**	bracelet	*arm*-*bant* **ARMBAND**
		brooch	*brosh*-*er* **BROSCHE**
good	*goot* **GUT**	chain	*ket*-*ter* **KETTE**
expensive	*price*-*goonstig* **PREISGÜNSTIG**	clip	*shpang*-*er* **SPANGE**
		earrings	*or*-*ringer* **OHRRINGE**
cheaper	*bil*-*ligger* **BILLIGER**	necklace	*halss*-*ketter* **HALSKETTE**
better	*bess*-*ser* **BESSER**	pendant	*an*-*henger* **ANHÄNGER**
smaller	*kliy*-*ner* **KLEINER**	ring	*ring* **RING**
larger	*grur*-*ser* **GRÖSSER**		
simpler	*iyn*-*fasher* **EINFACHER**	**MATERIALS** *mattairee*-*yarl*-*yern* **MATERIALIEN**	
alternative	*al*-*tairna*-*tee*-*ver* **ALTERNATIVE**	amber	*bairn*-*shtine* **BERNSTEIN**
		ceramic	*kair*-*rar*-*meek* **KERAMIK**
souvenir	*an*-*denkern* **ANDENKEN**	chromium	*krome* **CHROM**
present	*gur*-*shenk* **GESCHENK**	copper	*koop*-*fer* **KUPFER**
		crystal	*kree*-*stal* **KRISTALL**
real	*esht* **ECHT**	diamond	*deeya*-*mant* **DIAMANT**
carats	*ka*-*rart* **KARAT**	ebony	*ay*-*bern*-*holts* **EBENHOLZ**
very	*zair* **SEHR**	emerald	*smah*-*ragd* **SMARAGD**
old	*alt* **ALT**	enamel	*ay*-*my* **EMAIL**
new	*noy* **NEU**	(cut) glass	*(gur*-*shliff*-*erners) glass* **(GESCHLIFFENES) GLAS**
		gold (gold plate)	*golt (fair*-*gol*-*dert)* **GOLD (VERGOLDET)**
broken	*gur*-*brosh*-*ern* **GEBROCHEN**	ivory	*el*-*fern*-*bine* **ELFENBEIN**
cracked	*gur*-*shproong*-*ern* **GESPRUNGEN**	jade	*yar*-*der* **JADE**
		onyx	*oh*-*neex* **ONYX**
WATCH	*arm*-*bant*-*oor* **ARMBANDUHR**	pearl	*pair*-*ler* **PERLE**
alarm clock	*veck*-*er* **WECKER**	pewter	*har*-*tsin* **HARTZINN**
battery	*batta*-*ree* **BATTERIE**	platinum	*plah*-*teen* **PLATIN**
clock	*oor* **UHR**	ruby	*roo*-*been* **RUBIN**
glass	*glass* **GLAS**	sapphire	*zah*-*feer* **SAPHIR**
strap	*arm*-*bant* **ARMBAND**	silver	*zil*-*ber* **SILBER**
winder	*kroh*-*nern*-*owff*-*tsoog* **KRONENAUFZUG**	stainless steel	*rost*-*fryer shtarl* **ROSTFREIER STAHL**

colours: 28   more jewellry: 27

I	*ish* **ICH**		I would like	*ish* **mersh**-ter **ICH MÖCHTE**
my	*mine* **MEIN**		we would like	*veer* **mersh**-tern **WIR MÖCHTEN**
we	*veer* **WIR**		do you want	*vol-ern zee* **WOLLEN SIE**
our	*oon-ser* **UNSER**			
you	*zee* **SIE**		I have	*ish* **har**-ber **ICH HABE**
your	*eeyer* **IHR**		we have	*veer* **har**-bern **WIR HABEN**
			do you have	**har**-bern *zee* **HABEN SIE**
not	*nisht* **NICHT**			
no	*kine* **KEIN**		can I	*kan ish* **KANN ICH**
			can we	**ker**-nen *veer* **KÖNNEN WIR**
which	**vel**-shyer **WELCHER**		can you	**ker**-nen *zee* **KÖNNEN SIE**
where	*voh* **WO**			
when	*van* **WANN**		am	*bin* **BIN**
what	*vass* **WAS**		is	*isst* **IST**
what time	*uhm* vee-**feel** *ooer* **UM WIEVIEL UHR**		are	*zint* **SIND**
			is there	*gipt ess* **GIBT ES**
how long	*vee* **lang**-er **WIE LANGE**			
			change (job)	*veck-***serln** **WECHSELN**
near	*in dair* **nay**-er *fon* **IN DER NÄHE VON**		do	**mash**-ern **MACHEN**
here	*here* **HIER**		finish	*owf-***her**-rern **AUFHÖREN**
there	*dar* **DA**		have	**har**-bern **HABEN**
			like	**mer**-gurn **MÖGEN**
and	*oont* **UND**		start	**an**-fang-ern **ANFANGEN**
at	*an* **AN**		work	**ar**-bight-ern **ARBEITEN**
by	*by* **BEI**			
for	*foor* **FÜR**		studying	**shtoo**-dyum **STUDIUM**
in	*in* **IN**		training	*owss-*bildoong **AUSBILDUNG**
on	*owf* **AUF**		visiting	*ber-***soosh**-ern **BESUCHEN**
to	*tsoo* **ZU**			
			large	*gross* **GROSS**
name	**nar**-mer **NAME**		medium	*mit-erl-gross* **MITTELGROS**
address	*ad-***dress**-er **ADRESSE**		small	*kline* **KLEIN**

college	*hosh-shooler* **HOCHSCHULE**	mechanic	**MECHANIKER**
clinic	*klee-neek* **KLINIK**	musician	**MUSIKER**
		nurse	**KRANKENPFLEGER**
factory	*vairk* **WERK**	photographer	**PHOTOGRAPH**
		planner	**PLANER**
farm	*baoo-wern-horf* **BAUERNHOF**	policeman	**POLIZEIBEAMTE**
		politician	**POLITIKER**
hospital	*kran-kern-house* **KRANKENHAUS**	programmer	**PROGRAMMIERER**
		salesperson	**VERKÄUFER**
aboratory	*lah-bor* **LABOR**	scientist	**WISSENSCHAFTLER**
		secretary	**SEKTRETÄRIN**
office	*boo-roh* **BÜRO**	social worker	**FÜRSORGER**
		surveyor	**GUTACHTER**
school	*shoo-ler* **SCHULE**	teacher	**LEHRER**
		technician	**TECHNIKER**
shop	*gur-sheft* **GESCHÄFT**	waiter (ress)	**KELLNER(-IN)**
		writer	**SCHRIFTSTELLER**
varehouse	*lar-gur* **LAGER**	**INDUSTRY**	*shpar-ter* **SPARTE**
		aerospace	**LUFTFAHRT**
		airline	**FLUGGESELLSCHAFT**
overnment	*reh-gear-roong* **REGIERUNG**	banking	**BANKWESEN**
ocal govt.	*shtat-fair-valtoong* **STADTVERWALTUNG**	broadcasting	**FERNSEH UND RUNDFUNK**
		building materials	**BAUSTOFFE**
orivate co.	*pree-vart-feermar* **PRIVATFIRMA**	car	**AUTO**
		catering	**GASTRONOMIE**
state co.	*shtarts-oonter-naymern* **STAATSUNTERNEHMEN**	chemical	**CHEMIE**
		clothing	**KLEIDUNG**
employed	*iy-gurn-shtendig* **EIGENSTÄNDIG**	construction	**BAUWESEN**
		computer	**COMPUTER**
		domestic goods	**HAUSWAREN**
		electrical equipment	**ELEKTRO-GERÄTE**
JOB	*bair-roof* **BERUF**	electrical supply	**STROMVERSORGUNG**
		entertainment	**UNTERHALTUNG**
sual work	*gur-lay-gurn-heights-arbight* **GELEGENHEITSARBEIT**	electronics	**ELEKTRONIK**
		farming	**LANDWIRTSCHAFT**
		food processing	**LEBENSMITTELVERARBEITUNG**
housewife	**HAUSFRAU**	forestry	**FORSTWIRTSCHAFT**
retired	**PENSIONIERT**	furniture	**MÖBEL**
student	**STUDENT**	health	**GESUNDHEITSWESEN**
employed	**ARBEITSLOS**	hotel	**HOTEL**
worker	**ARBEITER**	insurance	**VERSICHERUNG**
accountant	**RECHNUNGSFÜHRER**	leisure	**FREIZEIT**
actor	**SCHAUSPIELER**	machinery	**MASCHINENBAU**
architect	**ARCHITEKT**	manufacturing	**HERSTELLUNG**
artist	**KÜNSTLER**	military	**MILITÄR**
ministrator	**VERWALTUNGSBEAMTE**	mining	**BERGBAU**
assembler	**MONTEUR**	newspapers	**ZEITUNGEN**
chef	**KÜCHENCHEF**	oil	**ÖL**
clerk	**BÜROGEHILFE**	paper	**PAPIER**
designer	**KONSTRUKTEUR**	plastics	**KUNSTSTOFF**
doctor	**ARZT**	postal service	**POSTWESEN**
driver	**FAHRER**	pottery	**TÖPFEREI**
electrician	**ELEKTROTECHNIKER**	printing	**DRUCK**
engineer	**INGENIEUR**	publishing	**VERLAGSWESEN**
inspector	**INSPEKTOR**	railways	**EISENBAHN**
journalist	**JOURNALIST**	retail industry	**KLEINHANDEL**
lawyer	**ANWALT**	road haulage	**SPEDITION**
librarian	**BIBLIOTHEKAR**	telecommunications	**NACHRICHTENWESEN**
linguist	**SPRACHENKUNDIGE**	textiles	**TEXTILIEN**
manager	**MANAGER**	timber	**HOLZ**

ther subjects: 86-87

I	*ish* **ICH**		I would like	*ish* **mersh**-ter **ICH MÖCHTE**
my	*mine* **MEIN**		we would like	*veer* **mersh**-tern **WIR MÖCHTEN**
we	*veer* **WIR**		do you want	*vol-ern* zee **WOLLEN SIE**
our	*oon-ser* **UNSER**			
you	*zee* **SIE**		I have	*ish* **har**-ber **ICH HABE**
it	*ess* **ES**		we have	*veer* **har**-bern **WIR HABEN**
			do you have	**har**-bern zee **HABEN SIE**
not	*nisht* **NICHT**			
no	*kine* **KEIN**		can I	*kan ish* **KANN ICH**
			can we	**ker**-nen veer **KÖNNEN WIR**
which	*vel-shyer* **WELCHER**		can you	**ker**-nen zee **KÖNNEN SIE**
where	*voh* **WO**			
when	*van* **WANN**		is	*isst* **IST**
what	*vass* **WAS**		are	*zint* **SIND**
what time	*uhm vee-**feel** ooer* **UM WIEVIEL UHR**		is there	*gipt ess* **GIBT ES**
			is this	*ist dass* **IST DAS**
how long	*vee* **lang**-er **WIE LANGE**		is it	*ist ess* **IST ES**
how often	*vee oft* **WIE OFT**			
how much is (that)	*vass* **koss**-tert *(das)* **WAS KOSTET (DAS)**		I must	*ish mooss* **ICH MUSS**
			we must	*veer* **moo**-sern **WIR MÜSSEN**
nearest	**nex**-ster **NÄCHSTER**			
here	*here* **HIER**		arrive	*an-kommern* **ANKOMMEN**
there	*dar* **DA**		change	*oom-shtigh-gurn* **UMSTEIGEN**
			depart	*ap-far-rern* **ABFAHREN**
at	*an* **AN**		get off	*owss-shtigh-gurn* **AUSSTEIGEN**
by	*by* **BEI**		go	*far-rern* **FAHREN**
for	*foor* **FÜR**		have	*har-bern* **HABEN**
from	*fon* **VON**		do you know	*viss-ern zee* **WISSEN SIE**
in	*in* **IN**		stop	*an-haltern* **ANHALTEN**
of	*fon* **VON**		tell me	*zar-gurn zee meer* **SAGEN SIE MIR**
on	*owf* **AUF**			
to	*narsh* **NACH**		STOP HERE PLEASE	*here bitter* **an**-hal-te **HIER BITTE ANHALTEN**

ticket	*far-shine* **FAHRSCHEIN**	this	*dee-zer* **DIESER**
book of tickets	*far-shine-heft* **FAHRSCHEINHEFT**	place	*ort* **ORT**
ticket machine	*far-shine-owtoh-mart* **FAHRSCHEINAUTOMAT**		
ꙍw does ... work?)	*vee foonk-tsio-neert ...* **WIE FUNKTIONIERT ...**	map	*kar-ter* **KARTE**
the fare	*dair far-price* **DER FAHRPREIS**	destination	*tseel* **ZIEL**
small change	*kline-gelt* **KLEINGELD**	(the) direction	*dee rish-toong* **(DIE) RICHTUNG**
		journey	*fart* **FAHRT**
single	*iyn-fash* **EINFACH**	number	*noo-mer* **NUMMER**
return	*hin oont tsoo-rook* **HIN UND ZURÜCK**		
		boat	*shiff* **SCHIFF**
reduction	*air-may-sigoong* **ERMÄSSIGUNG**	bus	*booss* **BUS**
group	*groo-per* **GRUPPE**	ferry	*fair-rer* **FÄHRE**
student	*shtoo-dent* **STUDENT**	overground metro	*ess-barn* **S-BAHN**
child	*kint* **KIND**	taxi	*tax-ee* **TAXI**
senior citizen	*zay-nyor* **SENIOR**	train	*tsoog* **ZUG**
identification	*owss-vice* **AUSWEIS**	tram	*shtrar-sern-barn* **STRASSENBAHN**
		trolley bus	*oh-ber-lightoongs-boos* **OBERLEITUNGSBUS**
first	*airst* **ERST**	underground metro	*oo-barn* **U-BAHN**
last	*letst* **LETZT**		
next	*next* **NÄCHST**	bus station	*booss-barn-horf* **BUSBAHNHOF**
		bus stop	*booss-halter-shteller* **BUSHALTESTELLE**
early	*frooh* **FRÜH**	fare stage	*tsoh-ner* **ZONE**
late	*shpayt* **SPÄT**	jetty	*shtayg* **STEG**
earlier	*froo-er* **FRÜHER**	left luggage lockers	*gur-peck-shlees-feshyer* **GEPÄCKSCHLIESSFÄCHER**
later	*shpay-ter* **SPÄTER**	left luggage office	*gur-peck-owf-ber-var-roong* **GEPÄCKAUFBEWAHRUNG**
		platform	*barn-shtiyg* **BAHNSTEIG**
every	*al-ler* **ALLE**	request stop	*beh-darfs-halter-shteller* **BEDARFSHALTESTELLE**
per	*pro* **PRO**	railway station	*barn-horf* **BAHN**
		taxi rank	*taxi-shtant* **TAXISTAND**
minutes	*min-oo-tern* **MINUTEN**	terminus	*ent-shtatsee-own* **ENDSTATION**
hour	*shtoon-der* **STUNDE**	ticket office	*far-kartern-shallter* **FAHRKARTENSCHALTER**
day	*targ* **TAG**	tram stop	*shtrar-sern-barn-halter-shteller* **STRASSENBAHNHALTESTELLE**

tourist places: 112-113   time & meeting: 122

I	*ish* **ICH**	I would like	*ish* **mersh**-ter **ICH MÖCHTE**
my	*mine* **MEIN**	we would like	*veer* **mersh**-tern **WIR MÖCHTEN**
we	*veer* **WIR**	do you want	*vol-ern* zee **WOLLEN SIE**
our	*oon-ser* **UNSER**		
you	*zee* **SIE**	I have	*ish* **har**-ber **ICH HABE**
it	*ess* **ES**	we have	*veer* **har**-bern **WIR HABEN**
		do you have	*har-bern* zee **HABEN SIE**
not	*nisht* **NICHT**		
no	*kine* **KEIN**	can I	*kan ish* **KANN ICH**
		can we	*ker-nen veer* **KÖNNEN WIR**
which	*vel-shyer* **WELCHER**	can you	*ker-nen zee* **KÖNNEN SIE**
where	*voh* **WO**		
when	*van* **WANN**	is	*isst* **IST**
what time	*uhm vvee-feel ooer* **UM WIEVIEL UHR**	are	*zint* **SIND**
		is there	*gipt ess* **GIBT ES**
how often	*vee oft* **WIE OFT**	is this	*ist dass* **IST DAS**
how long	*vee lang-er* **WIE LANG**	is it	*ist ess* **IST ES**
how much is (that)	*vass koss-tert (das)* **WAS KOSTET (DAS)**		
		arrive	*an-kommern* **ANKOMMEN**
near	*in dair nay-er fon* **IN DER NÄHE VON**	change	*oom-shtigh-gurn* **UMSTEIGEN**
next to	*nay-burn* **NEBEN**	depart	*ap-far-rern* **ABFAHREN**
here	*here* **HIER**	get off	*owss-shtigh-gurn* **AUSSTEIGEN**
there	*dar* **DA**	go	*far-rern* **FAHREN**
this	*dee-zer* **DIESER**	have	*har-bern* **HABEN**
		do you know	*viss-ern zee* **WISSEN SIE**
at	*an* **AN**	leave (things)	*lass-ern* **LASSEN**
by	*by* **BEI**	reserve	*rezzair-vee-rern* **RESERVIEREN**
for	*foor* **FÜR**		
from	*fon* **VON**	ticket	*far-karter* **FAHRKARTE**
in	*in* **IN**	reservation	*rez-air-vee-roong* **RESERVIERUNG**
on	*owf* **AUF**	single	*iyn-fash* **EINFACH**
to	*narsh* **NACH**	return	*hin oont tsoo-rook* **HIN UND ZURÜCK**

first class	*air-ster klass-er*	map	*kar-ter*
	ERSTER KLASSE		**KARTE**
second class	*tsvo-ter klass-er*	time table	*far-plarn*
	ZWOTER KLASSE		**FAHRPLAN**
		destination	*tseel*
			ZIEL
seat	*zits*	journey	*fart*
	SITZ		**FAHRT**
couchette	*lee-gur-zittzer*	number	*noo-mer*
	LIEGESITZE		**NUMMER**
sleeper berth	*shlarf-vargurn-bet*		
	SCHLAFWAGENBETT		
upper	*oh-ber-rer*	express bus	*fairn-booss*
	OBERER		**FERNBUS**
lower	*oon-ter-rer*	train	*tsoog*
	UNTERER		**ZUG**
		(luxury express)	*een-ter tsee-tee*
			INTER CITY
non-smoking	*nisht-rau-sher*	(express)	*day-tsoog*
	NICHTRAUCHER		**D-ZUG**
window	*fen-ster*	(fast local)	*iyl-tsoog*
	FENSTER		**EILZUG**
facing engine	*fart-reesh-toong*	local	*nar-fair-kairss-tsoog*
	IN FAHRTRICHTUNG		**NAHVERKEHRSZUG**

reduction	*air-may-sigoong*	baggage car	*gur-peck-vargurn*
	ERMÄSSIGUNG		**GEPÄCKWAGEN**
group	*groo-per*	carriage	*var-gurn*
	GRUPPE		**WAGEN**
student	*shtoo-dent*	dining car	*shpiy-zer-vargurn*
	STUDENT		**SPEISEWAGEN**
child	*kint*	sleeping car	*shlarf-vargurn*
	KIND		**SCHLAFWAGEN**
(age)	*al-ter*		
	ALTER		
senior citizen	*zay-nyor*	bus & coach station	*booss-barn-horf*
	SENIOR		**BUSBAHNHOF**
identification	*owss-vice*	information	*owss-koonft*
	AUSWEIS		**AUSKUNFT**
		left luggage lockers	*gur-peck-shleess-feshyer*
			GEPÄCKSCHLIESSFÄCHER
first	*airst*	left luggage office	*gur-peck-owf-ber-varoong*
	ERST		**GEPÄCKAUFBEWAHRUNG**
last	*letst*	luggage	*gur-peck*
	LETZT		**GEPÄCK**
next	*next*	lost property office	*foont-boo-roh*
	NÄCHST		**FUNDBÜRO**
earlier	*froo-er*	platform	*barn-shtiyg*
	FRÜHER		**BAHNSTEIG**
later	*shpay-ter*	train station	*barn-horf*
	SPÄTER		**BAHNHOF**
on time	*poonkt-lish*	ticket office	*far-kartern-shallter*
	PÜNKTLICH		**FAHRKARTENSCHALTER**
cancelled	*ent-felt*	toilet	*twal-let-ter*
	ENTFÄLLT		**TOILETTE**
		waiting room	*var-ter-tsimmer*
			WARTEZIMMER
minutes	*min-oo-tern*		
	MINUTEN		
hours	*shtoon-dern*	open	*owff*
	STUNDEN		**AUF**
days	*tar-gur*	closed	*tsoo*
	TAGE		**ZU**

I	*ish* **ICH**	I would like	*ish* **mersh**-*ter* **ICH MÖCHTE**
my	*mine* **MEIN**	we would like	*veer* **mersh**-*tern* **WIR MÖCHTEN**
we	*veer* **WIR**	do you want	*vol*-*ern zee* **WOLLEN SIE**
our	**oon**-*ser* **UNSER**		
you	*zee* **SIE**	I have	*ish* **har**-*ber* **ICH HABE**
your	*eeyer* **IHR**	we have	*veer* **har**-*bern* **WIR HABEN**
it	*ess* **ES**	do you have	**har**-*bern zee* **HABEN SIE**
not	*nisht* **NICHT**	can I	*kan* *ish* **KANN ICH**
no	*kine* **KEIN**	can we	**ker**-*nen veer* **KÖNNEN WIR**
		can you	**ker**-*nen zee* **KÖNNEN SIE**
which	**vel**-*shyer* **WELCHER**		
where	*voh* **WO**	is	*isst* **IST**
when	*van* **WANN**	are	*zint* **SIND**
what	*vass* **WAS**	is there	*gipt ess* **GIBT ES**
what time	*uhm* **vvee-feel** *ooer* **UM WIEVIEL UHR**	is it	*ist ess* **IST ES**
how many	**vee-fee**-*ler* **WIEVIELE**	get	*ber*-**kom**-*mern* **BEKOMMEN**
how much is (that)	*vass* **koss**-*tert (das)* **WAS KOSTET (DAS)**	have	**har**-*bern* **HABEN**
		do you know	*viss*-*ern zee* **WISSEN SIE**
nearest	**nex**-*ster* **NÄCHSTER**	pay	*tsar*-*lern* **ZAHLEN**
near	*in dair* **nay**-*er fon* **IN DER NÄHE VON**	return (*thing*)	*tsoo*-**rook**-*gay-bern* **ZURÜCKGEBEN**
here	*here* **HIER**	see	*zay*-*urn* **SEHEN**
there	*dar* **DA**	show me	**tsigh**-*gurn zee mee* **ZEIGEN SIE MIR**
		wrap	*iyn*-*packern* **EINPACKEN**
about	**oo**-*ber* **ÜBER**	each	**yay**-*der* **JEDER**
and	*oont* **UND**	receipt	**kvit**-*toong* **QUITTUNG**
by	*by* **BEI**	bag	**too**-*ter* **TÜTE**
for	*foor* **FÜR**		
in	*in* **IN**	open	*owf* **AUF**
of	*fo* **VON**	closed	*tsoo* **ZU**
to	*tsoo* **ZU**		

good	*goot* **GUT**	**BOOKSHOP**		**boosh**-hant-loong **BUCHHANDLUNG**
cheap	*bil-lig* **BILLIG**	**NEWSAGENT**		*tsigh-toongs-hentler* **ZEITUNGSHÄNDLER**
		NEWS-STAND		*tsigh-toongs-kiosk* **ZEITUNGSKIOSK**
cheaper	*bil-ligger* **BILLIGER**	atlas		*at-larss* **ATLAS**
better	*bess-ser* **BESSER**	book		*boosh* **BUCH**
alternative	*al-tairna-tee-ver* **ALTERNATIVE**	dictionary		*vur-ter-boosh* **WÖRTERBUCH**
bigger	*grur-ser* **GRÖSSER**	guide book		*foo-rer* **FÜHRER**
smaller	*kliy-ner* **KLEINER**	magazine		*tsight-shrift* **ZEITSCHRIFT**
		map		*lant-karter* **LANDKARTE**
		(bus & metro map)		*booss* oont *oo-barn-plarn* **BUS- UND U-BAHNPLAN**
OBACCONIST	ta-**back**-gur-sheft **TABAKGESCHÄFT**	(road map)		*shtrar-sern-karter* **STRASSENKARTE**
battery	*batta-ree* **BATTERIE**	(town map)		*shtat-plarn* **STADTPLAN**
cigar	*tsee-gar-rer* **ZIGARRE**	newspaper		*tsigh-toong* **ZEITUNG**
(box of cigars)	*kiss-ter tsee-gar-rern* **KISTE ZIGARREN**	paperback		*tash-ern-boosh* **TASCHENBUCH**
cigarettes	*tsee-gar-ret-tern* **ZIGARETTEN**	poster		*plah-kart* **PLAKAT**
(American)	*amairee-kar-nish* **AMERIKANISCH**	postcard		*posst-karter* **POSTKARTE**
(English)	*eng-glish* **ENGLISCH**	souvenir		*an-denkern* **ANDENKEN**
(German)	*doytch* **DEUTSCH**	travel guide		*riy-zer-foorer* **REISEFÜHRER**
(filter cigarettes)	*fil-ter-tsee-gar-ret-tern* **FILTERZIGARETTEN**			
(king size)	*ex-trar lang* **EXTRA LANG**	architecture		*arsheeteck-toor* **ARCHITEKTUR**
flints	*foy-yer-shtiyner* **FEUERSTEINE**	biography		*beeyo-grar-fee* **BIOGRAPHIE**
lighter	*foy-yer-tsoyg* **FEUERZEUG**	childrens'		*kin-der-* **KINDER-**
(fluid)	*ben-tseen* **BENZIN**	history		*gur-shishts-* **GESCHICHTS-**
(gas)	*garss* **GAS**	novel		*roh-marn* **ROMAN**
box of matches	*shash-terl shtriysh-hurl-tser* **SCHACHTEL STREICHHÖLZER**			
pipe	*pfiy-fer* **PFEIFE**	name		*nar-mer* **NAME**
pipe cleaners	*pfiy-fern-riy-nigger* **PFEIFENREINIGER**	author		*ow-tor* **AUTOR**
tobacco	*tah-back* **TABAK**	publisher		*fair-larg* **VERLAG**
		local		*fon dair gay-gurnt* **VON DER GEGEND**
strong	*shtark* **STARK**	national		*natseeyo-narl* **NATIONAL**
mild	*milt* **MILD**	English		*eng-glish* **ENGLISCH**
menthol	*men-tol* **MENTHOL**	German		*doytch* **DEUTSCH**

further subjects: 86 & 99 **sports: 116**

I	*ish* **ICH**		I would like	*ish* **mersh**-ter **ICH MÖCHTE**
my	*mine* **EIN**		do you want	*vol*-ern zee **WOLLEN SIE**
you	*zee* **SIE**			
your	*eeyer* **IHR**		I have	*ish* **har**-ber **ICH HABE**
it	*ess* **ES**		do you have	*har*-bern zee **HABEN SIE**
they	*zee* **SIE**			
			can I	*kan ish* **KANN ICH**
not	*nisht* **NICHT**		can you	*ker*-nen zee **KÖNNEN SIE**
no	*kine* **KEIN**			
			is	*isst* **IST**
which	***vel**-shyer* **WELCHER**		are	*zint* **SIND**
where	*voh* **WO**		is there	*gipt ess* **GIBT ES**
when	*van* **WANN**		is it	*ist ess* **IST ES**
what	*vass* **WAS**		are they	*zint zee* **SIND SIE**
what time	*uhm vee-**feel** ooer* **UM WIEVIEL UHR**			
			get	*ber-**kom**-mern* **BEKOMMEN**
how long	*vee **lang**-er* **WIE LANGE**		have	*har*-bern **HABEN**
how many	*vee-**fee**-ler* **WIEVIELE**		do you know	*viss*-ern zee **WISSEN SIE**
how much is (that)	*vass **koss**-tert (das)* **WAS KOSTET (DAS)**		pay	*tsar*-lern **ZAHLEN**
			process	*fair-**ar**-biy-tern* **VERARBEITEN**
near	*in dair **nay**-er fon* **IN DER NÄHE VON**		(and) print	*(mit) ap*-tsoo-gurn **(MIT) ABZÜGEN**
here	*here* **HIER**		will be ready	*veert **fair**-tig* **WIRD FERTIG**
there	*dar* **DA**		repair	*reppar-**ree**-rern* **REPARIEREN**
			see	*zay*-urn **SEHEN**
and	*oont* **UND**		show me	*tsigh*-gurn zee meer **ZEIGEN SIE MIR**
at	*an* **AN**		will take	*nimmt* **NIMMT**
by	*by* **BEI**		how does..work	*vee foonk-tseo-**neert** ..* **WIE FUNKTIONIERT ....**
for	*foor* **FÜR**			
from	*fon* **VON**		the cost	*dee **koss**-tern* **DIE KOSTEN**
in	*in* **IN**		included	*ent-**hal**-tern* **ENTHALTEN**
of	*fon* **VON**		receipt	*kvit*-toong **QUITTUNG**
to	*tsoo* **ZU**		deposit	*an*-tsarloong **ANZAHLUNG**

name	**nar**-*mer* **NAME**	**FILM**	*film* **FILM**	
good	*goot* **GUT**	110	**hoon**-*dert-tsayn* **HUNDERTZEHN**	
inexpensive	**price**-*goonstig* **PREISGÜNSTIG**	120	**hoon**-*dert-tsvantsig* **HUNDERTZWANZIG**	
cheaper	**bil**-*ligger* **BILLIGER**	135	**hoon**-*dert-foonf-oont-drysig* **HUNDERTFÜNFUNDDREISSIG**	
better	**bess**-*er* **BESSER**	620	*zex-hoondert-tsvantsig* **SECHSHUNDERTZWANZIG**	
alternative	*al-tairna-**tee**-ver* **ALTERNATIVE**	8mm	*asht* **mee**-*lee-mayter* **ACHT MILLIMETER**	
		super 8mm	*zoo-per asht* **SUPER ACHT**	
		16mm	*ze**sh**-tsayn* **mee**-*lee-mayter* **SECHZEHN MILLIMETER**	
broken	*gur-**brosh**-ern* **GEBROCHEN**	polaroid film	*polaroid-film* **POLAROID-FILM**	
jammed	*fair-**klemt*** **VERKLEMMT**	video cassette	*vee-dayoh-cassetter* **VIDEOKASSETTE**	
not working	*funkt-sio-**neert nisht*** **FUNKTIONIERT NICHT**			
			12 20 24 36	
		exposures	*owff-narmern* **AUFNAHMEN**	
now	*yetzt* **JETZT**			
later	**shpay**-*ter* **SPÄTER**	ASA/DIN	*arsar/deen* **ASA/DIN**	
		fast	**hurxt**-*emp-fin-dlish* **HÖCHSTEMPFINDLICH**	
QUIPMENT	*owss-**roostoong*** **AUSRÜSTUNG**	fine grain	*fine-corn* **FEINKORN**	
(auto) aperture	*(auto)* **blen**-*der* **(AUTO) BLENDE**	indoor	*in-nern* **INNEN**	
battery	*batta-**ree*** **BATTERIE**	outdoor	*drow-sern* **DRAUSSEN**	
cable release	**kar**-*burl-fair-shloss* **KABELVERSCHLUSS**			
camera	**cam**-*mair-rar* **KAMERA**	black & white	*shvarts-vice* **SCHWARZ-WEISS**	
(auto) exposure	*auto bell-**lish**-toong* **(AUTO) BELICHTUNG**	colour prints	*farp-ap-tsoogur* **FARBABZÜGE**	
filter	**fil**-*ter* **FILTER**	colour slides	*farp-deeyass* **FARBDIAS**	
flash gun	**blits**-*gur-rayt* **BLITZGERÄT**			
(auto) focus	*(auto)* **bren**-*poonkt* **(AUTO) BRENNPUNKT**	**PRINTS**	*ap-tsoogur* **ABZÜGE**	
lens	*ob-yek-**teef*** **OBJEKTIF**	negative	*neg-ateef* **NEGATIV**	
lightmeter	*ber-**lish**-toongs-messer* **BELICHTUNGSMESSER**	gloss finish	**hosh**-*glants* **HOCHGLANZ**	
movie camera	**film**-*cammair-rar* **FILMKAMERA**	matt finish	*matt* **MATT**	
vind mech'm	**rook**-*shpool-mecka-nissmoos* **RÜCKSPULMECHANISMUS**	size	**grur**-*ser* **GRÖSSE**	
self timer	**zelpst**-*aoos-ler-zer* **SELBSTAUSLÖSER**	enlargement	*fair-**grur**-seroong* **VERGRÖSSERUNG**	
shutter	*fair-**shlooss*** **VERSCHLUSS**			
tripod	*shta-**teef*** **STATIV**	lighter	**hel**-*ler* **HELLER**	
viewfinder	**zoossher** **SUCHER**	darker	**doonk**-*ler* **DUNKLER**	

I	*ish* **ICH**	I would like	*ish* **mersh**-ter **ICH MÖCHTE**	
my	*mine* **MEIN**	do you want	*vol*-ern zee **WOLLEN SIE**	
you	*zee* **SIE**			
your	*eeyer* **IHR**	I have	*ish* **har**-ber **ICH HABE**	
it	*ess* **ES**	do you have	*har*-bern zee **HABEN SIE**	
they	*zee* **SIE**			
		can I	*kan ish* **KANN ICH**	
not	*nisht* **NICHT**	can you	***ker**-nen zee* **KÖNNEN SIE**	
no	*kine* **KEIN**			
		is	*isst* **IST**	
where	*voh* **WO**	are	*zint* **SIND**	
when	*van* **WANN**	is there	*gipt ess* **GIBT ES**	
what	*vass* **WAS**	is it	*ist ess* **IST ES**	
what time	*uhm vee-feel ooer* **UM WIEVIEL UHR**			
		will arrive	*veer **an**-kommern* **WIRD ANKOMMEN**	
how long	*vee **lang**-er* **WIE LANGE**	go	*ap-gay-ern* **ABGEHEN**	
how many	*vee-**fee**-ler* **WIEVIELE**	have	*har-bern* **HABEN**	
how much is (that)	*vass **koss**-tert (das)* **WAS KOSTET (DAS)**	do you know	*viss-ern zee* **WISSEN SIE**	
how much will it cost	*ess veert vee-**feel koss**-tern* **ES WIRD WIEVIEL KOSTEN**	post	*tsoor post **bring**-er* **ZUR POST BRINGEN**	
		receive	*emp-**fang**-ern* **EMPFANGEN**	
		send	***shick**-ern* **SCHICKEN**	
near	***nar**-ur* **NAHE**	sign	*oonter-**tsiysh**-nern* **UNTERZEICHNEN**	
nearest	***nex**-ster* **NÄCHSTER**	will take	*nimmt* **NIMMT**	
and	*oont* **UND**	here	*here* **HIER**	
at	*an* **AN**	there	*dar* **DA**	
by	*pair* **PER**			
for	*foor* **FÜR**	post office	***posst**-amt* **POSTAMT**	
from	*fon* **VON**	post box	***brief**-kass-tern* **BRIEFKASTEN**	
in	*in* **IN**	open	*owf* **AUF**	
of	*fon* **VON**	closed	*tsoo* **ZU**	
to	*narsh* **NACH**	until	*biss* **BIS**	

first	*air*-ster **ERSTE**	air mail	*looft*-posst **LUFTPOST**
last	*let*-ster **LETZTE**	express	*iyl*-boat-ern **EILBOTEN**
next	*nex*-ster **NÄCHSTE**	letter post	*breef*-posst **BRIEFPOST**
		insured	*fair-zish*-ert **VERSICHERT**
days	*tar*-gur **TAGE**	registered mail	*iyn*-shriy-bern **EINSCHREIBEN**
weeks	*vosh*-ern **WOCHEN**	parcel post	*pah-kait*-posst **PAKETPOST**
today	*hoy*-ter **HEUTE**	surface mail	*gur-vern-lisher* posst **GEWÖHNLICHE POST**
tomorrow	*more*-gurn **MORGEN**		
morning	*for*-mittarg **VORMITTAG**	customs	*tsoll* **ZOLL**
afternoon	*narsh*-mittarg **NACHMITTAG**	delivery	*tsoo*-shtelloong **ZUSTELLUNG**
		international money order	*inter-natseeyo-nar*-ler *tsar*-loongs-shine **INTERNATIONALER ZAHLUNGSSCHEIN**
letter	*breef* **BRIEF**		
facsimile	*tay*-layfax **TELEFAX**	philatelic bureau	*fee-latter-lee*-shalter **PHILATELIESCHALTER**
form	*formoo-lar* **FORMULAR**	post restante /general delivery	*posst*-lar-gurnder *zen*-doongurn **POSTLAGERNDE SENDUNGEN**
mail	*posst* **POST**		
money order	*posst*-an-viyzoong **POSTANWEISUNG**		
parcel	*pah-kait* **PAKET**	country	*lant* **LAND**
post card	*posst*-karter **POSTKARTE**	in German	*owff doytch* **AUF DEUTSCH**
protective envelope	*shoots*-oom-shlarg **SCHUTZUMSCHLAG**		
stamp	*brief*-marker **BRIEFMARKE**	Australia	*owss-strar*-lyen **AUSTRALIEN**
telegram	*taylay*-gram **TELEGRAMM**	Britain	*gross-bree-tan*-yen **GROSSBRITANNIEN**
telex	*tay*-lex **TELEX**	Canada	*kan-nah-dah* **KANADA**
		Ireland	*eer*-lant **IRLAND**
each	*yay*-der **JEDER**	New Zealand	*noy-zay*-lant **NEUSEELAND**
per word	*pro vort* **PRO WORT**	South Africa	*sood-aff*-reekar **SÜDAFRIKA**
words	*ver*-ter **WÖRTER**	USA	*oo ess ar* **USA**
the cost	*dee koss*-tern **DIE KOSTEN**		
total	*inss*-gur-zamt **INSGESAMT**	photocopy service	*kop-peer*-deenst **KOPIERDIENST**

name	*nar*-mer **NAME**	**POSTLAGERNDE SENDUNGEN** =	POST RESTANTE/ GENERAL DELIVERY
address	*ad-dress*-ser **ADRESSE**	**BRIEFMARKEN** =	STAMPS
post code	*posst-light*-tsarl **POSTLEITZAHL**	**PAKETE** = **POSTANWEISUNGEN** =	PARCELS MONEY ORDERS

I	*ish* **ICH**		I would like	*ish mersh-ter* **ICH MÖCHTE**
my	*mine* **MEIN**		we would like	*veer mersh-tern* **WIR MÖCHTEN**
we	*veer* **WIR**		do you want	*vol-ern zee* **WOLLEN SIE**
our	*oon-ser* **UNSER**			
you	*zee* **SIE**		I have	*ish har-ber* **ICH HABE**
it	*ess* **ES**		we have	*veer har-bern* **WIR HABEN**
			do you have	*har-bern zee* **HABEN SIE**
not	*nisht* **NICHT**			
no	*kine* **KEIN**		can I	*kan ish* **KANN ICH**
			can we	*ker-nen veer* **KÖNNEN WIR**
which	*vel-shyer* **WELCHER**		can you	*ker-nen zee* **KÖNNEN SIE**
where	*voh* **WO**			
when	*van* **WANN**		is	*isst* **IST**
what	*vass* **WAS**		are	*zint* **SIND**
what time	*uhm vee-feel ooer* **UM WIEVIEL UHR**		is there	*gipt ess* **GIBT ES**
			is it	*ist ess* **IST ES**
how long	*vee lang-er* **WIE LANGE**			
how many	*vee-fee-ler* **WIEVIELE**		depart	*ap-far-rern* **ABFAHREN**
how much is (that)	*vass koss-tert (das)* **WAS KOSTET (DAS)**		go	*gay-ern* **GEHEN**
			have	*har-bern* **HABEN**
near	*in dair nay-er fon* **IN DER NÄHE VON**		do you know	*viss-ern zee* **WISSEN SIE**
here	*here* **HIER**		see	*zay-ern* **SEHEN**
there	*dar* **DA**		stay	*bligh-bern* **BLEIBEN**
			take photos	*bil-der mash-ern* **BILDER MACHEN**
and	*oont* **UND**		reserve	*rezzair-vee-rern* **RESERVIEREN**
at	*an* **AN**			
by	*by* **BEI**			
for	*foor* **FÜR**		entrance fee	*iyn-trits-gur-boor* **EINTRITTSGEBÜHR**
from	*fon* **VON**		ticket	*iyn-trits-karter* **EINTRITTSKARTE**
in	*in* **IN**		per	*pro* **PRO**
on	*owf* **AUF**		person	*pair-zone* **PERSON**
to	*narsh* **NACH**		hours	*shtoon-dern* **STUNDEN**
			days	*tar-gur* **TAGE**

reduction	*air-**may**-sigoong* **ERMÄSSIGUNG**		start	*an-fang* **ANFANG**
group	*groo-per* **GRUPPE**		finish	*en-der* **ENDE**
student	*shtoo-dent* **STUDENT**			
child	*kint* **KIND**		earlier	*froo-er* **FRÜHER**
age	*al-ter* **ALTER**		later	*shpay-ter* **SPÄTER**
senior citizen	*zay-nyor* **SENIOR**			
deposit	*an-tsarloong* **ANZAHLUNG**		longer	*leng-er* **LÄNGER**
			shorter	*koort-ser* **KÜRZER**
architectural	*arsheetek-toh-nish* **ARCHITEKTONISCH**		cheaper	*goon-stigger* **GÜNSTIGER**
general interest	*foor arl-gurmyner inter-ressern* **FÜR ALLGEMEINE INTERESSEN**		better	*bess-ser* **BESSER**
historical	*hee-stor-rish* **HISTORISCH**			
scenic	*lant-shaft-lish shurn* **LANDSCHAFTLICH SCHÖN**		meals	*ess-sern* **ESSEN**
			transport	*trarns-port-vay-zern* **TRANSPORTWESEN**
boat	*boat* **BOOT**		included	*ent-hal-tern* **ENTHALTEN**
bus	*booss* **BUS**			
(air-conditioned)	*klee-mattee-zeert* **KLIMATISIERT**		ticket office	*kass-ser* **KASSE**
walking	*laoo-fern* **LAUFEN**		tourist office	*frem-dern-fairkairs-booro* **FREMDENVERKEHRSBÜRO**
			(long) queue	*(lang-er) shlang-er* **(LANGE) SCHLANGE**
tour	*roont-fart* **RUNDFAHRT**		toilets	*twal-let-tern* **TOILETTEN**
trip	*owss-floog* **AUSFLUG**			
			open	*owff* **AUF**
whole day	*gants-targs* **GANZTAGS**		closed	*tsoo* **ZU**
half-day	*halp-targs* **HALBTAGS**			
.... hour	*...shtoon-digger* **.... STÜNDIGE**		entrance	*iyn-gang* **EINGANG**
			exit	*owss-gang* **AUSGANG**
now	*yetst* **JETZT**			
soon	*balt* **BALD**		guide	*fyoo-rer* **FÜHRER**
today	*hoy-ter* **HEUTE**		(English speaking)	*eng-glish shpresh-yernt* **ENGLISCH SPRECHEND**
tomorrow	*more-gurn* **MORGEN**		guide book	*riy-zer-foorer* **REISEFÜHRER**
morning	*for-mittarg* **VORMITTAG**		map	*lant-karter* **LANDKARTE**
afternoon	*narsh-mittarg* **NACHMITTAG**		catalogue	*katta-lorg* **KATALOG**
evening	*ar-bent* **ABEND**		(in English)	*in eng-glish* **IN ENGLISCH**

PLACES OF	*zay-erns-voordig-kiy-tern*	exhibition	*dee owss-shtell-loong*
INTEREST	**SEHENSWÜRDIGKEITEN**		**die AUSSTELLUNG**
		factory	*dee far-brick*
			die FABRIK
old	*alt*	farm	*dair baoo-ern-horf*
	ALT		**der BAUERNHOF**
new	*noy*	flea market	*dair flow-markt*
	NEU		**der FLOHMARKT**
		fountain	*dair broo-nern*
			der BRUNNEN
the:		fort	*dee fess-toong*
			die FESTUNG
abbey	*dass kloh-ster*	fun fair	*dair roo-merl-plats*
	das KLOSTER		**der RUMMELPLATZ**
amusem't pk	*der fairg-noo-goongs-park*	gardens	*dee groon-arn-largurn*
	der VERGNÜGUNGSPARK		**die GRÜNANLAGEN**
antiques fair	*dee antickfee-tay-tern-mess-er*	gate	*das tor*
	die ANTIQUITÄTENMESSE		**das TOR**
aquarium	*das ar-kvar-ree-yoom*	harbour	*dair har-fern*
	das AQUARIUM		**der HAFEN**
art gallery	*dee koonst-galler-ree*	historical site	*dee hiss-tor-risher shtet-*
	die KUNSTGALERIE		**die HISTORISCHE STÄTTE**
artists' quarter	*das koonst-ler-feer-terl*	house	*das house*
	das KÜNSTLERVIERTEL		**das HAUS**
botanical gdns	*dair bot-tar-nisher gar-tern*	industrial	*dee in-dooss-tree-elll-*
	der BOTANISCHE GARTEN	- archaeology	*arshay-ologisher shtet-*
bridge	*dee broo-ker*	- site	**die INDUSTRIELL-**
	die BRÜCKE		**ARCHÄOLOGISCHE STÄTTE**
building	*das gur-boy-der*	lake	*der zay*
	das GEBÄUDE		**der SEE**
business dist.	*das gur-shefts-feer-terl*	library	*dee bib-leeyo-take*
	das GESCHÄFTSVIERTEL		**die BIBLIOTHEK**
canal	*dair kan-narl*	market	*dair markt*
	der KANAL		**der MARKT**
castle	*das shloss /dee boorg*	monastery	*das kloh-ster*
	das SCHLOSS /die BURG		**das KLOSTER**
catacombs	*dee katta-kom-bern*	monument	*das denk-marl*
	die KATAKOMBEN		**das DENKMAL**
cathedral	*dee kattay-drar-ler /der dome*		
	die KATHEDRALE /der DOM	museum	*das moo-zay-oom*
cave	*dee her-ler*		**das MUSEUM**
	die HÖHLE	of:	*fon:*
cemetery	*dair freet-horf*		**VON:**
	der FRIEDHOF	(art)	*koonst*
circus	*der tseer-kooss*		**KUNST**
	der ZIRKUS	(culture)	*kool-toor*
city	*dee shtat*		**KULTUR**
	die STADT	(geology)	*gay-ollo-ghee*
city centre	*dee shtat-mitter*		**GEOLOGIE**
	die STADTMITTE	(industry)	*in-dooss-tree*
city hall	*dass rart-house*		**INDUSTRIE**
	das RATHAUS	(local history)	*lo-karl-gur-shish-ter*
city walls	*dee shtat-mau-ern*		**LOKALGESCHICHTE**
	die STADTMAUERN	(national hist.)	*lan-des-gur-shish-ter*
church	*dee keer-shyer*		**LANDESGESCHICHTE**
	die KIRCHE	(natural hist.)	*nar-toor-gur-shish-ter*
concert hall	*dee con-tsairt-har-ler*		**NATURGESCHICHTE**
	die KONZERTHALLE	(science)	*nar-toor-vissern-sharfter*
convent	*das non-nern-kloh-ster*		**NATURWISSENSCHAFTEN**
	das NONNENKLOSTER	(transport)	*trarns-port-vay-zern*
docks	*dee har-fern-arn-lar-gurn*		**TRANSPORTWESEN**
	die HAFENANLAGEN	(performing arts)	*dar-shtell-oondern*
downtown area	*dee in-nern-shtat*		*koon-stern*
	die INNENSTADT		**DARSTELLENDEN KÜNSTEN**

observatory	*das opzair-vah-tor-reeyum*
	das OBSERVATORIUM
old city	*dee alt-shtat*
	die ALTSTADT
open air mus	*das fry-lisht-moo-zay-oom*
	das FREILICHTMUSEUM
opera house	*das oh-pern-house*
	das OPERNHAUS
palace	*dair par-last*
	der PALAST
parliament bldg	*das par-lar-ments-gur-boyder*
	das PARLAMENTSGEBÄUDE
park	*dair park*
	der PARK
planetarium	*das plannay-tar-ree-yoom*
	das PLANETARIUM
president's hse	*das prezzee-den-tern-house*
	das PRÄSIDENTENHAUS
races	*dee ren-barn*
	die RENNBAHN
river	*der flooss*
	der FLUSS
ruins	*dee roo-ee-nern*
	die RUINEN
school	*dee shoo-ler*
	die SCHULE
ship	*das shiff*
	das SCHIFF
shopping ctr	*das iyn-kowfs-tsen-troom*
	das EINKAUFSZENTRUM
show	*dee owss-shtell-loong*
	die AUSSTELLUNG
site	*das gur-len-der*
	das GELÄNDE
stadium	*das shtar-deeyon*
	das STADION
statue	*dee shtar-too-er*
	die STATUE
(main) square	*dair (howpt) plats*
	der (HAUPT) PLATZ
synagogue	*dee zoonar-go-gur*
	die SYNAGOGE
telev'n tower	*dair fairn-zay-toorm*
	der FERNSEHTURM
theatre	*das tay-ar-ter*
	das THEATER
tomb	*dee grooft*
	die GRUFT
tower	*dair toorm*
	der TURM
town	*dee shtat*
	die STADT
town hall	*das rart-house*
	das RATHAUS
tunnel	*dair too-nerl*
	der TUNNEL
university	*dee oonee-vairzee-tate*
	die UNIVERSITÄT
village	*das dorf*
	das DORF
vineyard	*dair vine-bairg*
	der WEINBERG
zoo	*dair tsoh*
	der ZOO

EVENTS	*fair-an-shtal-toong-ern*
	VERANSTALTUNGEN
ceremony	*tsay-ray-moh-nee*
	ZEREMONIE
event	*fair-an-shtal-toong*
	VERANSTALTUNG
exhibition	*owss-shtell-loong*
	AUSSTELLUNG
fair *(trade etc)*	*mess-er*
	MESSE
festival	*fest*
	FEST
game	*shpeel*
	SPIEL
illuminations	*fest-ber-loysh-toong-gurn*
	FESTBELEUCHTUNGEN
parade	*par-rar-der*
	PARADE
race	*ren-nern*
	RENNEN
regatta	*ray-gat-tah*
	REGATTA
son et lumière	*lisht oont*
	klang-for-fooroong
	LICHT und
	KLANGVORFÜHRUNG
show	*owss-shtell-loong*
	AUSSTELLUNG

the top	*dee shpit-ser*
	DIE SPITZE
underground	*oon-ter-groont*
	UNTERGRUND
view	*owss-zisht*
	AUSSICHT
of	*oo-ber*
	ÜBER

cable car	*ziyl-shvay-ber-barn*
	SEILSCHWEBEBAHN
funicular	*ziyl-shee-nern-barn*
	SEILSCHIENENBAHN

somewhere	*eer-goont-voh*
	IRGENDWO
something	*et-vars*
	ETWAS
good	*goot*
	GUT
interesting	*in-tay-ress-sant*
	INTERESSANT
special	*ber-zon-ders*
	BESONDERS

I	*ish* **ICH**		I would like	*ish mersh-ter* **ICH MÖCHTE**
my	*mine* **MEIN**		we would like	*veer mersh-tern* **WIR MÖCHTEN**
me	*mish* **MICH**		do you want	*vol-ern zee* **WOLLEN SIE**
we	*veer* **WIR**			
our	*oon-ser* **UNSER**		I have	*ish har-ber* **ICH HABE**
us	*oonts* **UNS**		we have	*veer har-bern* **WIR HABEN**
you	*zee* **SIE**		do you have	*har-bern zee* **HABEN SIE**
your	*eeyer* **IHR**			
it	*ess* **ES**		can I	*kan ish* **KANN ICH**
			can we	*ker-nen veer* **KÖNNEN WIR**
not	*nisht* **NICHT**		can you	*ker-nen zee* **KÖNNEN SIE**
no	*kine* **KEIN**			
			is	*isst* **IST**
which	*vel-shyer* **WELCHER**		are	*zint* **SIND**
where	*voh* **WO**		is there	*gipt ess* **GIBT ES**
when	*van* **WANN**		is it	*ist ess* **IST ES**
what	*vass* **WAS**			
what's on	*vass gipt ess* **WAS GIBT ES**		get	*ber-kom-mern* **BEKOMMEN**
what time	*uhm vee-feel ooer* **UM WIEVIEL UHR**		go	*gay-ern* **GEHEN**
			have	*har-bern* **HABEN**
how long	*vee lang-er* **WIE LANGE**		hire	*mee-tern* **MIETE**
how many	*vee-fee-ler* **WIEVIELE**		do you know	*viss-ern zee* **WISSEN SIE**
ow much is (that)	*vass koss-tert (das)* **WAS KOSTET (DAS)**		like	*mer-gurn* **MÖGEN**
			play	*shpee-lern* **SPIELEN**
at	*an* **AN**		repair	*reppar-ree-rern* **REPARIEREN**
by	*bay* **BEI**		rescue	*ret-ern* **RETTEN**
for	*foor* **FÜR**		reserve	*rezair-vee-rern* **RESERVIEREN**
from	*fon* **VON**		show me	*tsigh-gurn zee meer* **ZEIGEN SIE MIR**
in	*in* **IN**		take part	*tile-nay-mern* **TEILNEHMEN**
on	*owf* **AUF**		teach me	*lair-rern zee mish* **LEHREN SIE MICH**
to	*narsh* **NACH**		teach us	*lair-rern zee oonts* **LEHREN SIE UNS**
with	*mit* **MIT**		watch	*tsoo-zayern* **ZUSEHEN**

somewhere	*eer-goond-voh* **IRGENDWO**	reduction	*air-may-sisgoong* **ERMÄSSIGUNG**
nearest	*nex-ster* **NÄCHSTER**	group	*groo-per* **GRUPPE**
near	*in dair nay-er fon* **IN DER NÄHE VON**	student	*shtoo-dent* **STUDENT**
here	*here* **HIER**	child	*kint* **KIND**
there	*dar* **DA**	age	*al-ter* **ALTER**
		senior citizen	*zay-nyor* **SENIOR**
conditions	*ber-ding-oong-ern* **BEDINGUNGEN**	identification	*owss-vice* **AUSWEIS**
good	*goot* **GUT**		
safe	*oon-gur-fair-lish* **UNGEFÄHRLICH**	lesson	*lair-shtoonder* **LEHRSTUNDE**
dangerous	*gur-fair-lish* **GEFÄHRLICH**	instructor	*lair-rer* **LEHRER**
easy	*liysht* **LEICHT**		
difficult	*shveer-ig* **SCHWIERIG**	beginner	*an-feng-er* **ANFÄNGER**
		average	*mit-terl-maysig* **MITTELMÄSSIG**
crowded	*oober-foolt* **ÜBERFÜLLT**	experienced	*air-far-rern* **ERFAHREN**
(long) queue	*(lang-er) shlang-er* **(LANGE) SCHLANGE**	professional	*pro-fee* **PROFI**
quiet	*roo-wig* **RUHIG**	player	*shpee-ler* **SPIELER**
		team	*man-shaft* **MANNSCHAFT**
open	*owff* **AUF**		
closed	*tsoo* **ZU**	course	*barn* **BAHN**
start	*an-fang* **ANFANG**	courts	*shpeel-pletser* **SPIELPLÄTZE**
finish	*shlooss* **SCHLUSS**	lake	*zay* **SEE**
entrance	*iyn-gang* **EINGANG**	race track	*ren-barn* **RENNBAHN**
exit	*owss-gang* **AUSGANG**	river	*flooss* **FLUSS**
		sauna	*zow-ner* **SAUNA**
ticket	*iyn-tritts-karter* **EINTRITTSKARTE**	sports centre	*shport-tsen-troom* **SPORTZENTRUM**
the charge	*dair price* **DER PREIS**	sports ground	*shport-anlargur* **SPORTANLAGE**
deposit	*an-tsarloong* **ANZAHLUNG**	sports shop	*shport-gesheft* **SPORTGESCHÄFT**
per	*pro* **PRO**	swimming pool	*shvim-bad* **SCHWIMMBAD**
person	*pair-zone* **PERSON**		
session	*payree-yo-der* **PERIODE**	tournament	*vett-kampf* **WETTKAMPF**
hour	*shtoon-der* **STUNDE**	race	*ren-nern* **RENNEN**
day	*targ* **TAG**	match / game	*shpeel* **SPIEL**

SPORTS	*shport*	keep fit	*trim dish*	
	SPORT		**TRIMM DICH**	
American football	*amairee-kar-nisher* *fooss-bal*	lacrosse	*la-cross*	
	AMERIKANISCHER FUSSBALL		**LACROSSE**	
archery	*bo-gurn-shee-sern*	martial arts	*kampf-shport*	
	BOGENSCHIESSEN		**KAMPFSPORT**	
athletics	*liysht-atlay-teek*	motor racing	*ow-toh-rennern*	
	LEICHTATHLETIK		**AUTORENNEN**	
badminton	*fay-der-bal*	motorcycle racing	*mo-tor-rard-rennern*	
	FEDERBALL		**MOTORRADRENNEN**	
baseball	*base-bal*	motocross	*mo-toh-cross*	
	BASEBALL		**MOTOCROSS**	
basket ball	*bass-ket-bal*	net ball	*nets-bal-shpeel*	
	BASKETBALL		**NETZBALLSPIEL**	
billiards	*beel-yad*	parachuting	*fal-sheerm-shpring-ern*	
	BILLARD		**FALLSCHIRMSPRINGEN**	
BMX	*BMX*	polo	*po-lo*	
	BMX		**POLO**	
bowling	*kay-gurln*	pot holing	*her-lern-forshern*	
	KEGELN		**HÖHLENFORSCHEN**	
boxing	*box-ern*	roller skating	*rol-shoe-laoofern*	
	BOXEN		**ROLLSCHUHLAUFEN**	
canoeing	*pad-erln*	rowing	*roo-dern*	
	PADDELN		**RUDERN**	
climbing	*bairg-shtigh-gurn*	rugby	*rugby*	
	BERGSTEIGEN		**RUGBY**	
cricket	*cree-kit*	running	*laoof-ern*	
	KRICKET		**LAUFEN**	
curling	*ice-shee-sern*	sailing	*zay-gurln*	
	EISSCHIESSEN		**SEGELN**	
cycling	*rard-far-rern*	scuba diving	*shport-taoosh-ern*	
	RADFAHREN		**SPORTTAUCHEN**	
fencing	*fesh-tern*	skiing	*shee-laoofern*	
	FECHTEN		**SKILAUFEN**	
fishing	*ang-gurln*	shooting	*shee-sern*	
	ANGELN		**SCHIESSEN**	
football	*fooss-bal*	snooker	*snooker (art **bill**-yard shpe*	
	FUSSBALL		**SNOOKER (art Billardspiel)**	
flying	*flee-gurn*	snorkelling	*shnor-sherln*	
	FLIEGEN		**SCHNORCHELN**	
gliding	*zay-gurl-flee-gurn*	speedboat racing	*shnel-boat-rennern*	
	SEGELFLIEGEN		**SCHNELLBOOTRENNEN**	
go-cart racing	*go-cart-rennern*	squash	*skvosh*	
	GO-KART-RENNEN		**SQUASH**	
golf	*golf*	surfing	*vel-lern-right-ern*	
	GOLF		**WELLENREITEN**	
gymnastics	*toor-nern*	swimming	*shvim-ern*	
	TURNEN		**SCHWIMMEN**	
hang gliding	*drash-ern-flee-gurn*	table tennis	*tish-tennis*	
	DRACHENFLIEGEN		**TISCHTENNIS**	
hockey	*hock-ee*	tennis	*tennis*	
	HOCKEY		**TENNIS**	
horse racing	*pfair-der-rennern*	volley ball	*vol-ley-bal*	
	PFERDERENNEN		**VOLLEYBALL**	
horse riding	*right-ern*	walking	*van-dern*	
	REITEN		**WANDERN**	
hunting	*yargd*	water polo	*vass-ser-bal*	
	JAGD		**WASSERBALL**	
ice skating	*shlitt-shoe-laoofern*	water skiing	*vass-ser-shee-laoofern*	
	SCHLITTSCHUHLAUFEN		**WASSERSKILAUFEN**	
judo	*yoo-doh*	windsurfing	*surf-ern*	
	JUDO		**SURFEN**	
		wrestling	*ring-ern*	
			RINGEN	

winter sports: 132   countryside: 36

EQUIPMENT	*owss-rooss-toong*	sail board	*vint-surf-bret*
	AUSRÜSTUNG		**WINDSURFBRETT**
air mattress	*looft-mattrat-ser*	shoes	*shoo-er*
	LUFTMATRAZE		**SCHUHE**
anorak	*an-norak*	shuttlecock	*fed-der-bal*
	ANORAK		**FEDERBALL**
aqualung	*tau-sher-loong-gur*	snorkel	*shnor-sherl*
	TAUCHERLUNGE		**SCHNORCHEL**
ball	*bal*	stick	*shlair-gur*
	BALL		**SCHLÄGER**
bat	*shlay-gur*	sun glasses	*zon-nern-briller*
	SCHLÄGER		**SONNENBRILLE**
bicycle	*far-rart*	sun shade	*zon-nern-sheerm*
	FAHRRAD		**SONNENSCHIRM**
binoculars	*fairn-glarss*	surf board	*surf-bret*
	FERNGLAS		**SURFBRETT**
boat	*boat*	swimming costume	*bar-der-antsoog*
	BOOT		**BADEANZUG**
boots	*shtee-ferl*	towel	*hant-toosh*
	STIEFEL		**HANDTUCH**
bowls	*koo-gurln*	trainers	*shport-shoo-er*
	KUGELN		**SPORTSCHUHE**
canoe	*canoe*	visor	*viz-zeer*
	KANU		**VISIER**
clothing	*kliy-doong*	water skis	*vass-ser-shee-er*
	KLEIDUNG		**WASSERSCHIER**
compass	*komm-pass*	wet suit	*tao-sher-anzoog*
	KOMPASS		**TAUCHERANZUG**
fishing rod	*ang-gurl-rooter*	wind break	*vint-shoots*
	ANGELRUTE		**WINDSCHUTZ**
fishing tackle	*ang-gurl-gur-ret*		
	ANGELGERÄT		
flip flops	*goo-mee-latchern*		
	GUMMILATSCHEN		
gloves	*hant-shoo-er*	BEACH	*shtrant*
	HANDSCHUHE		**STRAND**
goggles	*shoots-briller*	private	*erf-ernt-leesh*
	SCHUTZBRILLE		**ÖFFENTLICH**
golf club	*golf-shlay-gur*	public	*pree-vat*
	GOLFSCHLÄGER		**PRIVAT**
hat	*hoot*		
	HUT		
headband	*shteern-bant*	sea	*mair*
	STIRNBAND		**MEER**
helmet	*shoots-helm*	high-tide	*floot*
	SCHUTZHELM		**FLUT**
ice skates	*shlit-shoo-er*	low-tide	*eb-ber*
	SCHLITTSCHUHE		**EBBE**
life jacket	*shvim-vester*	deep	*teef*
	SCHWIMMWESTE		**TIEF**
net	*nets*	shallow	*ziysht*
	NETZ		**SEICHT**
overtrousers	*oober-hoze-er*	currents	*shtrer-mer*
	ÜBERHOSE		**STRÖME**
paddle	*pad-erl*	waves	*vel-lern*
	PADDEL		**WELLEN**
racquet	*shlay-gur*		
	SCHLÄGER		
roller skates	*rol-shoo-er*	the sand	*der zant*
	ROLLSCHUHE		**DER SAND**
rope	*zile*	jellyfish	*kval-ler*
	SEIL		**QUALLE**
rucksack	*rook-sack*	lifeguard	*ret-toongs-shvimmer*
	RUCKSACK		**RETTUNGSSCHWIMMER**

I	*ish* **ICH**		I would like	*ish* **mersh**-ter **ICH MÖCHTE**
my	*mine* **MEIN**		we would like	*veer* **mersh**-tern **WIR MÖCHTEN**
we	*veer* **WI**		do you want	*vol*-ern *zee* **WOLLEN SIE**
you	*zee* **SIE**			
your	*eeyer* **IHR**		I have	*ish* **har**-ber **ICH HABE**
it	*ess* **ES**		we have	*veer* **har**-bern **WIR HABEN**
			do you have	**har**-bern *zee* **HABEN SIE**
not	*nisht* **NICHT**			
no	*kine* **KEIN**		can I	*kan ish* **KANN ICH**
			can we	**ker**-nen *veer* **KÖNNEN WIR**
which	*vel-shyer* **WELCHER**		can you	**ker**-nen *zee* **KÖNNEN SIE**
where	*voh* **WO**			
when	*van* **WANN**		is	*isst* **IST**
what	*vass* **WAS**		are	*zint* **SIND**
what time	*uhm* vee-**feel** *ooer* **UM WIEVIEL UHR**		is there	*gipt ess* **GIBT ES**
			is it	*ist ess* **IST ES**
how many	vee-**fee**-ler **WIEVIELE**			
how much is (that)	*vass* **koss**-tert *(das)* **WAS KOSTET (DAS)**		get	ber-**kom**-mern **BEKOMMEN**
			have	**har**-bern **HABEN**
nearest	**nex**-ster **NÄCHSTER**		pay	tsar-lern **ZAHLEN**
near	*in dair* **nay**-er *fon* **IN DER NÄHE VON**		return (thing)	tsoo-**rook**-gay-bern **ZURÜCKGEBEN**
here	*here* **HIER**		see	**zay**-ern **SEHEN**
there	*dar* **DA**		show me	**tsigh**-gurn *zee meer* **ZEIGEN SIE MIR**
			wrap	**iyn**-packern **EINPACKEN**
and	*oont* **UND**			
at	*an* **AN**		open	*owff* **AUF**
by	*by* **BEI**		closed	*tsoo* **ZU**
for	*foor* **FÜR**			
in	*in* **IN**		each	**yay**-der **JEDER**
of	*fon* **VON**		receipt	**kvit**-toong **QUITTUNG**
on	*owf* **AUF**			
to	*tsoo* **ZU**		THAT'S FINE	*das ist* **ord**-noong **DAS IST ORDNUNG**

good	*goot* **GUT**	**STATIONERY**	*shriyp-var-rern* **SCHREIBWAREN**
cheap	*bil-lig* **BILLIG**	ball point pen	*koo-gurl-shriyber* **KUGELSCHREIBER**
		carbon paper	*dursh-shlarg-pappeer* **DURCHSCHLAGPAPIER**
cheaper	*bil-ligger* **BILLIGER**	cellophane tape	*klay-ber-bant* **KLEBEBAND**
better	*bess-ser* **BESSER**	chalks	*kriy-der-shtifter* **KREIDESTIFTE**
alternative	*al-tairna-tee-ver* **ALTERNATIVE**	computer discs	*diss-ket-tern* **DISKETTEN**
		drawing pins	*rice-tsveck-ern* **REISSZWECKEN**
bigger	*grur-ser* **GRÖSSER**	envelopes	*oom-shlay-gur* **UMSCHLÄGE**
smaller	*kliy-ner* **KLEINER**	eraser	*ra-deer-goo-mee* **RADIERGUMMI**
thicker	*dick-er* **DICKER**	file	*map-per* **MAPPE**
thinner	*doo-ner* **DÜNNER**	fountain pen	*fool-fayder-hal-ter* **FÜLLFEDERHALTER**
wider	*brigh-ter* **BREITER**	felt-tip pen	*filts-shtift* **FILZSTIFT**
narrower	*shmar-ler* **SCHMALER**	glue	*clayp-shtoff* **KLEBSTOFF**
		(bottle of) ink	*flasher tin-ter* **(FLASCHE) TINTE**
RT SUPPLIES	*koon-stler-berdarf* **KÜNSTLERBEDARF**	labels	*ettee-ket-er* **ETIKETTE**
acrylic paints	*ack-rool-farbern* **AKRYLFARBEN**	notebook	*no-teets-heft* **NOTIZHEFT**
canvas	*line-vant* **LEINWAND**	note paper	*breef-pappeer* **BRIEFPAPIER**
charcoal	*tsiy-shyern-coal-er* **ZEICHENKOHLE**	paper	*pap-peer* **PAPIER**
coloured paper	*boont-pappeer* **BUNTPAPIER**	pencil	*bligh-shtift* **BLEISTIFT**
coloured pencils	*farp-shtifter* **FARBSTIFTE**	pencil sharpener	*bligh-shtift-shpit-ser* **BLEISTIFTSPITZER**
crayons	*boont-shifter* **BUNTSTIFTE**	printer ribbon	*droo-ker-far-bant* **DRUCKERFARBBAND**
drawing paper	*tsiy-shyern-pappeer* **ZEICHENPAPIER**	playing cards	*shpeel-kartern* **SPIELKARTEN**
easel	*shtaffer-ligh* **STAFFELEI**	refill for biro	*mee-ner* **MINE**
fixative	*fix-eer-mitterl* **FIXIERMITTEL**	rubber	*goo-mee* **GUMMI**
(coloured) ink	*(farp) tin-ter* **(FARB) TINTE**	rubber bands	*goo-mee-ben-ter* **GUMMIBÄNDER**
oil	*erl* **ÖL**	ruler	*leenay-yarl* **LINEAL**
oil paints	*erl-farbern* **ÖLFARBEN**	self adhesive labels	*zelbst-hafternder ettee-ket-er* **SELBSTHAFTENDE ETIKETTE**
paint box	*marl-kastern* **MALKASTEN**	string	*shnoor* **SCHNUR**
paint brush	*pin-zerl* **PINSEL**	tissue paper	*ziy-dern-pappeer* **SEIDENPAPIER**
pastels	*pah-stell-shtifter* **PASTELLSTIFTE**	typewriter	*shriyp-masheener* **SCHREIBMASCHINE**
turpentine	*tairpen-teen* **TERPENTIN**	typewriter ribbon	*farp-bant* **FARBBAND**
water colours	*vass-ser-farbern* **WASSERFARBEN**	wrapping paper	*pack-pappeer* **PACKPAPIER**

minerals: 97   fabrics: 28   colours: 28

Public phone boxes are operated by coins. A green sign "AUSLAND" indicates boxes from which international calls can be made. Coin-feeding for long distance calls can be avoided by making such calls from Post Offices where payment is made at the counter afterwards. In German, phone numbers are stated in pairs, eg: 2386 would be *twenty-three, eighty-six*, but single numbers will probably be understood.

I	*ish* **ICH**		I would like	*ish* **mersh**-*ter* **ICH MÖCHTE**
my	*mine* **MEIN**			
me	*mish* **MICH**		I have	*ish* **har**-*ber* **ICH HABE**
you	*zee* **SIE**		do you have	**har**-*bern zee* **HABEN SIE**
who	*vair* **WER**			
			can I	*kan ish* **KANN ICH**
not	*nisht* **NICHT**		can you	**ker**-*nen zee* **KÖNNEN SIE**
no	*kine* **KEIN**		I cannot	*ish kan nisht* **ICH KANN NICHT**
where	*voh* **WO**		is	*isst* **IST**
what	*vass* **WAS**		is there	*gipt ess* **GIBT ES**
what time	*uhm vee-**feel** ooer* **UM WIEVIEL UHR**			
			call again	*tsoo-**rook**-roofern* **ZURÜCKRUFEN**
how long	*vee **lang**-er* **WIE LANGE**		(later)	*(**shpay**-ter)* **(SPÄTER)**
how much is (that)	*vas **koss**-tert (das)* **WAS KOSTET (DAS)**		dial (direct)	**vay**-*lern (deer-**reckt**)* **WÄHLEN (DIREKT)**
how much was (that)	*vass **koss**-terter (das)* **WAS KOSTETE (DAS)**		get me	*vairbindern zee mish mit* **VERBINDEN SIE MICH MIT**
			have	**har**-*bern* **HABEN**
near	*in dair **nay**-er fon* **IN DER NÄHE VON**		do you know	*viss-sern zee* **WISSEN SIE**
here	*here* **HIER**		make	**foor**-*rern* **FÜHREN**
there	*dar* **DA**		speak	**spresh**-*ern* **SPRECHEN**
this	**dee**-*zer* **DIESER**		tell me	**zar**-*gurn zee meer* **SAGEN SIE MIR**
			use	*fair-**ven**-dern* **VERWENDEN**
and	*oont* **UND**			
at	*an* **AN**		telephone call	**fairn**-*gur-shpresh* **FERNGESPRÄCH**
for	*foor* **FÜR**		international call	*owss-lants-gur-**shpresh*** **AUSLANDSGESPRÄCH**
from	*fon* **VON**		morning call	**veck**-*an-roof* **WECKANRUF**
in	*in* **IN**		person to person call	*gur-**shpresh** mit for-**ran**-mel-doong* **GESPRÄCH MIT VORANMELDUNG**
of	*fon* **VON**			
to	*mit* **MIT**		reverse charge call	*err-gur-**shpresh*** **R-GESPRÄCH**

place name pronunciations in Austria Germany & Switzerland: 32-33

the code	*dee **for**-varl*	Australia	*owss-**strar**-lyen*
	DIE VORWAHL		**AUSTRALIEN**
the name	*dair **nar**-mer*	Britain	*gross-bree-**tan**-yen*
	DER NAME		**GROSSBRITANNIEN**
he tel. number	*dee **roof**-noomer*	Canada	*kan-nadda*
	DIE RUFNUMMER		**KANADA**
wrong number	*dee **fal**-sher **noo**-mer*	Ireland	*eer-lant*
	DIE FALSCHE NUMMER		**IRLAND**
		New Zealand	*noy-**zay**-lant*
			NEUSEELAND
the charge	*dair price*	South Africa	*sood-**aff**-ree-kar*
	DER PREIS		**SÜDAFRIKA**
per minute	*pro **mee-noo**-ter*	United states	*oo ess ar*
	PRO MINUTE		**USA**

extension	*dair appa-**rart***	
	DER APPARAT	
the operator	*dee fair-**mit**-loong*	0 *nool*
	DIE VERMITTLUNG	1 *iynts*
telephone	*taylay-**phone***	2 *tsvoh*
	TELEFON	3 *drigh*
telephone box	*taylay-**phone**-tseller*	4 *fear*
	TELEFONZELLE	5 *foonf*
phone directory	*taylay-**phone**-boo<u>sh</u>*	6 *zex*
	TELEFONBUCH	7 *zee-bern*
small change	***kline**-ghelt*	8 *a<u>sh</u>t*
	KLEINGELD	9 *noyn*

Do you speak English?	*<u>sh</u>pre<u>sh</u>-ern zee **eng**-lish*
	SPRECHEN SIE ENGLISCH?
Does anyone there speak English?	*<u>sh</u>pri<u>sht</u> **yay**-mant **eng**-lish*
	SPRICHT JEMAND ENGLISCH?
Please speak very slowly	*<u>sh</u>pre<u>sh</u>-ern zee **bit**-ter zair **lang**-zam*
	SPRECHEN SIE BITTE SEHR LANGSAM
I don't understand	*i<u>sh</u> fair-**shtay**-er ni<u>sht</u>*
	ICH VERSTEHE NICHT
Say again very slowly	*no<u>sh</u> marl **bit**-ter - zair **lang**-zam*
	NOCH MAL BITTE - SEHR LANGSAM

THE OPERATOR OR PERSON AT THE OTHER END MIGHT SAY:	
***hal**-lo*	Hello
*gur-**shpre<u>sh</u>** foor zee*	Telephone call for you
*vel-<u>sh</u>yer **noo**-mer **mer<u>sh</u>**-tern zee?*	What number do you want?
*vee ist eer **nar**-mer?*	What's your name?
*vel-<u>sh</u>yer **noo**-mer **har**-bern zee?*	What's your number?
***bliy**-bern zee dran*	Hold the line
***bit**-ter **shpre<u>sh</u>**-ern*	Go ahead please
*dee **leen**-yer ist ber-**zetst***	The line's engaged
*ess **mel**-dert zi<u>sh</u> **nee**-mant*	There's no reply
*zee **har**-bern zi<u>sh</u> fair-**vaylt***	Wrong number

EMERGENCY PHONE NUMBERS:

Austria	fire - 122	police - 133
Germany	fire - 112	police - 110
Switzerland	fire - 118	police - 117

payment: 47   alphabet pronunciation: 141

I	*ish*	I would like	*ish* **mer**-shter
	ICH		**ICH MÖCHTE**
me	*mish*	he/she would like	*air / zee* **mersh**-ter
	MICH		**ER/SIE MÖCHTE**
he	*air*	we would like	*veer* **mersh**-tern
	ER		**WIR MÖCHTEN**
she	*zee*	do you want	*vol-ern zee*
	SIE		**WOLLEN SIE**
him	*een*		
	IHN		
her	*zee*	I have	*ish* **har**-ber
	SIE		**ICH HABE**
we	*veer*	he / she has	*air / zee hat*
	WIR		**ER/SIE HAT**
us	*oonts*	we have	*veer* **har**-bern
	UNS		**WIR HABEN**
you	*zee*	do you have	**har**-bern *zee*
	SIE		**HABEN SIE**
they / them	*zee*		
	SIE		
it	*ess*	can I	*kan ish*
	ES		**KANN ICH**
		can he / she	*kan air / zee*
			KANN ER/SIE
not	*nisht*	can we	**ker**-nen *veer*
	NICHT		**KÖNNEN WIR**
no	*kine*	can you	**ker**-nen *zee*
	KEIN		**KÖNNEN SIE**
where	*voh*	I cannot	*ish kan nisht*
	WO		**ICH KANN NICHT**
when	*van*	he/she cannot	*air / zee kan nisht*
	WANN		**ER/SIE KANN NICHT**
what	*vass*	we cannot	*veer* **ker**-nern *nisht*
	WAS		**WIR KÖNNEN NICHT**
what time	*uhm vee-***feel** *ooer*	you cannot	*zee* **ker**-nern *nisht*
	UM WIEVIEL UHR		**SIE KÖNNEN NICHT**
how long	*vee* **lang**-*er*	I must	*ish mooss*
	WIE LANGE		**ICH MUSS**
how many	*vee-***fee**-*ler*	we must	*veer* **moo**-sern
	WIEVIELE		**WIR MÜSSEN**
		you must	*zee* **moo**-sern
			SIE MÜSSEN
and	*oont*		
	UND		
at	*an*	am	*bin*
	AN		**BIN**
by	*by*	is	*isst*
	BEI		**IST**
for	*foor*	are	*zint*
	FÜR		**SIND**
from	*fon*	is there	*gibt ess*
	VON		**GIBT ES**
in	*in*	is it	*ist ess*
	IN		**IST ES**
on	*owf*	it is	*ess ist*
	AUF		**ES IST**
to	*tsoo*		
	ZU		
too	*owsh*	let's	**vol**-*lern veer*
	AUCH		**WOLLEN WIR**

arrange	*ap-shtimmern* **ABSTIMMEN**		first	*airst* **ERST**
arrive	*an-kommern* **ANKOMMEN**		next	*next* **NÄCHST**
cancel	*rook-ghen-gig ma**sh**-ern* **RÜCKGÄNGIG MACHEN**		last	*letst* **LETZT**
come	*kom-mern* **KOMMEN**			
depart	*ap-far-rern* **ABFAHREN**		now	*yetst* **JETZT**
go	*far-rern* **FAHREN**		soon	*balt* **BALD**
have	*har-bern* **HABEN**		early	*froo* **FRÜH**
do you know	*viss-ern zee* **WISSEN SIE**		late	*shpayt* **SPÄT**
meet	*tref-fern* **TREFFEN**		earlier	*froo-er* **FRÜHER**
will be ready	*veert **fair**-tig* **WIRD FERTIG**		later	*shpay-ter* **SPÄTER**
return	*tsoo-**rook**-kommern* **ZURÜCKKOMMEN**			
postpone	*fair-**shee**-bern* **VERSCHIEBEN**		before	*for* **VOR**
I'm sorry	*ess toot meer light* **ES TUT MIR LEID**		after	*nar**sh*** **NACH**
stay	*bligh—bern* **BLEIBEN**		until	*biss* **BIS**
will take	*nimmt* **NIMMT**		during	*vair-runt* **WÄHREND**
telephone	*taylay-fon-**neer**-rern* **TELEPHONIEREN**		since	*zight* **SEIT**
tell me	*zar-gurn zee meer* **SAGEN SIE MIR**		ago	*for* **VOR**
tell us	*zar-gurn zee oonts* **SAGEN SIE UNS**			
wait	*var-tern* **WARTEN**		start	*an-fang-ern* **ANFANGEN**
write down	*shriy-bern* **SCHREIBEN**		finish	*ber-en-dern* **BEENDEN**
			open	*owff* **AUF**
nearest	*nex-ter* **NÄCHSTER**		closed	*tsoo* **ZU**
near	*in dair **nay**-er fon* **IN DER NÄHE VON**			
here	*here* **HIER**		name	*nar-mer* **NAME**
there	*dar* **DA**		address	*ad-**dress**-er* **ADRESSE**
the time	*dee tsight* **DIE ZEIT**		(a) delay	*(iyner) fair-**tsur**-gur-roong* **(EINE) VERZÖGERUNG**
the date	*dass **dar**-toom* **DAS DATUM**		delayed	*fair-**shpay**-tert* **VERSPÄTET**
			cancelled	*shtor-**neert*** **STORNIERT**
appointment	*tair-**meen*** **TERMIN**		postponed	*fair-**show**-bern* **VERSCHOBEN**
meeting	*fair-**ap**-pray-doong* **VERABREDUNG**			
birthday	*gur-**boort**-starg* **GEBURTSTAG**			

hours, days & months etc.: overleaf ☞   clock face: overleaf ☞

yesterday	*guest-ern* **GESTERN**	January	*yan-noo-ar* **JANUAR**
today	*hoy-ter* **HEUTE**	February	*feb-roo-ar* **FEBRUAR**
tomorrow	*more-gurn* **MORGEN**	March	*mairts* **MÄRZ**
		April	*ap-ril* **APRIL**
morning	*for-mittarg* **VORMITTAG**	May	*my* **MAI**
this morning	*hoy-ter mor-gurn* **HEUTE MORGEN**	June	*yoo-nee* **JUNI**
midday	*mit-targ* **MITTAG**	July	*yoo-lee* **JULI**
afternoon	*narsh-mittarg* **NACHMITTAG**	August	*ow-goost* **AUGUST**
this afternoon	*hoy-ter narsh-mittarg* **HEUTE NACHMITTAG**	September	*zep-tem-ber* **SEPTEMBER**
evening	*ar-bent* **ABEND**	October	*ock-toh-ber* **OKTOBER**
this evening	*hoy-ter ar-bent* **HEUTE ABEND**	November	*no-vem-ber* **NOVEMBER**
night	*narsht* **NACHT**	December	*day-tsem-ber* **DEZEMBER**
tonight	*hoy-ter ar-bent* **HEUTE ABEND**		
midnight	*mit-ter-narsht* **MITTERNACHT**	Sunday	*zon-targ* **SONNTAG**
		Monday	*morn-targ* **MONTAG**
seconds	*zeck-koon-dern* **SEKUNDEN**	Tuesday	*deens-targ* **DIENSTAG**
minutes	*mee-noo-tern* **MINUTEN**	Wednesday	*mit-vosh* **MITTWOCH**
quarter of an hour	*feer-terl-shtoonder* **VIERTELSTUNDE**	Thursday	*don-ners-targ* **DONNERSTAG**
half an hour	*hal-ber shtoon-der* **HALBE STUNDE**	Friday	*fry-targ* **FREITAG**
three quarters of an hour	*drigh-feer-terl-shtoonder* **DREIVIERTELSTUNDE**	Saturday	*zams-targ* **SAMSTAG**
hour	*shtoon-der* **STUNDE**		
hours	*shtoon-dern* **STUNDEN**	day off	*fry-yer targ* **FREIE TAG**
day	*targ* **TAG**	holiday	*fiy-yer-targ* **FEIERTAG**
days	*tar-gur* **TAGE**	school holidays	*shool-fay-ree* **SCHULFERIEN**
week	*vosh-er* **WOCHE**	weekday	*vosh-ern-targ* **WOCHENTAG**
weeks	*vosh-ern* **WOCHEN**	weekend	*vosh-ern-end* **WOCHENENDE**
month	*moh-nart* **MONAT**	working day	*vairk-targ* **WERKTAG**
months	*moh-narter* **MONATE**		
year	*yar* **JAHR**	*the* Spring	*der froo-ling* **DER FRÜHLING**
years	*yar-rer* **JAHRE**	*the* Summer	*der som-mer* **DER SOMMER**
decade	*yar-tsaint* **JAHRZEHNT**	*the* Autumn	*der hairpst* **DER HERBST**
century	*yar-hoon-dert* **JAHRHUNDERT**	*the* Winter	*der vin-ter* **DER WINTER**

	PUBLIC HOLIDAYS					
January 1	**New Year's Day**	A	S	WG	EG	A = Austria
January 2			S			S = Switzerland
January 6	**Epiphany**	A				WG = West Germany
May 1	**Labour Day**	A		WG	EG	EG = East Germany
June 17	**National Unity Day**			WG		
August 1	**National Day**		S			
August 15	**Assumption Day**	A				
October 7	**Foundation Day of GDR**				EG	
October 26	**National Day**	A				
November 1	**All Saints' Day**	A				
December 8	**Immaculate Conception**	A				
December 25	**Christmas Day**	A	S	WG	EG	
December 26	**St Stephen's Day**	A	S	WG	EG	
	Good Friday		S	WG	EG	
	Easter Monday	A	S	WG		
	Ascension Day	A	S	WG		
	Whit Monday	A	S	WG	EG	
	Corpus Christi	A				

SIMPLE WAY OF SAYING TIME

at	5.05	= *oom 5 oor 5*
at	5.30	= *oom 5 oor 30*
at	6.00	= *oom 6 oor*
at	18.00	= *oom 18 oor*
at midnight 25		= *25 nar<u>sh</u> **mit**-ter-narsht*

I	*ish* **ICH**		I would like	*ish* **mersh**-*ter* **ICH MÖCHTE**
my	*mine* **MEIN**		we would like	*veer* **mersh**-*tern* **WIR MÖCHTEN**
we	*veer* **WIR**		do you want	*vol*-*ern zee* **WOLLEN SIE**
our	*oon*-*ser* **UNSER**			
you	*zee* **SIE**		I have	*ish* **har**-*ber* **ICH HABE**
your	*eeyer* **IHR**		we have	*veer* **har**-*bern* **WIR HABEN**
it	*ess* **ES**		do you have	**har**-*bern zee* **HABEN SIE**
not	*nisht* **NICHT**		can I	*kan ish* **KANN ICH**
no	*kine* **KEIN**		can we	*ker*-*nen veer* **KÖNNEN WIR**
			can you	*ker*-*nen zee* **KÖNNEN SIE**
which	*vel*-*shyer* **WELCHER**			
where	*voh* **WO**		is	*isst* **IST**
when	*van* **WANN**		are	*zint* **SIND**
what	*vass* **WAS**		is there	*gipt ess* **GIBT ES**
what time	*uhm vee*-**feel** *ooer* **UM WIEVIEL UHR**		is it	*ist ess* **IST ES**
how far	*vee vight* **WIE WEIT**		come back	*tsoo*-**rook**-*kommern* **ZURÜCKKOMMEN**
how long	*vee* **lang**-*er* **WIE LANGE**		drive	*far*-*rern* **FAHREN**
how many	*vee*-**fee**-*ler* **WIEVIELE**		explain	*air*-**clair**-*rern* **ERKLÄREN**
how much is (that)	*vass* **koss**-*tert (das)* **WAS KOSTET (DAS)**		go	*far*-*rern* **FAHREN**
			have	**har**-*bern* **HABEN**
nearest	**nex**-*ster* **NÄCHSTER**		hire	**mee**-*tern* **MIETEN**
near	*in dair* **nay**-*er fon* **IN DER NÄHE VON**		leave (vehicle)	**lass**-*ern* **LASSEN**
			how do...work	*vee foonk-tseo-**nee**-*rern* **WIE FUNKTIONIEREN ....**
and	*oont* **UND**		pay	**tsar**-*lern* **ZAHLEN**
at	*an* **AN**		ride	*mit*-**far**-*rern* **MITFAHREN**
for	*foor* **FÜR**		show me	*tsigh*-**gurn**-*zee meer* **ZEIGEN SIE MIR**
from	*fon* **VON**		take	**nay**-*mern* **NEHMEN**
in	*in* **IN**			
to	*narsh* **NACH**		here	*here* **HIER**
with	*mit* **MIT**		there	*dar* **DA**

the charge	*dair price* **DER PREIS**	cheaper	*goon-stigger* **GÜNSTIGER**	
total cost	*gur-zamt-kostern* **GESAMTKOSTEN**	better	*bess-ser* **BESSER**	
deposit	*an-tsar-loong* **ANZAHLUNG**			
credit card	*kred-deet-karter* **KREDITKARTE**	small	*kline* **KLEIN**	
		medium	*mit-terl-gross* **MITTELGROSS**	
iving license	*foo-rer-shine* **FÜHRERSCHEIN**	large	*gross* **GROSS**	
dentification	*owss-vice* **AUSWEIS**	automatic	*mit owtoh-mar-teek* **MIT AUTOMATIK**	
		manual	*mit hant-shall-toong* **MIT HANDSCHALTUNG**	
name	*nar-mer* **NAME**	air conditioning	*kleematee-zattsee-own* **KLIMATISATION**	
address	*ad-dress-ser* **ADRESSE**			
		bicycle	*far-rard* **FAHRRAD**	
taxes	*shtoy-ern* **STEUERN**	car	*ow-toh* **AUTO**	
kilometerage	*keelo-may-ter-gur-boor* **KILOMETERGEBÜHR**	moped	*moh-far* **MOFA**	
ll) insurance	*fol-ler fair-zish-eroong* **(VOLLE) VERSICHERUNG**	motorcycle	*moh-tor-rard* **MOTORRAD**	
included	*ent-hal-tern* **ENTHALTEN**	van	*lee-fer-vargurn* **LIEFERWAGEN**	
necessary	*ner-tig* **NÖTIG**			
extra	*ex-trar* **EXTRA**	brakes	*brem-zern* **BREMSEN**	
		diesel	*dee-zerlerl* **DIESELÖL**	
per	*pro* **PRO**	gears	*shall-toong* **SCHALTUNG**	
		lights	*lishter* **LICHTER**	
hour	*shtoon-der* **STUNDE**	petrol / gas	*ben-tseen* **BENZIN**	
hours	*shtoon-dern* **STUNDEN**	reverse	*rook-vairts-gang* **RÜCKWÄRTSGANG**	
day	*targ* **TAG**	tank	*tank* **TANK**	
days	*tar-gur* **TAGE**	(full)	*foll* **VOLL**	
week	*vosh-er* **WOCHE**	washers	*shigh-bern-vash-an-largur* **SCHEIBENWASCHANLAGE**	
weeks	*vosh-ern* **WOCHEN**	wipers	*shigh-bern-visher* **SCHEIBENWISCHER**	
kilometer(s)	*keelo-may-ter* **KILOMETER**	husband	*man* **MANN**	
		wife	*frow* **FRAU**	
longer	*leng-er* **LÄNGER**	son	*zone* **SOHN**	
shorter	*nisht zoh lang* **NICHT SO LANG**	daughter	*tosh-ter* **TOCHTER**	
time	*tair-mee-ner* **TERMINE**	friend	*froynt* **FREUND**	

I	*ish* **ICH**		I would like	*ish mersh-ter* **ICH MÖCHTE**
we	*veer* **WIR**		we would like	*veer mersh-tern* **WIR MÖCHTEN**
you	*zee* **SIE**		do you want	*vol-ern zee* **WOLLEN SIE**
your	*eeyer* **IHR**			
it	*ess* **ES**		I have	*ish har-ber* **ICH HABE**
			we have	*veer har-bern* **WIR HABEN**
not	*nisht* **NICHT**		do you have	*har-bern zee* **HABEN SIE**
no	*kine* **KEIN**			
			can I	*kan ish* **KANN ICH**
which	*vel-shyer* **WELCHER**		can we	*ker-nen veer* **KÖNNEN WIR**
where	*voh* **WO**		can you	*ker-nen zee* **KÖNNEN SIE**
when	*van* **WANN**			
what	*vass* **WAS**		is	*isst* **IST**
what time	*uhm vee-feel ooer* **UM WIEVIEL UHR**		are	*zint* **SIND**
			is there	*gipt ess* **GIBT ES**
how long	*vee lang-er* **WIE LANGE**		is it	*ist ess* **IST ES**
how many	*vee-fee-ler* **WIEVIELE**			
how much is (that)	*vass koss-tert (das)* **WAS KOSTET (DAS)**		arrive	*an-kommern* **ANKOMMEN**
			fix	*reppar-ree-rern* **REPARIEREN**
nearest	*nex-ster* **NÄCHSTER**		go	*far-rern* **FAHREN**
near	*in dair nay-er fon* **IN DER NÄHE VON**		have	*har-bern* **HABEN**
here	*here* **HIER**		leave (things)	*lass-ern* **LASSEN**
there	*dar* **DA**		rent	*mee-tern* **MIETEN**
			reserve	*rezzair-vee-rern* **RESERVIEREN**
and	*oont* **UND**		show me	*tsigh-gurn zee meer* **ZEIGEN SIE MIR**
by	*by* **BEI**		stay	*bligh-bern* **BLEIBEN**
for	*foor* **FÜR**		use	*fair-ven-dern* **VERWENDEN**
from	*fon* **VON**		how does..work	*vee foonk-tseo-neert .* **WIE FUNKTIONIERT ...**
in	*in* **IN**			
on	*owf* **AUF**		furnished	*mer-bleert* **MÖBLIERT**
to	*tsoo* **ZU**		flat	*vo-noong* **WOHNUNG**
too	*owsh* **AUCH**		villa	*iyn-fam-meelyern-hou* **EINFAMILIENHAUS**

available	*fair-foog-bar* VERFÜGBAR	electricity	*shtrome* STROM
now	*yetzt* JETZT	fuses	*zish-er-roong-ern* SICHERUNGEN
eckout time	*ap-farts-tsight* ABFAHRTSZEIT	garage	*ga-rar-djer* GARAGE
		garden	*gar-tern* GARTEN
name	*nar-mer* NAME	gas	*garz* GAS
address	*ad-dress-ser* ADRESSE	grocer shop	*lay-berns-mitterl-gur-sheft* LEBENSMITTELGESCHÄFT
ephone no.	*roof-noomer* RUFNUMMER	heating	*high-tsoong* HEIZUNG
		keys	*shloo-serl* SCHLÜSSEL
rent	*mee-ter* MIETE	kitchen	*koosh-yer* KÜCHE
includes	*shleest iyn* SCHLIESST EIN	lamp	*lam-per* LAMPE
rvice charge	*ber-dee-noong* BEDIENUNG	light bulb	*gloo-beerner* GLÜHBIRNE
taxes	*shtoy-ern* STEUERN	living room	*vone-tsimmer* WOHNZIMMER
deposit	*an-tsar-loong* ANZAHLUNG	lock	*shloss* SCHLOSS
receipt	*kvit-toong* QUITTUNG	mattress	*mar-trart-ser* MATRAZE
		pillow	*kopf-kissern* KOPFKISSEN
extra	*tsoo-zets-lish* ZUSÄTZLICH	pillow case	*kopf-kissern-ber-tsoog* KOPFKISSENBEZUG
better	*bess-ser* BESSER	plug *(basin)*	*shtop-fern* STOPFEN
dirty	*shmoot-zig* SCHMUTZIG	plug *(electrical)*	*shteck-er* STECKER
broken	*kah-poot* KAPUTT	refrigerator	*kool-shrank* KÜHLSCHRANK
not working	*foonk-tseeyo-neert nisht* FUNKTIONIERT NICHT	sheet	*lar-kern* LAKEN
		shower	*doosh-er* DUSCHE
bath	*bard* BAD	sink	*shpoo-ler* SPÜLE
bathroom	*bar-der-tsimmer* BADEZIMMER	table	*tish* TISCH
bed	*bet* BETT	tap	*vass-ser-harn* WASSERHAHN
bedroom	*shlarf-tsimmer* SCHLAFZIMMER	telephone	*tay-lay-phone* TELEFON
blanket	*deck-er* DECKE	television	*fairn-zay-apparrat* FERNSEHAPPARAT
car	*ow-toh* AUTO	toilet	*twal-let-ter* TOILETTE
chair	*shtool* STUHL	vacuum cleaner	*shtowb-zowgur* STAUBSAUGER
cooker	*haird* HERD	wash basin	*vash-beckern* WASCHBECKEN
curtains	*for-henger* VORHÄNGE	(drinking) water	*(trink)* *vass-ser* (TRINK) WASSER
door	*toor* TÜR	water heater	*vass-ser-high-tser* WASSERHEIZER
duvet	*fay-der-bet* FEDERBETT	window	*fen-ster* FENSTER

ousehold utensils: 16-17   cleaning: 22

north	*nort* **NORD**	do you know	*viss-ern zee* **WISSEN SIE**
south	*zood* **SÜD**	if	*op* **OB**
east	*ost* **OST**	it	*ess* **ES**
west	*vest* **WEST**	will	*veert* **WIRD**
		will be	*veert zine* **WIRD SEIN**
		there will be	*ess veert zine* **ES WIRD SEIN**
		is	*ist* **IST**
		is it	*ist ess* **IST ES**
it	*ess* **ES**		
		clear up	*froynt-lishyer vair-dern* **FREUNDLICHER WERDEN**
not	*nisht* **NICHT**	continue	*bligh-bern* **BLEIBEN**
no	*kine* **KEIN**	have	*har-bern* **HABEN**
		improve	*bess-er vair-dern* **BESSER WERDEN**
which	*vel-shyer* **WELCHER**	rain	*rayg-nern* **REGNEN**
when	*van* **WANN**	snow	*shniy-ern* **SCHNEIEN**
what	*vass* **WAS**	worsen	*shlesh-ter vair-dern* **SCHLECHTER WERDEN**
what time	*uhm vee-feel ooer* **UM WIEVIEL UHR**		
		maybe	*fee-liysht* **VIELLEICHT**
how long	*vee lang-er* **WIE LANGE**	very	*zair* **SEHR**
how many	*vee-fee-ler* **WIEVIELE**	good	*goot* **GUT**
how often	*vee oft* **WIE OFT**	bad	*shlesht* **SCHLECHT**
		lovely	*shurn* **SCHÖN**
and	*oont* **UND**	severe	*shtark* **STARK**
by	*biss* **BIS**		
for	*foor* **FÜR**	more	*mair* **MEHR**
from	*ap* **AB**	less	*vay-nigger* **WENIGER**
if	*op* **OB**	lots of	*feel* **VIEL**
on	*am* **AM**		
or	*oh-der* **ODER**	soon	*balt* **BALD**
too	*owsh* **AUCH**	later	*shpay-ter* **SPÄTER**
with	*mit* **MIT**	after	*narsh* **NACH**

English	Pronunciation	German
forecast for	*for-**hair**-zargur foor*	VORHERSAGE FÜR
today	*hoy-ter*	HEUTE
tomorrow	*more-gurn*	MORGEN
next few days	*nex-ster tar-gur*	NÄCHSTE TAGE
this morning	*hoy-ter more-gurn*	HEUTE MORGEN
afternoon	*narsh-mittarg*	NACHMITTAG
this afternoon	*hoy-ter narsh-mittarg*	HEUTE NACHMITTAG
evening	*ar-bent*	ABEND
this evening	*hoy-ter ar-bent*	HEUTE ABEND
night	*narsht*	NACHT
tonight	*hoy-ter ar-bent*	HEUTE ABEND
morrow morning	*more-gurn froo*	MORGEN FRÜH
temperature	*temper-ra-toor*	TEMPERATUR
hot	*zair varm*	SEHR WARM
hotter	*vair-mer*	WÄRMER
warm	*varm*	WARM
mild	*milt*	MILD
cool	*kool*	KÜHL
cold	*kallt*	KALT
colder	*kel-ter*	KÄLTER
freezing	*freert*	FRIERT
..... degrees (C)	*grard*	GRAD
humidity	*foysh-tig-kight*	FEUCHTIGKEIT
high	*hosh*	HOCH
low	*nee-drig*	NIEDRIG
moderate	*may-sig*	MÄSSIG
depression	*teef*	TIEF
anticyclone	*hosh*	HOCH
changeable	*veck-serl-haft*	WECHSELHAFT
cloud	*vol-ker*	WOLKE
cloudy	*vol-kig*	WOLKIG
dry	*trock-ern*	TROCKEN
fog	*nay-berl*	NEBEL
foggy	*nay-blig*	NEBLIG
frosty	*fross-tig*	FROSTIG
haze	*doonst*	DUNST
hazy	*dee-zig*	DIESEG
humid	*shviy-ool*	SCHWÜL
ice	*ice*	EIS
icy	*iy-zig*	EISIG
mist	*fiy-ner nay-berl*	FEINER NEBEL
misty	*liysht nay-blig*	LEICHT NEBLIG
rain	*ray-gurn*	REGEN
rainy	*rayg-nerish*	REGNERISCH
snow	*shnay*	SCHNEE
snowy	*shnay-ig*	SCHNEEIG
storm	*shtoorm*	STURM
stormy	*shtoor-mish*	STÜRMISCH
(thunder storm)	*gur-vit-ter*	GEWITTER
sun	*zon-ner*	SONNE
sunny	*zon-nig*	SONNIG
wet	*nass*	NASS
wind	*vint*	WIND
windy	*vin-dig*	WINDIG
direction of	*rish-toong*	RICHTUNG
strength of	*shtair-ker*	STÄRKE
very	*zair*	SEHR
strong	*shtark*	STARK
force.....	*shtair-ker ....*	STÄRKE

I	*ish* **ICH**	I would like	*ish mersh-ter* **ICH MÖCHTE**
my	*mine* **MEIN**	we would like	*veer mersh-tern* **WIR MÖCHTEN**
we	*veer* **WIR**	do you want	*vol-ern zee* **WOLLEN SIE**
our	*oon-ser* **UNSER**		
you	*zee* **SIE**	I have	*ish har-ber* **ICH HABE**
your	*eeyer* **IHR**	we have	*veer har-bern* **WIR HABEN**
it	*ess* **ES**	do you have	*har-bern zee* **HABEN SIE**
not	*nisht* **NICHT**	can I	*kan ish* **KANN ICH**
no	*kine* **KEIN**	can we	*ker-nen veer* **KÖNNEN WIR**
		can you	*ker-nen zee* **KÖNNEN SIE**
which	*vel-shyer* **WELCHER**		
where	*voh* **WO**	is	*isst* **IST**
when	*van* **WANN**	are	*zint* **SIND**
what	*vass* **WAS**	is there	*gipt ess* **GIBT ES**
what time	*uhm vee-feel ooer* **UM WIEVIEL UHR**	is it	*ist ess* **IST ES**
how far	*vee vight* **WIE WEIT**	adjust	*rish-tig iyn-shtell-ern* **RICHTIG EINSTELLEN**
how high	*vee hosh* **WIE HOCH**	buy	*kow-fern* **KAUFEN**
how long	*vee lang-er* **WIE LANGE**	do	*mash-ern* **MACHEN**
how deep	*vee teef* **WIE TIEF**	go	*gay-urn* **GEHEN**
		have	*har-bern* **HABEN**
how many	*vee-fee-ler* **WIEVIELE**	hire	*mee-tern* **MIETEN**
how much is (that)	*vass koss-tert (das)* **WAS KOSTET (DAS)**	learn	*ler-nern* **LERNEN**
		repair	*reppar-ree-rern* **REPARIEREN**
and	*oont* **UND**	rescue	*ret-ern* **RETTEN**
at	*an* **AN**	search	*zoo-shern* **SUCHEN**
for	*foor* **FÜR**	sharpen	*shair-fern* **SCHÄRFEN**
from	*fon* **VON**	show me	*tsigh-gurn zee meer* **ZEIGEN SIE MIR**
in	*in* **IN**	ski	*shee-lau-fern* **SCHILAUFEN**
on	*owf* **AUF**	traverse	*travair-zee-rern* **TRAVERSIEREN**
to	*narsh* **NACH**	wait	*var-tern* **WARTEN**

nearest	*nex-ter* **NÄCHSTER**	ski run	*pee-ster* **PISTE**
near	*in dair **nay**-er fon* **IN DER NÄHE VON**	(green)	*groon* **GRÜN**
here	*here* **HIER**	(blue)	*blaoo* **BLAU**
there	*dar* **DA**	(red)	*roh-t* **ROT**
		(black)	*shvarts* **SCHWARZ**
day ticket	*tar-gez-karter* **TAGESKARTE**	(nursery slope)	*eedee-**oh**-tern-hoogurl* **IDIOTENHÜGEL**
3-day ticket	*dry-tar-gez-karter* **DREITAGESKARTE**	off piste	*ap-zites dair pee-ster* **ABSEITS DER PISTE**
weekly ticket	*vosh-ern-karter* **WOCHENKARTE**		
..... - run ticket	*.....-er-karter* **.....-ER KARTE**	button lift	*lift mit tell-er* **LIFT MIT TELLER**
return ticket	*rook-far-karter* **RÜCKFAHRKARTE**	cable car	*ziyle-barn* **SEILBAHN**
ski pass	*shee-pass* **SKIPASS**	chair lift	*zess-sel-lift* **SESSELLIFT**
		T bar lift	*lift mit kvair-rer-shtanger* **LIFT MIT QUERSTANGE**
person	*pair-zone* **PERSON**		
people	*loy-ter* **LEUTE**	top station	*ghipfel-statsee-yohn* **GIPFELSTATION**
reduction	*air-may-sigoong* **ERMÄSSIGUNG**	middle station	*bairk-statsee-yohn* **BERGSTATION**
group	*groo-per* **GRUPPE**	bottom station	*tarl-statsee-yohn* **TALSTATION**
insurance	*fair-zish-eroong* **VERSICHERUNG**	the operator	*dair ber-dee-noongs-man* **DER BEDIENUNGSMAN**
		queue	*shlang-er* **SCHLANGE**
lesson	*lair-shtoonder* **LEHRSTUNDE**		
ski instructor	*shee-lair-rer* **SKILEHRER**	aprés ski	*ap-ray skee* **APRES SKI**
guide	*foo-rer* **FÜHRER**	bar	*bar* **BAR**
		restaurant	*restau-rang* **RESTAURANT**
beginner	*an-feng-er* **ANFÄNGER**	sports shop	*shport-gur-sheft* **SPORTGESCHÄFT**
average	*mit-terl-maysig* **MITTELMÄSSIG**	tourist office	*frem-dern-fair-kairsbooro* **FREMDENVERKEHRSBÜRO**
experienced	*air-far-rern* **ERFAHREN**		
		open	*owff* **AUF**
skating	*shlit-shoe-laufern* **SCHLITTSCHUHLAUFEN**	closed	*tsoo* **ZU**
skiing	*shee-lauf-ern* **SKILAUFEN**		
oss country skiing	*lang-lauf* **LANGLAUF**	start	*shtart* **START**
ski jumping	*shee-springern* **SKISPRINGEN**	finish	*tseel* **ZIEL**
downhill racing	*ap-farts-rennern* **ABFAHRTSRENNEN**	entrance	*iyn-gang* **EINGANG**
tobogganing	*shlit-tern-far-rern* **SCHLITTENFAHREN**	exit	*owss-gang* **AUSGANG**

other sports: 116   conditions, terrain, equipment & clothing: overleaf

CONDITIONS	*ber-**ding**-oongurn* **BEDINGUNGEN**	TEMPERATURE	*tempera-**toor*** **TEMPERATUR**
very	*zair* **SEHR**	warm	*varm* **WARM**
		mild	*milt* **MILD**
crowded	*oo-ber-foolt* **ÜBERFÜLLT**	cold	*kalt* **KALT**
quiet	*roo-ig* **RUHIG**	freezing	*freert* **FRIERT**
avalanche	*la-**vee**-ner* **LAWINE**	TERRAIN	*gur-**len**-der* **GELÄNDE**
blocked	*block-**eert*** **BLOCKIERT**	glacier	*glet-sher* **GLETSCHER**
crevasse	*gletsher-**shpall**-ter* **GLETSCHERSPALTE**	hill	*hoo-gurl* **HÜGEL**
dangerous	*gur-**fair**-li<u>sh</u>* **GEFÄHRLICH**	hut	*hoo-ter* **HÜTTE**
detour	*oom-veg* **UMWEG**	mountain	*bairg* **BERG**
difficult	*shveer-rig* **SCHWIERIG**	pass	*pass* **PASS**
easy	*liy<u>sht</u>* **LEICHT**	path	*vayg* **WEG**
frost	*frost* **FROST**	peak	*ghip-fel* **GIPFEL**
frosty	*fross-tig* **FROSTIG**	ridge	*kam* **KAMM**
good	*goot* **GUT**	rocks	*fel-sern* **FELSEN**
ice	*ice* **EIS**	slope	*ap-hang* **ABHANG**
icy	*iy-zig* **EISIG**	(facing north)	*owf dair **nort**-zight* **AUF DER NORDSEITE**
possible	***mer**-gli<u>sh</u>* **MÖGLICH**	(facing south)	*owf dair **zood**-zigh* **AUF DER SÜDSEITE**
(with care)	*mit **zor**-gur* **MIT SORGE**	steep	*shtile* **STEIL**
safe	*oon-gur-fair-li<u>sh</u>* **UNGEFÄHRLICH**	valley	*tarl* **TAL**
slippery	*glat* **GLATT**	view	*owss-zi<u>sht</u>* **AUSSICHT**
slush	*shnay-match* **SCHNEEMATSCH**		
snow	*shnay* **SCHNEE**	up	*oh-bern* **OBEN**
(breakable crust)	*liy<u>sht</u> fair-**harsht*** **LEICHT VERHARSCHT**	down	*oon-tern* **UNTEN**
(deep powder snow)	***tee**-fer **pool**-ver-shnay* **TIEFER PULVERSCHNEE**	left	*links* **LINKS**
(granular snow)	*kur-**nig**-shnay* **KÖRNIGSCHNEE**	right	*re<u>sht</u>s* **RECHTS**
(spring snow)	***pap**-shnay* **PAPPSCHNEE**	straight ahead	*guh-**rar**-der-owss* **GERADEAUS**
(sticky snow)	***pap**-shnay* **PAPPSCHNEE**		
snow drift	*shnay-fair-vay-oong* **SCHNEEVERWEHUNG**	altitude	***her**-er* **HÖHE**
thawing	***tau**-vetter* **TAUWETTER**	high	*ho<u>sh</u>* **HOCH**
windy	***vin**-dig* **WINDIG**	low	*nee-**drig*** **NIEDRIG**

English	Pronunciation	German
QUIPMENT	*owss-roo-stoong*	**AUSRÜSTUNG**
bindings	*bin-doong*	**BINDUNG**
bob sleigh	*bop*	**BOB**
boots	*shtee-ferl*	**STIEFEL**
clip (on boot)	*shnall-er*	**SCHNALLE**
clip (on ski)	*hal-ter-reemern*	**HALTERIEMEN**
compact ski	*compact-shee*	**KOMPAKT-SKI**
compass	*kom-pass*	**KOMPASS**
crampons	*shtiyg-eye-zern*	**STEIGEISEN**
ss-cross-country ski	*lang-lauf-shee*	**LANGLAUF-SKI**
orward release	*owss-ler-zoong narsh forn*	**AUSLÖSUNG NACH VORN**
full-length ski	*lang-er shee*	**LANGER SKI**
goggles	*shnay-briller*	**SCHNEEBRILLE**
heel piece	*fair-zern-tile*	**FERSENTEIL**
heel release	*fair-zen-owtoh-martik*	**FERSENAUTOMATIK**
helmet	*shoots-helm*	**SCHUTZHELM**
ice axe	*ice-pickerl*	**EISPICKEL**
mid-length ski	*mit-ler-rer shee*	**MITTLERER SKI**
pole	*shtock*	**STOCK**
rope	*zile*	**SEIL**
short ski	*koorts-er shee*	**KURZER SKI**
skates	*shlit-shoo-er*	**SCHLITTSCHUHE**
ski	*shee*	**SKI**
skis	*shee-er*	**SKIER**
nning surface)	*lauf-flesher*	**LAUFFLÄCHE**
deways release	*owss-ler-zoong tsoor ziy-ter*	**AUSLÖSUNG ZUR SEITE**
ski boots	*shee-shteeferl*	**SKISTIEFEL**
(high back)	*mit hoh-em shafft*	**MIT HOHEM SCHAFT**
(inner boot)	*in-nern-shoo*	**INNENSCHUH**
ski pole	*shee-shtock*	**SKISTOCK**
sleigh	*shlit-tern*	**SCHLITTEN**
snow shoe	*shnay-shoo-er*	**SCHNEESCHUHE**

English	Pronunciation	German
stick	*shtock*	**STOCK**
toboggan	*row-derl-shlit-tern*	**RODELSCHLITTEN**
toe piece	*tsay-ern-tile*	**ZEHENTEIL**
touring bindings	*too-rern-bind-oong*	**TOURENBINDUNG**
visor	*viz-zeer*	**VISIER**
CLOTHES	*kliy-doong*	**KLEIDUNG**
anorak	*an-orak*	**ANORAK**
balaclava	*cap-oots-ser*	**KAPUZE**
cagoule	*vint-hemt*	**WINDHEMD**
ear flaps	*or-rern-clap-ern*	**OHRENKLAPPEN**
hat	*hoot*	**HUT**
jacket	*yak-ker*	**JACKE**
leggings	*gam-mash-ern*	**GAMASCHEN**
long johns	*lang-er oon-ter-hozer*	**LANGE UNTERHOSE**
mittens	*faust-hant-shoo-er*	**FAUSTHANDSCHUHE**
overtrousers	*oo-ber-hozer*	**ÜBERHOSE**
sweater	*pull-oh-ver*	**PULLOVER**
ski pants	*shee-hozer*	**SKIHOSE**
ski suit	*shee-ant-soog*	**SKIANZUG**
socks	*zoc-kern*	**SOCKEN**
sunglasses	*zon-ern-brill-er*	**SONNENBRILLE**
thermal underwear	*vair-mer oon-tervesher*	**WÄRME-UNTERWÄSCHE**
ACCESSORIES	*tsoo-ber-her*	**ZUBEHÖR**
belt	*goor-tel*	**GÜRTEL**
buckle	*shnal-ler*	**SCHNALLE**
elastic	*goo-mee-tsoog*	**GUMMIZUG**
laces	*shnoor-zen-kerl*	**SCHNÜRSENKEL**
ski wax	*shee-vax*	**SKIWACHS**
strap	*ree-men*	**RIEMEN**
zip	*rice-fair-shlooss*	**REISSVERSCHLUSS**

other clothing: 26   other sports equipment: 117

I	*ish* **ICH**	I would like	*ish* **mersh**-ter **ICH MÖCHTE**
my	*mine* **MEIN**	we would like	*veer* **mersh**-tern **WIR MÖCHTEN**
we	*veer* **WIR**	do you want	*vol*-ern *zee* **WOLLEN SIE**
our	*oon*-ser **UNSER**		
you	*zee* **SIE**	I have	*ish* **har**-ber **ICH HABE**
your	*eeyer* **IHR**	we have	*veer* **har**-bern **WIR HABEN**
it	*ess* **ES**	do you have	**har**-bern *zee* **HABEN SIE**
not	*nisht* **NICHT**	can I	*kan ish* **KANN ICH**
no	*kine* **KEIN**	can we	**ker**-nen *veer* **KÖNNEN WIR**
		can you	**ker**-nen *zee* **KÖNNEN SIE**
which	**vel**-shyer **WELCHER**		
where	*voh* **WO**	is	*isst* **IST**
when	*van* **WANN**	are	*zint* **SIND**
what	*vass* **WAS**	is there	*gipt ess* **GIBT ES**
what time	*uhm* vee-**feel** *ooer* **UM WIEVIEL UHR**	is it	*ist ess* **IST ES**
how long	*vee* **lang**-er **WIE LANGE**	buy	**kow**-fern **KAUFEN**
how many	vee-**fee**-ler **WIEVIELE**	clean	*zow*-ber-**mash**-ern **SAUBERMACHEN**
how much is (that)	*vass* **koss**-tert *(das)* **WAS KOSTET (DAS)**	come back	tsoo-**rook**-kommern **ZURÜCKKOMMERN**
		cook	**kosh**-ern **KOCHEN**
near	*in dair* **nay**-er *fon* **IN DER NÄHE VON**	dry	**trock**-nern **TROCKNEN**
here	*here* **HIER**	go	**far**-rern **FAHREN**
		have	**har**-bern **HABEN**
and	*oont* **UND**	hire	**mee**-tern **MIETEN**
at	*an* **AN**	join	**mit**-gleed **vair**-dern **MITGLIED WERDEN**
for	*foor* **FÜR**	leave *(things)*	**lass**-ern **LASSEN**
from	*fon* **VON**	pay	**tsar**-lern **ZAHLEN**
in	*in* **IN**	reserve	rezzair-**vee**-rern **RESERVIEREN**
of	*owf* **AUF**	stay	**bligh**-bern **BLEIBEN**
to	*tsoo* **ZU**	tidy	**owff**-roy-mern **AUFRÄUMEN**
with	*mit* **MIT**	wash	**vash**-ern **WASCHEN**

name	*nar*-mer	meals	*ess*-ern	
	NAME		**ESSEN**	
address	ad-*dress*-ser	breakfast	*froo*-shtook	
	ADRESSE		**FRÜHSTÜCK**	
membership card	*yoo*-goont-hairbairg-*owss*-vice	lunch	*mit*-targ-essern	
	JUGENDHERBERGAUSWEIS		**MITTAGESSEN**	
		dinner	*ar*-bent-essern	
			ABENDESSEN	
per	*pro*	snack	*imm*-biss	
	PRO		**IMBISS**	
night	*narsht*			
	NACHT			
nights	*nesh*-ter	room	*tsim*-mer	
	NÄCHTE		**ZIMMER**	
week	*vosh*-er	bed	*bet*	
	WOCHE		**BETT**	
		number	*noo*-mer	
			NUMMER	
early	*froo*			
	FRÜH			
now	*yetst*	bath	*bard*	
	JETZT		**BAD**	
later	*shpay*-ter	bathroom	*bar*-der-tsimmer	
	SPÄTER		**BADEZIMMER**	
before	*for*	blanket	*deck*-er	
	VOR		**DECKE**	
after	*narsh*	clothes	*kliy*-doong	
	NACH		**KLEIDUNG**	
		dormitory	*shlarf*-zarl	
			SCHLAFSAAL	
open	*owff*	dining room	*shpiy*-zer-zarl	
	AUF		**SPEISESAAL**	
closed	*tsoo*	duty *(job)*	*owff*-garber	
	ZU		**AUFGABE**	
		entrance door	*iyn*-gangs-toor	
			EINGANGSTÜR	
all day	den *gant*-sern targ	groceries	*lay*-berns-mitterl	
	DEN GANZEN TAG		**LEBENSMITTEL**	
today	*hoy*-ter	key	*shloo*-serl	
	HEUTE		**SCHLÜSSEL**	
tonight	*hoy*-ter *narsht*	kitchen	*koosh*-yer	
	HEUTE NACHT		**KÜCHE**	
tomorrow	*more*-gurn	lights	*lish*-ter	
	MORGEN		**LICHTER**	
morning	*for*-mittarg	locker	*shleess*-fash	
	VORMITTAG		**SCHLIESSFACH**	
afternoon	*narsh*-mittarg	lounge	*owf*-ent-halts-roaoom	
	NACHMITTAG		**AUFENTHALTSRAUM**	
evening	*ar*-bent	pillow	*kopf*-kissern	
	ABEND		**KOPFKISSEN**	
		security safe	*tray*-zor	
			TRESOR	
alternative	al-tairna-*tee*-ver	shower	*doosh*-er	
	ALTERNATIVE		**DUSCHE**	
quieter	*roo*-wigger	sleeping bag	*shlarf*-zack	
	RUHIGER		**SCHLAFSACK**	
extra	*tsoo*-zets-lish	sleeping sheet	*liy*-nern-shlarf-zack	
	ZUSÄTZLICH		**LEINENSCHLAFSACK**	
		mens' toilet	*men*-ner-twal-letter	
			MÄNNERTOILETTE	
on	*iyn*	womens' toilet	*dar*-mern-twal-letter	
	EIN		**DAMENTOILETTE**	
off	*owss*	valuables	*vairt*-zashern	
	AUS		**WERTSACHEN**	

household utensils: 16-17   bedding: 129

ABBREVIATIONS

ACS	**AUTOMOBIL-CLUB DER SCHWEIZ**	Swiss Automobile Association
ADAC	**ALLGEMEINER DEUTSCHER AUTOMOBIL-CLUB**	General Automobile Association of Germ
a.M.	**AM MAIN.**	On the River Main
a.Rh	**AM RHEIN**	On the River Rhine
AvD	**AUTOMOBILCLUB VON DEUTSCHLAND**	Automobile Club of Germany
Bhf	**BAHNHOF**	Railway station
BRD	**BUNDESREPUBLIK DEUTSCHLAND**	West Germany
DB	**DEUTSCHE BUNDESBAHN**	Federal German Railways
DDR	**DEUTSCHE DEMOKRATISCHE REPUBLIK**	East Germany
FD -Zug	**FERNSCHNELLZUG**	Long distance express
Frl	**FRÄULEIN**	Miss
G	**GASSE**	Lane
Hbf	**HAUPTBAHNHOF**	Central railway station
Hr	**HERR**	Mr
LKW	**LASTKRAFTWAGON**	Lorry
nachm.	**NACHMITTAGS**	In the afternoon / pm
n.Chr	**NACH CHRISTUS**	A.D.
ÖAMTC	**ÖSTERREICHISCHER AUTOMOBIL-MOTORRAD- UND TOURING-CLUB**	Austrian Automobile, Motorcycle and Touring Association
ÖBB	**ÖSTERREICHISCHE BUNDESBAHNEN**	Austrian Railways
p.A	**PER ADRESSE**	Care of, c/o
Pl	**PLATZ**	Square
PTT	**POST, TELEPHON und TELEGRAPH**	Post & Telephone office
qm	**QUADRATMETER**	Square meter
SB	**SELBSTBEDIENUNG**	Self-service
SBB	**SCHWEIZERISCHE BUNDESBAHNEN**	Swiss Federal Railways
St	**STOCK**	Floor
st	**STUNDE**	Hour
Str	**STRASSE**	Street
TCS	**TOURING-CLUB DER SCHWEIZ**	Swiss Touring Club
v.Chr	**VOR CHRISTUS**	B.C.
vorm	**VORMITTAGS**	In the morning / am

DISTANCE/SPEED

kms	miles
10	6
20	12
30	19
40	25
50	31
60	37
70	44
80	50
90	56
100	62
110	68
120	75
130	81
140	87
150	93
160	99
170	106
180	112
190	118
200	124
300	186
400	248
500	310
1000	620

TEMPERATURE

°C	°F
-15	5
-10	14
-5	23
0	32
5	41
10	50
15	59
20	68
25	77
30	86
35	95
40	104
45	113
50	122
55	131
60	140
65	149
70	158
75	167
80	176
85	185
90	194
95	203
100	212

FLUID MEASURE

litres	gal
5	1.1
10	2.2
15	3.3
20	4.4
25	5.5
30	6.6
35	7.7
40	8.8
45	9.9
50	11.0

WEIGHT

kgs	lbs
1	2.2
2	4.4
3	6.6
4	8.8
5	11.0
6	13.2
7	15.4
8	17.6
9	19.8
10	22.0

LENGTH

metres	feet
1	3.3
2	6.6
3	9.9
4	13.1
5	16.4
6	19.7
7	23.0
8	26.2
9	29.5
10	32.9

cm	inches
1	0.4
2	0.8
3	1.2
4	1.6
5	2.0
6	2.4
7	2.8
8	3.2
9	3.5
10	4.0
11	4.3
12	4.7

clothes sizes: 29

Here are the meanings of a few gestures you may come across in Germany, Austria and Switzerland which may not be familiar to you, or have different meanings to those you are used to. The precise meanings and degree of use can vary from area to area. Where alternatives are given, the first is the more common.

FINGER KISS
= Good!

BACKHAND V-SIGN
= Victory
(not an insult)

TOOTH FLICK
= Anger

CHIN FLICK
= Not Interested

CHEEK STROKE
= Looks Ill

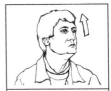

BACKWARD HEAD TOSS
= Come here

BACKHAND WIPE
= Go away!

FOREARM JERK
= Strong! / or Sexy!

EYE PULL
= Watch out!

FINGER PURSE
= Emphasis

TWO-FINGERED RING
= Good!/OK

THUMB POKE
= Sexy!

0	*nool*
	NULL
1	*iynts*
	EINS
2	*tsvigh*
	ZWEI
3	*drigh*
	DREI
4	*fear*
	VIER
5	*foonf*
	FÜNF
6	*zex*
	SECHS
7	*zee-bern*
	SIEBEN
8	*asht*
	ACHT
9	*noyn*
	NEUN
10	*tsayn*
	ZEHN
11	*elf*
	ELF
12	*tsverlf*
	ZWÖLF
13	*drigh-tsayn*
	DREIZEHN
14	*fear-tsayn*
	VIERZEHN
15	*foonf-tsayn*
	FÜNFZEHN
16	*zesh-tsayn*
	SECHZEHN
17	*zeep-tsayn*
	SIEBZEHN
18	*asht-tsayn*
	ACHTZEHN
19	*noyn-tsayn*
	NEUNZEHN
20	*tsvan-tsig*
	ZWANZIG
21	*iyn-oon-tsvantsig*
	EINUNDZWANZIG
22	*tsvigh-oont-tsvantsig*
	ZWEIUNDZWANZIG
23	*drigh-oont-tsvantsig*
	DREIUNDZWANZIG
24	*fear-oont-tsvantsig*
	VIERUNDZWANZIG
25	*foonf-oont-tsvantsig*
	FÜNFUNDZWANZIG
26	*zex-oont-tsvansig*
	SECHSUNDZWANZIG
27	*zee-bern-oont-tsvantsig*
	SIEBENUNDZWANZIG
28	*asht-oont-tsvantsig*
	ACHTUNDZWANZIG
29	*noyn-oont-tsvantsig*
	NEUNUNDZWANZIG
30	*drigh-sig*
	DREISSIG
40	*fear-tsig*
	VIERZIG

50	*foonf-tsig*
	FÜNFZIG
60	*zesh-tsig*
	SECHZIG
70	*zeep-tsig*
	SIEBZIG
80	*ash-tsig*
	ACHTZIG
90	*noyn-tsig*
	NEUNZIG
100	*hoon-dert*
	HUNDERT
101	*hoon-dert-iynts*
	HUNDERTEINS
200	*tsvigh-hoon-dert*
	ZWEIHUNDERT
1000	*tauw-zoont*
	TAUSEND
1100	*tauw-zoont-iyn-hoondert*
	TAUSENDEINHUNDERT
2000	*tsvigh-tauw-zoont*
	ZWEITAUSEND
100 000	*hoon-dert-tauw-zoont*
	HUNDERTTAUSEND
1 000 000	*iyn-er mill-yown*
	EINE MILLION

1st	*air-ster*
	ERSTE
2nd	*tsvigh-ter*
	ZWEITE
3rd	*drit-ter*
	DRITTE
4th	*fear-ter*
	VIERTE
5th	*foonf-ter*
	FÜNFTE
6th	*zex-ter*
	SECHSTE
7th	*zeeb-ter*
	SIEBTE
8th	*ash-ter*
	ACHTE
9th	*noyn-ter*
	NEUNTE
10th	*tsayn-ter*
	ZEHNTE
11th	*elf-ter*
	ELFTE
12th	*tsverlf-ter*
	ZWÖLFTE
13th	*drigh-tsayn-ter*
	DREIZEHNTE
20th	*tsvan-tsig-ster*
	ZWANZIGSTE
last	*letz-ter*
	LETZTE

once	*iyn*-*marl*	A	*ar*
	EINMAL		
twice	*tsvigh*-*marl*	Ä	*air*
	ZWEIMAL		
..... times	.....*marl*	B	*bay*
	.....**MAL**		
		C	*tsay*
an eight	*iyn* **a<u>sh</u>**-*terl*	D	*day*
	EIN ACHTEL		
a quarter	*iyn* **fear**-*terl*	E	*ay*
	EIN VIERTEL		
a third	*iyn* **drit**-*terl*	F	*eff*
	EIN DRITTEL		
a half	*iyn*-*er* **helf**-*ter*	G	*gay*
	EINE HÄLFTE		
two thirds	*tsvigh*-*drit*-*terl*	H	*har*
	ZWEI DRITTEL		
three quarters	**dry**-*fear*-*terl*	I	*ee*
	DREIVIERTEL		
seven eighths	*zee*-*bern*-**ar<u>sh</u>**-*terl*	J	*yot*
	SIEBENACHTEL		
		K	*kah*
example:	**fear**-*iyn*-**fear**-*terl*	L	*ell*
4¼	**VIEREINVIERTEL**		
	(four, a quarter)	M	*em*
		N	*en*
%	*pro*-**tsent**	O	*oh*
	PROZENT		
example:		Ö	*er*
20% of 100	*tsvan*-*tsig* *pro*-**tsent** *fon* **hoon**-*dert*		
	ZWANZIG PROZENT VON HUNDERT	P	*pay*
	(twenty percent of hundred)		
		Q	*koo*
+	*plooss*	R	*er*
	PLUS		
−	**mee**-*nooss*	S	*ess*
	MINUS		
x	*marl*	ß	*ess*-*tset*
	MAL		
÷	*doy<u>sh</u>*	T	*tay*
	DURCH		
=	*gliy<u>sh</u>*	U	*oo*
	GLEICH		
		Ü	*oo*
		V	*fow*
	in German a comma is used	W	*vay*
	for the decimal point:		
example:		X	*iks*
4.5	4 *comma* 5		
	4,5	Y	**oop**-*seelon*
	dates are said as follows:	Z	*tset*
example:			
1989	*noyn*-*tsayn*-*hoondert*-		
	noyn-*oont*-**a<u>sh</u>**-*tsig*		
	NEUNZEHNHUNDERT-		
	NEUNUNDACHTZIG		
	(nineteen hundred, eighty nine)		

departures	**ABFAHRT**		cold drinks	**KALTE GETRÄNKE**
departure times	**ABFAHRTSZEITEN**		tickets	**KARTEN**
department (of store)	**ABTEILUNG**		cash desk	**KASSE**
take care	**ACHTUNG**		no exit	**KEIN AUSGANG**
admissions / arrivals	**ANKUNFT**		basement	**KELLER**
Sundays &	**AN SONN und**		empty	**LEER**
- Bank holidays free	**- FEIERTAGEN FREI**		men	**MÄNNER**
lounge	**AUFENTHALTSRAUM**		VAT tax	**MEHRWERTSTEUER**
lift	**AUFZUG**		coin change	**MÜNZWECHSLER**
exit	**AUSGANG**		do not touch	**NICHT ANGREIFEN**
exit	**AUSFAHRT**		do not touch	**NICHT BERÜHREN**
information / enquiries	**AUSKUNFT**		no smoking	**NICHT RAUCHEN**
sale	**AUSVERKAUF**		don't speak	**NICHT MIT DEM FAHRE**
reduced	**AUSVERKAUFSPREISE**		- to driver	**-SPRECHEN**
out of order / not in use	**AUSSER BETRIEB**		emergency exit	**NOTAUSGANG**
sold out	**AUSVERKAUFT**		pedestrians only	**NUR FÜR FUSSGÄNGER**
car hire	**AUTOMIETE**		open (until / daily)	**OFFEN (BIS / TÄGLICH)**
no bathing	**BADEN VERBOTEN**		opening hours	**ÖFFNUNGSZEITEN**
platform	**BAHNSTEIG**		police notice	**POLIZEIMELDUNG**
service (not) included	**BEDIENUNG (NICHT)**		private	**PRIVAT**
	-INBEGRIFFEN		no smoking	**RAUCHEN VERBOTEN**
messages	**BESCHEIDE**		smoking permitted	**RAUCHER**
occupied / no vacancies	**BESETZT**		closing down sale	**RÄUMUNGSVERKAUF**
trespassers will be	**BETRETEN BEI STRAFE**		travel office	**REISEBÜRO**
-prosecuted	**-VERBOTEN**		reserved	**RESERVIERT**
press button to get	**BEI VERSAGEN KNOPF**		press to reject	**RÜCKGABEKNOPF**
- money back	**-DRÜCKEN**		tour	**RUNDFAHRT**
beware of dog	**BISSIGER HUND**		sale	**SCHLUSSVERKAUF**
please ring	**BITTE KLINGELN**		while you wait	**SCHNELLDIENST**
boats for hire	**BOOTSVERLEIH**		swimming pool	**SCHWIMMBAD**
letters	**BRIEFE**		self-service	**SELBST**
conducted coach	**BUSRUNDFAHRTEN**		self-service	**SELBSTBEDIENUNG**
- tours	**-MIT FÜHRUNG**		bargains	**SONDERANGEBOTE**
ladies	**DAMEN**		late performance	**SPÄTVORSTELLUNG**
in	**EIN**		24 hours	**24 STUNDEN**
way in	**EINFAHRT**		day excursions	**TAGESAUSFLÜGE**
entrance	**EINGANG**		day tours	**TAGESTOUREN**
admission (free)	**EINTRITT (FREI)**		arrivals	**TREFFPUNKT**
no entrance	**ENTRITT VERBOTEN**		drinking water	**TRINKWASSER**
ground floor	**ERDGESCHOSS**		bed & breakfast	**ÜBERNACHTUNG und**
reductions	**ERMÄSSIGUNGEN**			**-FRÜHSTÜCK**
adults	**ERWACHSENE**		changing room	**UMKLEIDERAUM**
ticket	**FAHRAUSWEIS**		subway passage	**UNTERFÜHRUNG**
excess fares	**FAHRGELDZUSCHLAG**		accommodation	**UNTERKUNFT**
ticket office	**FAHRKARTENAUSGABE**		.... forbidden	**.....VERBOTEN**
fare	**FAHRPREIS**		sales & service	**VERKAUFS**
fire escape	**FEUERLEITER**		- und KUNDENDIENST	
women	**FRAUEN**		tourist office	**VERKEHRSAMT**
free	**FREI**		delayed	**VERSPÄTET**
room to let	**FREMDENZIMMER**		full	**VOLL**
cloakroom	**GARDEROBE**		caution	**VORSICHT**
charges	**GEBÜHREN**		booking office	**VORVERKAUFSSTELLE**
danger	**GEFAHR**		wait for coin	**WARTEN BIS**
dangerous currents	**GEFÄHRLICHE STRÖMUNGEN**		- to drop	**- MÜNZE FÄLLT**
insert coin	**GELDEINWURF**		waiting room	**WARTEZIMMER**
have exact money	**GENAUEN BETRAG**		money change	**WECHSELGELD**
- ready	**-BEREITHALTEN**		bureau de change	**WECHSELSTUBE**
hours of business	**GESCHÄFTSZEITEN**		room to let	**ZIMMER FREI**
closed	**GESCHLOSSEN**		chambermaid	**ZIMMERMÄDCHEN**
turn handle	**GRIFF DREHEN**		accom. bureau	**ZIMMERNACHWEIS**
gentlemen	**HERREN**		room service	**ZIMMERSERVICE**
wait here	**HIER WARTEN**		rooms to let	**ZIMMER ZU VERMIETEN**
pay here	**HIER ZAHLEN**		fare stage	**ZONE**
information desk	**INFORMATIONSSCHALTER**		closed	**ZU**